THE CULTURE OF
SOUTH-EAST ASIA

by the same author

BUDDHIST ART IN SIAM
AN ASIAN ARCADY
SIAMESE TALES, OLD AND NEW
THE COINAGE OF SIAM

Fig. 43. Mask of Buddha in Stucco. Môn. (Author's collection)

THE CULTURE OF
SOUTH-EAST
ASIA

THE HERITAGE OF INDIA

— ❦ —

REGINALD _Stuart_ LE MAY

PH.D. (CANTAB.)

Vice-President, Royal India, Pakistan and Ceylon Society
Silver Medallist, Royal Society of Arts
Honorary Member, Siam Society

FOREWORD BY
THE RT. HON. R. A. BUTLER
P.C., M.A., M.P.

LONDON
GEORGE ALLEN & UNWIN LTD

First published in 1954

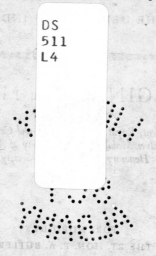
*Printed in Great Britain
in 12 point Bembo type by
Unwin Brothers Limited
Woking and London*

THIS BOOK
IS BY KIND PERMISSION
RESPECTFULLY DEDICATED
TO
PUNDIT JAWAHARLAL NEHRU
PRIME MINISTER OF INDIA

FOREWORD

In this study of the Culture of South-Eastern Asia Dr. le May has added notably to the services he has already performed by his earlier writings. It is more important than ever in this generation that we in the West should fully comprehend the characteristics of our neighbours in the East, and in pursuing this aim we must never neglect the cultural and historical background to the political and economic facts that confront us. Dr. le May's devoted research, which has been carried out over a quarter of a century, gives him special authority. His book will be of the greatest value.

R. A. BUTLER

Chairman of the Council,
Royal India, Pakistan and Ceylon Society

NOTE

The present name of Siam is Thailand, but as the general reader is, perhaps, still unfamiliar with that name, it has been thought convenient to keep to the old designation, Siam, throughout the text.

CONTENTS

After page 220

Map of Asia showing Sea Routes between India
    and South-East Asia

Map of South-East Asia

Illustrations

ILLUSTRATIONS

FIGURE

33. Stone standing Buddha, Gupta period, from India. (Brit. Mus.)
34. Stone standing Buddha, Gupta style, early Môn, outside Temple at Bangkok
35. Stone seated Buddha, Gupta style, early Môn, at P'rapatom, Lower Central Siam
36. Stone Bas-Relief of Buddha and Devotees, Gupta style, early Môn, from P'rapatom, Lower Central Siam. (Nat. Mus., Bangkok)
37. Stone 'Wheel of the Law,' early Indian style, early Môn, from P'rapatom. (Nat Mus., Bangkok)
38. Stone Deer (to represent Buddha), from P'rapatom, early Môn. (Nat. Mus., Bangkok)
39. Stupa at P'rapatom, North Indian style
40. Quartz Head of Buddha, early Môn. (Author's collection)
41. Stone standing Buddha, Môn. (Nat. Mus., Bangkok)
42. Stone Head of Buddha, Môn. (Author's collection)
44. Head of Buddha in Terra Cotta, Môn. (Nat. Mus., Bangkok)
45. Stone seated Buddha on Nāga King, late Môn period. (Nat. Mus., Bangkok)
46. Bronze standing Buddha, Môn. (Nat. Mus., Bangkok)

KINGDOM OF ÇRIVIJAYA

47. Bronze standing Buddha, Gupta period, from Kedah, Malay Peninsula
48. Stone standing Viṣnu, pure Indian style, from Region of Jaya, South Siam
49. Stone Brahmanic deities, Pallavā style, from Region of Takūapā, South Siam
50. Stone Brahmanic deity
51. Stone standing Viṣnu, Pallavā style. (Nat. Mus., Bangkok)
52. Bronze Torso of Lokeçvara, Pāla style. (Nat. Mus., Bangkok)
53. Stone seated Lokeçvara, Pāla period, from Bodhgaya, Bihar
54. Bronze standing Lokeçvara, Pāla style. (Nat. Mus., Bangkok)
55. Bronze seated Buddha, on Nāga King, Môn-Khmer style. (Nat. Mus., Bangkok)

JAVA

56. Arjuna group of Temples, Dieng Plateau, Java
57. Chandi Bhima, Dieng Plateau, Java
58. Monster Mask used on lintel of doorway at Chandi Arjuna
59. Bronze Çiva and Parvati, from Dieng Plateau
60. Stupa of Borobodur, Central Java
61. Circular platform with ring of small stupas, Borbodour
62. Gateway to Stupa, Borobodur
63. Stone relief portraying life of Buddha. Gallery at Borobodur
64. Stone relief portraying previous life of Buddha. Gallery at Borobodur
65. Typical stone Buddha at Borobodur
66. Chandi Kalasan, south-west of Prambanan
67. Chandi Mendoet, near Borobodur
68. Stone Buddha inside Chandi Mendoet, Gupta style

CHAPTER I

INTRODUCTORY

THIS is the first attempt, I believe, in any language, to bring together a comprehensive study of the culture of South-Eastern Asia.

The late Dr. Coomaraswamy in 1927 published a HISTORY OF INDIAN AND INDONESIAN ART, but naturally the Indonesian part took second place, and at that time he had not the material at his disposal which is available now.

I was Economic Adviser to the Siamese Government for a good many years before the Second World War, having also previously spent fourteen years in H.M. Consular Service in Siam and French Indo-China. I have travelled throughout all the countries dealt with in this book for the purpose of study, so that I am fully conversant with the political and economic problems confronting the peoples of that region today; but, since I retired from official service, my mind has been more and more drawn to a study of the cultural background of the countries which go to form South-Eastern Asia.

So now I have set out to piece together a mosaic, or weave a tapestry picture of all the forces which have gone to mould the culture of South-Eastern Asia, and in this Introductory chapter I would like to speak to the reader of the underlying principles of Buddhist and other culture of a spiritual nature which derives from India.

I am aware that to many Western eyes much of Indian art is repellent and, for reasons which are not at all clear to me, it appears that many English people refuse to have images of the Buddha in their homes on the ground that they are terribly unlucky. In itself this inhibition is unintelligible, since the historic Buddha was possibly the kindest man who ever lived, and I have often, while travelling in the north of Siam in years gone by, slept in his temple and laid my head beneath his watchful and beneficent care.

What I wish to do here is to try and explain the difference between the Eastern and Western approach to art and culture in general, since this seems to me to be of immense importance if we are to derive any feeling of satisfaction from a contemplation of Buddhist art. First of all, Buddhist religious art is almost entirely symbolic; that is to say, the artist in delineating the image of the Buddha is trying to create something over and beyond and above himself—a kind of super-man. In India and to a lesser extent in those countries influenced by India, he is bound by the rules of religious art, the *silpa-sastras*, and in all probability the function of the artist was carried on by succeeding generations of the same family. I personally derive a strong spiritual feeling from the best creations of Buddhist art—though I am not a Buddhist—and the effect that a masterpiece can have, even on an untrained English mind, is well illustrated by the story of my Cambridge landlady (with whom I did *not* discuss Buddhist art) saying to me one day at breakfast, as she pointed to the Môn head of Buddha (Fig. 42), which was standing on a cabinet in my rooms: 'Every morning I ask him for orders:' And when I, most astonished, asked her 'Why?', she thought for some moments and then said quite simply, 'He knows everything.' This is the greatest tribute paid to a work of art that I personally have ever heard.

Secondly, the use of symbolism, rather than of representational art, derives from the fact that, unlike his Western counterpart, the Eastern artist never takes a model. I have visited the studio of a Siamese who was 'producing' *ancient* stone sculpture and even he was not copying a genuine work of art: he was 'creating' them out of his own consciousness. The Eastern artist is aware that he cannot reproduce the actual or real object either in stone or on canvas: his aim is to try and reproduce the idea behind the object. In short he is the agent of the universal as opposed to that of the individual soul, whom the West upholds so fiercely; and this, to my mind, is in truth what Kipling meant when he said 'East is East and West is West, and never the twain shall meet.' It is obvious to all that the cleavage is great, but to 'missionaries' like myself this only makes the task of interpreting the one to the other more attractive, if at the same time more arduous.

It will not, therefore, be out of place to repeat what I said in my Introduction to BUDDHIST ART IN SIAM, since that book has probably not been in the hands of the general public, for whom this work is written.

Before we can appreciate the beauties of an alien art, it is essential to understand wherein it differs from our own. Fundamentally no doubt all mankind is one, but each branch of the human race has evolved its own system of culture and its own modes of expression, chiefly according to its geographical situation and to its own inherent strength, whether it can be influenced by exterior forces brought to bear upon it or whether it is strong enough to resist them. And here we are faced with an apparent paradox, for the practical, strong, dominating race may be the most receptive of culture from outside, while the politically weak may be the most resistant to it.

England, the world power, except in the territories which it has colonized, has influenced nobody in the world of art: on the contrary it owes its own chief architectural glories to France, its furniture and gardens largely to Italy, while Holland, France and Italy have all profoundly affected its sculpture and painting. China, on the other hand, which from an early period has been overrun and politically conquered by alien races—Huns, Tartars, Manchus and the like—has never failed to absorb them all, and to turn them culturally into good Chinese citizens, so strong is the inherent force of its culture. In India, while Persian (Achaemenid) and quasi-Hellenistic influences both made a strong attack upon the native art in its infancy and certainly left their mark upon it for a time, yet in the end these foreign influences were thrown off and a purely Indian art appeared, whether Hindu, Buddhist or Jain. India, indeed, once it recovered its independence of outlook, about the second century of the Christian era, began to exercise a profound cultural influence on its neighbours to the eastward—Burma, Siam, Malaya, Cambodia, Java and Ceylon all falling beneath its sway. And this, as far as one may judge, almost entirely as a result of trading and peaceful penetration by missionaries and others, and not by force of arms.

Indian religious art and culture seem naturally to have exercised an extraordinary fascination over the indigenous peoples of all these territories, no doubt owing to the attractions offered by Buddhism and Hinduism, while Chinese art, not bearing any particular religious message, apparently made but little impression, in spite of the fact that the Chinese, too, sailed the southern seas in search of trade from very early times.

For reasons as yet unexplained, perhaps too deep for explanation, from the dawn of European history, at least from the time of the beginnings of Greek art more than 2,500 years ago, the mental conceptions underlying Western and Eastern art seem to have been as the poles apart. Whereas the European, whether Greek or Roman, was content to cling to the earth in his desire to give expression to his aesthetic tastes, and to lavish all his skill on representations of the animal and plant kingdoms, the aim of the Eastern was to reach out after something unattainable, to try and define something beyond and above himself. Although no doubt in ancient India secular art was not lacking among the general population, yet the highest forms of religious art which have remained above ground for our admiration appear to me to possess a spirituality not to be found in Western art.

This seems to me to be the great inherent difference between Eastern and Western art. In the matter of technique too, a most important difference is seen. In the Eastern artist (whether Chinese, Indian, or Egyptian) there is an innate feeling for economy of line in delineating his subject. The Western artist, with his intense individualism, wishes the spectator to see the form, or the scene, exactly as he sees it, down to the very last detail, but the Eastern artist is content, in his simplicity, to give just the very essentials of the subject-matter and to leave it to the spectator to fill in the background and all inessential details from the resources of his own imagination and experience. A perfect example of this economy of line, which will explain my meaning better than any words to the true artistic eye, may be seen in a Chinese plate of Ting ware of the Sung period, from the collection of Sir Percival David. The scene incised on the plate is that of 'Two ducks in a lotus-pond,' and the whole picture is accomplished in about two dozen sure strokes of the instrument: but the essentials of the scene are there and nothing but the spectator's imagination is needed to fill in the background. It is, indeed, one of the most finished works of art that I know and can never be forgotten by anyone who has seen it with his 'inner' eye. The truth is that the Chinese artist has realized that no two pairs of eyes ever 'see' the same picture, and that the artist's chief aim should be to give full rein to the spectator's own imagination.

These ingredients, a spiritual aim and economy of line, combined with an intense feeling for form, make up the reason why the highest forms of Eastern art are to me so immeasurably more satisfying than their compeers of the West. If only the youthful artist of Europe will take these lessons to heart—a spiritual aim, economy of line, coupled with true simplicity and sincerity of heart—what may the future not produce?

It is only because I believe he is striving to do so that I feel the urge to write these words. Why is that great artist, Holbein, so completely satisfying? Because he, too, whether consciously or unconsciously, adopted the Eastern precept of 'economy of line,' and because, if one looks at those wonderful portraits of John Fisher or Thomas More, one sees a simplicity, a sincerity and a spirituality which appeal direct to the heart and the mind.

Chinese art has in some respects maintained its simplicity and serenity almost up to the present day, but the later forms of Hindu, Burmese and Siamese art are entirely decadent, grossly overladen with ornament and, indeed, running riot in an orgy of decoration. I am, however, writing of the earlier and formative periods up to the end of the fifteenth century A.D.

An account of my own 'conversion' in the matter of Eastern art may be useful to record, especially as I have reason to believe that the modern European artist is coming more and more to realize the truth of what I am about to say. Having been brought up from my youth to admire classical Greek art, I found, when first I went to the East, little or nothing of beauty in Siamese or Indian sculptural art. The general treatment in Eastern art is nearly always symbolical, 'natural form' being of little account, while in classical Greek art it is just that 'natural form' of the human body that the student is taught to study and that the critic is taught, as a European, to admire. But during a residence of twenty-five years in the East and a constant study of Indian, Sinhalese, Chinese, Cambodian, Siamese, Japanese and Javanese art, I gradually and imperceptibly found myself, so to speak, changing front—and I think now that I know the reason why. It is just the spiritual appeal in Eastern art, to which something universal and deep within one responds, and which is lacking in all Greek art except the very earliest. So that now, when I stand and look at the Elgin Marbles, for instance, or the sculptures from the altar of Pergamum, although I can and do admire the perfection of the human and equine forms portrayed, still I come away with part of me unsatisfied. I see the beauty of the form, but it is a physical beauty of a particular European type, and there it ends. There is nothing universal in its appeal, and it touches none of the deeper chords of one's nature. But when I gaze at the finest examples of Eastern art (for example, at the pottery Lohan of the T'ang Dynasty in the Chinese Exhibition or the similar figure in the British Museum), I find that my spirit is satisfied as well as my more superficial senses. My inner eye sees beyond the form as it is intended to do, and I experience something more than the sensation of enjoying the sight of physical beauty, or, in the case mentioned, of an example of the highest form of the potter's art. It is true that the best examples of Byzantine and also of early medieval European art also satisfy the spirit, but they again owe their inspiration to Eastern forms.

On the subject of 'treatment' Coomaraswamy has written words which must surely give the clue to any student wishing to understand the significance of form in Eastern art:

> It cannot be too clearly understood that the mere representation of nature is never the aim of Indian art. Probably no truly Indian sculpture has been wrought from a living model, or any religious painting copied from the life. Possibly no Hindu artist of the old schools ever drew from nature at all. His store of memory pictures, his power of visualization and his imagination were for his purpose finer means: for he desired to suggest the Idea behind sensuous appearance, not to give the detail of the seeming reality, that was in truth but *Maya*, illusion.... To mistake the *Maya* for reality were error indeed. 'Men of no understanding think of Me, the unmanifest, as having manifestation, knowing not My higher being to be changeless, supreme.' (BHAGAVAD GITA, vii. 24.)

In one sense Eastern art has an advantage over its Western sister in that it is nearly always devoted to religious ends, and may therefore be expected to show an attempt to inspire religious feelings, but the same criticism as I have made above would apply with almost equal force to a comparison between Eastern and Renaissance religious art. There is, for me, very little spiritual appeal in the figures of our Lord and of the Madonna that adorn Italian churches, in spite of an obvious attempt to endow them with such, and I wonder how many of the artistic souls who admire them are filled with any spiritual inspiration. Indeed, with a few notable exceptions such as works by Giotto and Cimabue, Simone Martini of Siena and Fra Angelico, although they may be works of great artistic merit, these figures fill my spirit with neither devotion nor peace of mind, nor do they give my inner vision any sense of glory. In some cases I feel something almost akin to repulsion, in others the reaction is more physically satisfying than is intended. As an example of my meaning, I personally love the subject of Lippo Lippi's Madonna, Lucrezia Buti, but not, alas, for the reason I ought to do so. I love her for the same reason as that which induced him to carry her off from a nunnery. The early Flemish artists, such as Van Eyck and Rogier van der Weyden, do imbue their work with a strong spiritual quality.

Those pictures which inspire in me the most religious feeling are the earliest, and they again are Byzantine or Eastern in origin. The reason for this is not easy to explain. It is not that I lean more towards Buddhism than towards Christianity, for I do not. No, if it is to be explained at all,

I think the difference lies in this. The Buddhist artist painted his picture or fashioned his image to represent a Being far more exalted than himself purely for religious edification and not as a conscious work of art, while the Western artist was chosen to adorn the churches of Italy, France, Germany and England mainly because he was an expert painter or sculptor and *not* because he was a man of ardent spiritual feeling who happened to be a skilled artist. I am told that in ancient days in Siam many of the images of the Buddha were made by the priests themselves within closed walls, so that no profane or curious prying eyes should watch or disturb them at their work. If they happened to be skilful in the art, their images would naturally be of a high artistic order; if they were not skilful, the result would be mediocre or even poor, artistically. But what counted was the spiritual atmosphere in which the image was created, and not the degree of skill that went to its making.

The European, on the other hand, is averse from symbolism and a purely spiritual appeal. He cannot forget that 'God made man in His own image,' and he prefers to see his own manly form portrayed in all its glory.

However heretical this confession may seem to some, I am not ashamed to admit it, because it gives, I believe, the clue to the fundamental difference between the Eastern and Western outlook, and it is only by an appreciation of what the Eastern mind is striving to convey that the Western mind can come into harmonious contact with it. The late E. B. Havell, who was artistic to his finger-tips, strove to preach the same gospel, but he was too fanatical and too bitter in his attacks on what he considered Western Philistinism ever to make much impression upon his hard-headed fellow-countrymen. If one is to bring about an understanding between East and West, it is, first of all, necessary to eradicate from Western minds the feeling, if it still exists, that there is something inherently 'heathenish' or unnatural in Eastern religious art.

One has to realize that there are other peoples in the world who have not the same modes of thought as oneself, and to try and understand what is the fundamental basis of their thoughts. It is a trite saying '*tout comprendre, c'est tout pardonner*,' but it is true nevertheless, and it is my belief that human ideals all over the world are in essence the same, only that different people approach them by different roads and by different forms of conveyance. I therefore wish to plead for an open, tolerant spirit and for a genuine desire to understand the meaning of what is to us an alien form of art.

It is not pretended that this work is exhaustive. I have deliberately chosen the period which it covers of about one thousand years, from A.D. 500 to 1500, and I call it 'The Formative Period,' since after the close of the fifteenth century no important change took place to disturb the settled cultural state of the lands with which this book deals. Burma and Siam remained Burmese and Siamese respectively as well as Buddhist. The Indianized States of Indo-China, Lao-land and Cambodia, even if they changed hands politically, still contained the same people and practised the same religion, Buddhism. Malaya had become the home of the Malays, who had embraced Islam, and the same applies to the Indonesians who occupied Java and the Islands. Asia, or at least Indianized Asia, then adopted the role of Rip Van Winkle and went peacefully to sleep.

Now, thanks to the restless energy and driving force of the West, we have succeeded, perhaps to our alarm, certainly to our astonishment, in reawakening her, and, although this book contains no cure for present ills and no suggestions for future mutual benefit, yet, if we are to form a true picture of the needs of South-Eastern Asia, it is essential that we should possess an intimate knowledge of her past.

As far as Siam and Malaya are concerned, the chapters relating to them constitute, with the kind permission of the Cambridge University Press, a revised reprint of BUDDHIST ART IN SIAM, and all the illustrations to those chapters have been selected from that book, as being fully representative of the cultural background of those countries during the period chosen.

The illustrations for the chapter on Burma have been kindly provided by the Archaeological Survey of Burma: those for Java and Bali by the late Dr. Krom and Dr. J. P. Vogel, still happily with us; and those for Cambodia by the École Française d'Extrême-Orient in Hanoi, and the Musée Guimet in Paris. To all of them my thanks are gratefully offered.

It will be noted that there are no footnotes to the work, and that no authorities are quoted except in the text. I have omitted them purposely as I wish the general reader to be able to read the book continuously, without his attention being distracted by interruptions which such references require. At the end of the book will be found an adequate selected bibliography which, it is hoped, will satisfy any reader who wishes to dive more deeply into the subject.

CHAPTER II

A GENERAL SURVEY

THE subject-matter of this book is so wide that just before the outbreak of war, in the early months of 1939, I gave a series of ten lectures to London University covering the whole field of Burma, Siam, Malaya, French Indo-China, Java and Sumatra. In this chapter, without going into detail, I shall try and paint a broad picture, so that the reader will gain some idea of its scope and will come to realize how deep are the roots of Indian culture in all the countries with which it deals. He will thus, it is hoped, be prepared to understand the more readily the detailed chapters which follow.

On the map of Asia there is a range of mountains running down the spine of Annam in French Indo-China, and this range marks the boundary or dividing line between Chinese and Indian culture. Everything north and east of this range is culturally based on China, while everything west and south is based on India, and the two neither overlap nor clash. At least, up to now they have not done so, and even the large bodies of Chinese residing today in Siam and Malaya have always lived in perfect amity with the local population. In Siam in particular they have inter-married to a large extent, and the *lūk chin* as he or she is called, has proved to be of excellent stock.

The beginnings of Indian colonization overseas eastward go back a very long way in time and it is almost certain that the results seen today were, in the main, not achieved by military expeditions, but by peaceful trading and religious teaching—and thereby all the more permanent.

I shall treat of the planting of Indian culture in each country in turn, and the reader will, I believe, be surprised at the range and quality of religious objects which have been found there dating from those early times, and due to the fusion of the Indian and the local genius.

As it is obviously impossible for me to deal with every facet of Indian culture and religion in the homeland itself, I must assume, in presenting this general survey of the culture of South-Eastern Asia, that the reader is conversant to some degree with Indian art in general, and devote my attention to giving a brief outline of the conditions prevailing in each of those countries which go to form this region, at the same time endeavouring to indicate those parts of India from which the local inspiration has been drawn in each case.

In spite of the efforts and discoveries made by scholars and archaeologists during recent years, my task has proved and still remains a very difficult one, and to show you how little was thought or known only thirty years ago of early colonization by Indian peoples in Indonesia, I have but to say that in the whole of the 649 pages of Vol. I of the CAMBRIDGE HISTORY OF INDIA, which was published in 1922 and which takes us up to the middle of the first century A.D., no attempt has been made to treat of colonization at all. In a few of the relatively late instances, such as the Pāla (Bengal) influence on Burma in the eleventh century A.D., the connexion with India is clear, but generally speaking the early links are still weak if not entirely missing.

There is one fact, however, which I would like to impress upon the reader at the outset, namely, that, of whatever race the original colonists may have been and from whatever parts of India they may have come to the different lands of Indonesia, whether Burma, Siam, Malaya, Java, Cambodia or Ancient Champa, the treatment and execution of the sculpture and architecture imported from India has rapidly taken on a definite local form in each of those countries, in many cases comparable with, and in some cases, as in Cambodia and Java, excelling the standards set by the parent art itself. He must be a very insensitive being who can look at the magnificent grandeur of Angkor or the still beauty of Borobodur without a feeling of awe and wonder at the marvellous inspiration and skill in execution vouchsafed to their builders.

The chief object of my present researches has been to find a *terminus a quo*, a starting-point beyond which no light is at present visible. It is well known that the great Emperor Açoka is reputed to have sent the Buddhist missionaries Sona and Uttara into the 'Land of Gold,' which is probably represented by modern Indonesia. Nothing has yet been found in Burma or Siam or Malaya which could be remotely connected with his period, i.e. with Mauryan art. It is, however, an interesting fact that Açoka claimed to have brought the Cholas in the south and the Andhras of Telingana on the east coast within the Buddhist fold. Now Paloura at the southern end of the Chilka Lake in the Ganjam district just south of Puri (not at the mouth of the Ganges where Ptolemy placed it), was the point well known to early mariners as that at which it was safe to turn eastward; and Amarāvatī at the mouth of the Kistna river was an early port of embarkation for missionaries and traders. It is quite possible, therefore, that at the beginning of the Christian era, or even before it, Indian traders and other colonists were seeking their fortunes overseas eastwards, more especially perhaps in the second and third centuries A.D., when Amarāvatī was an important centre for the dissemination of Buddhism.

R. C. Majumdar, the well-known Indian scholar and archaeologist, has recently summed up the evidence of Schmidt and other scholars in favour of the Malay race having originally come from India, where the Mālaya-Māllava tribe was widely spread, and of their original emigration to Sumatra and the Archipelago having taken place in what he called 'prehistoric' times. He says that, if this were accepted, the cumulative effect of these researches would be to push back the first phase of Indian colonization in the Far East to a time prior to the Aryan or Dravidian conquest of India, and that it would not be rash to imagine that this colonization was, partly at least, the result of Dravidian and Aryan settlements in India dislodging the primitive inhabitants and forcing them to find a new home across the seas.

This assumption is based chiefly on the evidence of linguistic affinities existing between certain primitive tribes of India such as the *Munda* and *Khāsi* with *Môn-Khmer* and allied languages, grouped together in the family called Austro-Asiatic and their further connexion with the Austro-Nesian family to which the Malays belong. Schmidt regards the peoples of Indo-China and Indonesia as belonging to the same stock as the *Munda* and allied tribes of Central India, and the *Khāsi* of Assam in North-Eastern India.

Krom, the Dutch archaeologist, however, basing himself on Hornell's theory, believed that it was Indonesians who colonized India in pre-historic times, and that the later Aryan colonization of the Far East was merely the reverse of that process. Moreover, Schmidt's linguistic theories have been seriously challenged, notably by G. de Hevesy, who denies the existence of the Austro-Asiatic family of languages altogether. It will thus be seen that this subject is still highly speculative and controversial, and beyond mentioning it, I do not propose in this chapter to discuss it further; except to say that, if the Malays originally came from India, it is not surprising that they readily accepted the Indian religious influences when these flowed back in later times.

It is somewhat remarkable to find that the oldest sculptural remains hitherto unearthed in Sumatra are *Menhirs* very similar to those of the Han period in China, as are also the form of the Cist Graves and the paintings on the inner walls. It is suggested by Loeb and Heinegeldern that these were erected by settlers from Tonkin and North Annam between the years 300 B.C. and A.D. 100. It is credibly reported that the Chinese came at a very early date to the Malay Archipelago in their search for tin and this may account for such Chinese settlements. It is also suggested that the island of Suvarnadvipa, i.e. Sumatra, was known to the Indians in the first century A.D. at the latest, although no traces of this period are yet known. If this is true, we have in Sumatra the earliest meeting of India and China in Indonesia—at its southernmost point.

From the evidence available it seems that colonists from India began to cross the seas, and enter the lands of Indonesia from the beginning of the Christian era onwards, and it would appear that we have three different routes to consider for this emigration overseas. It looks as if the earliest settlers embarked at the port of Amāravatī and landed probably at the port of Martaban in Burma, though Coomaraswamy quotes Ptolemy as saying that the chief port of embarkation in India for 'The Land of Gold' was Guduru (Koddura) at the mouth of the Goda-vari river. Some would settle in the region of Thatôn and the delta of the Salwīn river; and later on, in that of the Irawadi round about Pegu. Others would push on southwards through the 'Three Pagodas' pass and finally find a resting-place in the fertile rice plains of Siam. Like the Chinese coolies who, hundreds of years later, came to seek their fortunes in Siam, it is easy to imagine that those immigrants never regretted leaving the dusty soil of India for the green and smiling lands of Burma and Siam, where the finest rice in the world is grown, and one has only to lie on one's back and wait for the bananas to fall into one's mouth. Compared with the local inhabitants they were probably already of a much higher standard of civilization and would bring with them their own culture and religion as well as images whether Brahman or Buddhist.

Later on, in Gupta times, when the capital of Northern India was at Pataliputra (Patna) it is likely that missionaries and traders travelling to Indonesia would use the port of Tamralipti (or Tamluk) on the Hugli river, even as the Chinese pilgrim, Fa-Hsien, did when he re-embarked for China in the early years of the fifth century A.D. These emigrants would make equally for Martaban, unless they were bound for Akyab and Arakan on the west coast of Burma, since Thatôn was already established as the seat of Môn culture in Burma, and Martaban was a useful port either for that country or for Siam.

Thirdly, in Pallava times, we have the southern route from Kānchi-puram either straight across to Mergui and Tenasserim or slightly south-wards to Takūa-pā and Puket Island (Junk Ceylon) or Trang in the Siamese portion of the Malay Peninsula, or again southwards through the Straits of Malacca to Sumatra, Java and Borneo. Yet another route carried travellers and merchants to Palembang and Java via the open sea south-west of Sumatra.

There is, of course, a fifth route to consider, the entire sea-route round the island of Singapore and either up the Gulf of Siam to where Bangkok now stands or across the China Sea to ancient Funan and Champa. From the finds already made in the Malay Peninsula it seems probable, however, that this was not in general use, and that there was a well-trodden route across the peninsula from Takūa-pā (the ancient Takola of Ptolemy) to Jaya and the bay of Bandon on the east coast, as well as from Trang to Patalung, which I have traversed myself on a good metalled road.

Quaritch Wales has travelled along the route to Jaya and mapped it accurately in his book TOWARDS ANGKOR. On an Island in the harbour of Takūa-pā, Wales found the remains of an ancient sanctuary, accom-panied by many sherds of early Chinese and Persian pottery; and twelve miles up the Takūa-pā river visited the well-known spot where still rest, embedded in the trunks of trees which have grown over them, three Brahmanic statues of pure Indian handiwork but made of a local schist. These images are Pallava in style and may be attributed to the seventh or eighth century A.D., as near by were found schist slabs one of which bore an inscription in eighth-century Tamil.

This brings us to a question to which as yet no definite answer can be given, namely, whether Brahmanism or Buddhism came first to Indo-nesia. It is an interesting (if not a very important) question, since it would indicate from which part of India the earliest colonists came. The probability is that both religions were imported more or less simultaneously and that, while Brahmanism remained the religion of certain well-defined bodies of colonists and was also a necessary adjunct to all the local courts, if only for horological purposes, it never appealed to the general mass of the peoples of Further India, who found the simpler teaching of Hinayana Buddhism more congenial.

As regards the Malay Peninsula, one of the earliest references to its colonization, presumably from India, is to be found in the Chinese annals of the history of Liang, dating from the sixth century A.D., where it is stated that among the vassal states of Funan (an ancient empire

whose capital was situated in modern Cochin-China) was one called
Lang-ya-Hsiu, now identified as occupying Kedah and Perak, which
sent an embassy to China in A.D. 515 and reported that 'our people say
that the Kingdom was founded more than 400 years ago,' that is to say,
in the first century A.D. Also, according to the same Chinese history,
Funan itself received its Indian influences in art and culture from the
ancient state of P'an-P'an, which is generally agreed now to have been
situated in the region of the Bay of Bandon (in Siam) on the east coast
of the Malay Peninsula. According to Coedès, there was also another
ancient state colonized from India in the same region named Tambralinga
as early as the second century A.D.

Turning to Central Siam, some light has been shed in recent years by
excavations at a small village called Pong-Tük about ten miles along the
road to Kānburi from the station of Bān Pong, where the railway from
Bangkok turns south for the peninsula and Penang. Here, in a banana
garden, was unearthed the plinth of a temple sanctuary, with the steps
leading up to it. The style of this plinth is similar to the early style of
platform found at Anurādhapura in Ceylon, which owed its earliest
Buddhist buildings to the great centre of Amarāvatī in India. In conjunction with this were found, first a Graeco-Roman bronze lamp of
Pompeian style attributed by Coedès to the second century A.D. and
secondly a small bronze Buddha image of the Amarāvatī type, which
he also ascribed to the second century A.D. though it must be said that
Sir John Marshall considers it to be as late as the fifth century A.D.
Similar images, though of much more finished execution, have been
found both in North-Eastern Siam and as far east as Dong Duang in
Annam. Whatever the date of the statue, the find of the Roman lamp
would seem to show that there was a settlement at Pongtük in the early
centuries of the Christian era, as well as sufficient intercourse with the
outside world for important foreign objects to find their way there.
Moreover, the statue of the Buddha is undoubtedly of the Amarāvatī
type and does not appear to have been locally made, since it shows the
so-called 'Greek' drapery in the robe which it wears. We have here then,
whether in the second or fifth century A.D., the earliest known tangible
contact between India and the territory of Siam.

From Siam we go to Burma and so little has been done in that country
in the way of archaeological research that Harvey, in his HISTORY OF
BURMA (published in 1925) could only fill the first three or four pages
of his work with conjectural matter concerning the first five hundred
years of the Christian era. Some important discoveries have been made

since 1925 by Duroiselle, the late Director of Archaeology, but the early history is still very obscure. For instance, during the past twenty-five years there have been important finds in Siam of sculpture made by the Môn settlers there, based on Gupta models from Northern India, but as far as I know, none have ever been found in Burma to compare with these, although the centre of Môn culture lay in the districts of Pegu and Thatôn in Southern Burma. Here I cannot help remarking, as I pointed out to Lord Zetland when he came to visit the exhibition of my collection of ancient sculpture at India House in 1938, that, although the French in Indo-China have always shown a deep interest in ancient connexions between Siam and what is now French Indo-China, the British, in both Burma and Malaya, have never exhibited the slightest interest in the cultural relations of these countries with Siam. This is hardly creditable either to our neighbourly or to our archaeological sense.

According to Harvey, the decisive factor for Burma was the rise in the fifth century A.D. of a great Hinayana Buddhist centre at Conjee-verām (ancient Kānchipuram) near Madras, under the commentator Dhammapāla, since ancient Môn writings frequently mention Dham-mapala and Conjeeverām, and the earliest Môn inscription is in the Pallavā alphabet used there in his time.

Turning to Java and Sumatra, Loeb and Heinegeldern state that the oldest stone image of Buddha, which was found near Palembang, can-not be dated earlier than the second half of the fifth century A.D., which places it in the Gupta period, and anterior to the Çrivijaya period of Sumatra. But Coedès, in his HISTOIRE ANCIENNE DES ÉTATS HIN-DOUISÉS D'EXTRÊME-ORIENT (to which reference will often be made) says that Buddhist images of the Amarāvatī period have been found in the Celebes, in the east of Java, and near Palembang in Sumatra. These would antedate anything of the Gupta period. Stone figures of Bod-hisattvas, e.g. Lokeçvara, have also been found which are related to the Pallava period. There are also some sculptural and architectural remains connected with Çaivism, but no date is assigned to these.

For Malaya the position is much the same as when Coedès wrote in 1928 that the archaeology of the peninsula presents problems which the evidence at present available is not enough to resolve. Recent research in ancient Wieng Sra, near Jaya, and its neighbourhood has led to the discovery of Brahmanic and Buddhist sculptures representing a variety of types. Some of these are very near to pure Indian prototypes, others by their complicated head-dresses recall the sculptures of Kānheri and

Aurangabad in North-Western Hyderabad of the sixth and seventh centuries A.D.

The earliest Buddhist images so far found in the peninsula whether in British or Siamese Malaya, are in the Gupta style, and are probably not earlier than the fifth or sixth century A.D. They are akin to those of the Môn kingdom found in Siam in that period but those from the peninsula seem to me to be nearer to the Indian prototype than those from Siam proper. A small bronze statue found at Pongtük is locally made but certainly Gupta in style.

Later on from the eighth century onwards we find in the peninsula another type of Indo-Malaysian sculpture which is connected with Çrivijaya, a kingdom which is believed to have arisen in the sixth or seventh century A.D. with its capital at Palembang in Sumatra and to have spread its wings over most of the Malay Peninsula. This sculpture is clearly of a Mahayana Buddhist type, and, although the subject of its provenance (or that of its prototypes) is still controversial, I believe that its origin will eventually be found among the Pālas of Bihar and Bengal, at any rate after the close of the eighth century. This kingdom of Çrivijaya later became known as Jāvaka, or Zābag, to the Arab traders.

When we turn to Siam proper, as distinct from the peninsula, we have to recall a fact which always astonishes me when I think of it. In a work on Brahmanical gods in Burma Nihar Ranjan Ray states that 'In Siam, which is professedly Buddhist, finds of Brahmanical Deities in considerable numbers testify to the existence of a large Brahmanical population,' and later that 'Brahmanism preceded Buddhism in that country.' Ranjan Ray may be referring to the finds in the peninsula which I have been discussing, in which case I do not feel by any means certain that Brahmanism preceded Buddhism in that part of the country, but there is another region of Siam, where images of Brahmanic deities have been found, which may well lend truth to his statement. In the heart of Siam, remote from all the principal waterways, at an ancient site called Çri-tep (Çri-Deva) in the valley of the Pā-Sak river, north of the modern town of Petchabūn, have been unearthed some of the most remarkable statues ever found in Further India, all of Brahmanic deities, together with a fragment of an inscription in Sanskrit which Finot assigns to the fifth or sixth century A.D.

During his tour Wales visited this ancient site and has given a clear picture of it in TOWARDS ANGKOR. How this Indian colony or state came to be formed in such a remote region is a mystery. Wales accounts for it by imagining that people of Ancient Funan (now in French Indo-

China) expanded their dominions by 'following the River Mekōng for some distance, thence going westward along the valley of the Mūn river, then through a gap in the mountainous escarpment that borders the plateau of Eastern Siam, then across the valley of the unnavigable Pāsak river, and finally to the fertile plains of the Menam valley.' But Çri-Deva is not in the fertile plains of the Menam valley, and the inevitable question presents itself: 'Why stop and build your capital at an absolute dead-end, on an unnavigable river, far remote from the centre of your kingdom, from the sea, and from all the principal trading centres?' I cannot find an answer to this question.

The ancient city (not including a larger area added by the Khmer later) was surrounded by a moat and ramparts, with six gates or entrances, the four principal ones being at the cardinal points of the compass, and the area enclosed was about a square mile. There are the ruins of four temples still standing in the centre of the city together with a lake, tanks, and a terraced structure.

Of the four temples, only one was found in a reasonable state of preservation, and consisted of a brick tower about 40 feet high, standing on a laterite pyramidal base which raised it a further 20 feet from the ground. Wales believed that he was looking at the oldest known Hindu temple in Indo-China. From the photograph given it is difficult to judge clearly of its architectural conception, but the mention of a laterite base gives rise to some doubt in my mind as to whether one can ascribe it to so early a period. Laterite is a kind of grey stone of ferruginous clay, very soft when it is cut or dug out, but when exposed to the air and sun, turning red and hardening to a rock-like substance, full of holes like Gruyère cheese. It was much in use in Khmer times for construction work of all descriptions, especially roads, and it is true that it was used in the early buildings discovered at Pong-tük, but the Funan and early Khmer people used brick for buildings, and whether the early Hindu settlers of Çri-Deva knew of the use of laterite certainly raises a question. When, too, this is reinforced by the mention of false porches and niches inside, resembling windows, the whole seems to me to smack strongly of Khmer architecture. There was a later Khmer settlement at Çri-Deva, as Khmer images have been found there too, and Wales refers to this later occupation which he ascribes to the eleventh century A.D. after the city had lain desolate for a long period. But for the moment this is by the way, as the city has undoubtedly yielded splendid stone statues of Vishnu and other Brahmanic gods which are probably not later in date than the fifth or sixth century A.D.

C

Going back to Central Siam and passing over the finds of Amarāvatī images at Pongtük, we begin to tread on firmer ground since the last thirty years have revealed a considerable number of Buddhist sculptures in bluish limestone, which may, I think, be ascribed without any doubt to Gupta prototypes. These sculptures were the work of Môn artists and can be dated back to the sixth century, if not earlier, since stone 'Wheels of the Law' and figures of 'The Deer' (which were symbols of the Buddha before his images were made), have been found in Central Siam as well as images seated in the so-called European fashion. For the moment we can say then that, even if early Brahmanic as compared with Buddhist remains are few and far between in Central Siam, the finds in Southern and North-Eastern Siam certainly indicate their presence there at an early date.

Now we must turn to Burma. The earliest inhabitants of Burma of which any record exists were the Pyu, a Tibeto-Burman tribe, and although the Pyu are now extinct as an entity, having been absorbed by the Burmese, a certain number of their inscriptions have been found from which it is clear that they were Buddhists by religion and had long had contact with India. This is also confirmed by the Chinese chronicles of the Tang dynasty. Their principal city, Old Prome (Hmawza) on the Irawadi, was $8\frac{1}{2}$ miles in circumference, twice as large as Mandalay, and the area enclosed was $5\frac{1}{2}$ square miles. Harvey, the historian, says that Buddhism existed side by side with Brahmanism and that what the excavator finds in Burma is often Hindu rather than Buddhist. As a comparative statement I hesitate to accept this dictum, but there is no doubt that, in view of the discovery in some numbers of Brahmanic images at Hmawza, Mergui and in Arakan, as well as coins and terra-cotta tablets, there must have been settlements of Indian colonists living among the Buddhist population, with special Brahman temples for their own worship, in exactly the same way as Hindus live and practise their religion today among the Burmese and Siamese. The provenance of these Brahmanic images or of their prototypes is at present not at all clear, but the earliest writing found in Old Prome can, according to Finot and Duroiselle, be traced to Southern Indian alphabets as its immediate source, as in the case of certain gold plates inscribed with Pali texts, which are in an archaic script like the Kadamba script of the fifth century A.D.

This rather points to Harvey's conclusion that the rise of Hinayana Buddhism in Burma was due to the great movement centred at Conjeeveram on the Madras coast in the fifth century A.D.

North of Prome in Old Pagān there seems to have grown up a very debased form of Tantric Mahayanism, practised by the Ari cult, but in the south of Burma we find the Môn, or Talaing as they are called today, with their centres at Thatôn and Pegu. When the Môn, who are linguistically allied to the Khmer, first settled in Lower Burma cannot be fixed for certain nor when they received the teaching of the Hinayana school. That they must have arrived fairly early in the Christian era is clear since they had reached Lamp'un in Northern Siam by the seventh or eighth century A.D. and the conversion of that country to Hinayana Buddhism had begun.

A few images of the Buddha, showing traces of a Gupta style, have been found at Hmawza, and some of these have inscriptions in Pyu and Sanskrit; but I do not yet know of any similar images of the Buddha having been found either at Pegu or Thatôn, which could afford us any clue as to their date or provenance. Finot suggests that the soundest inference to draw at present is that both Sanskrit and Pali, with their respective forms of religion, were more or less concurrent in the Môn country from an early but still unspecified date.

Before we leave Burma I should add that from the eleventh century onward, when the first Burmese kings of Pagān had such intimate dealings with Bodhgaya in Bihar, we are on firm ground and can trace the Buddhist art of Burma directly back to the school of Nalandā.

There we must leave Burma, and in this brief survey, travel across land and sea to ancient Funan and Khmerland.

Practically all we know historically of Funan is due to the researches of Pelliot who unearthed and translated a large number of references to this State in the early Chinese annals. From these it appears that Funan occupied the modern province of Cochin-China and a part of Cambodia, and that its capital was situated a little south of modern Pnompenh. There is a tradition that an Indian named Kaundinya came from the west in the first century A.D. and it is related further that between A.D. 240 and 245 a successor of Kaundinya named Fan-Chan sent an embassy to India.

After this we hear of no further connexion with India until the end of the fourth century A.D. when another Indian Brahman, also named Kaundinya, in response to 'A voice from Heaven' travelled to Funan from the State of P'an-P'an in the Malay Peninsula and was received with open arms by the people who immediately elected him their king. He completely changed the customs to those of India.

At the end of the fifth century A.D. a member of the same family was still on the throne, under the name of Kaundinya Jayavarman (this is the first mention of Varman in Indo-China) and by this time Buddhism had apparently also arrived, but whether from India or China is not absolutely clear. In A.D. 484 the king sent an Indian priest named Nagasena to the imperial court of China who reported to the emperor that 'the custom of his country was to render service to the god Maheçvara (Çiva) but that the Bodhisattva practised his mercy also. Indeed the reforming influence of Buddhism extended over ten regions.' From this it might appear that the Buddhism practised was a form of Mahayanism (as in China) but, whether this be so or not, here we have the first mention of a custom which has been in use in Indonesia from that day to this, where the court was surrounded by Brahman priests while the people were embracing the more congenial religion of Buddhism.

The Buddhist art of Funan (or at least of pre-Angkor Cambodia) is similar to the art of Dvāravatī, as the old kingdom of Central Siam occupied by the Môn people was called, and it is possible that this early style of Buddhist art was brought to Funan through the intermediary of Dvāravatī. From the history of Funan it does not seem likely that that country was often in direct contact with India, but rather that it received its Indian character through the Indian states of the Malay Peninsula and, as far as this type of art is concerned, from the Môn state of Dvāravatī.

The last king of Funan mentioned in the Chinese annals is Rudravarman, who was ruling in the first half of the sixth century and who is reported in A.D. 539 to have offered the emperor of China a hair of the Buddha 12 feet long. In the second half of that century, Funan was conquered by its northern vassal state of Chen-la, and the rise of the great Khmer empire had begun. At this time, Chen-la was split up into two parts, Chen-la of the water (i.e. the great lake and the lower reaches of the Mekōng) and Chen-la of the earth (i.e. the Lao states to the west of Annam). It was not until the end of the eighth century A.D. that the northern part obtained control over the whole of Cambodia.

After Chen-la had conquered Funan, a capital was established at Vyadhapura (Angkor-Borei) between Pnompenh and Chaudoc to the south of it, but apparently the capital of Southern Chen-la had previously been situated at Çambhupura (Sambhor) on the Mekōng river due east of the great Lake. Here are found the earliest types of Khmer temples all dedicated to the Brahman religion.

Maspero placed the capital of Chen-la of the earth at a place now called Pāk-hǐn-bŭn on the Mekōng, but Seidenfaden states that there are no Khmer ruins to be found there, and that the capital was probably at Ta-k'ek (opposite Nakon-Panom) slightly to the south where there are still the remains of a considerable city to be seen. In modern colloquial Siamese 'Ta-k'ek' would mean 'The Indian landing-place,' but the original meaning of *k'ek* is not 'Indian' but 'a guest' or 'a stranger.' In Siamese a drawing-room is 'hong rap k'ek' or 'room for receiving visitors.' I hesitate to draw any conclusions from this name, but it is interesting all the same.

What are probably the earliest sculptured remains in Northern Chenla were, I will not say, discovered (for they were previously seen by Prince Damrong, Lunet de Lajonquière, and Aymonier) but closely examined and photographed by myself in 1929. There is a noted temple, to which pilgrimages are still made by the devout, at Tāt-Panom, halfway between the towns of Nakon-Panom and Mukdahān to the south, and the base of the *stupa* in the temple grounds is constructed of large rectangular red bricks, whose surface is covered with spirited carving. Here I saw, greatly to my astonishment, a large figure of the Buddha seated on a lotus-throne turning the Wheel of the Law or 'preaching the first sermon.' The style reminded me of the Amarāvatī school, but whether this is so or not, the figures show a clear relationship to early Indian forms and cannot be later than the sixth or seventh century A.D. The other scenes represented were most lively figures of elephants with riders, men on galloping horses, and men walking in procession, all apparently in a proto-Khmer style. I think that we can safely say that here are the earliest Buddhist sculptures so far discovered in ancient Chen-la.

According to Parmentier the architecture of this first early period of Khmer art, from the fifth to the eighth century A.D., is a reproduction in brick of the original timber structures introduced into Funan by Indianised colonists. He draws this conclusion from the fact that none of the very early buildings have survived. All the indications at present show that the Brahmanic architecture of this early period was due to Pallavā influences. Curved roofs were employed as shown in the bas-reliefs on *ratha* at Mamallapuram. Decorative motives, such as the head of a monster flanked by *makaras*, heads in arched niches without pillars, and panels with standing figures either with or without niches, are all common to early Cambodia and the Pallavā State as well as to Java.

The sculpture of this early Khmer period still maintains the style of Funan and remains true to its Indian prototypes; but with the rise of the Khmer comes also the rise of the cult of the Buddha seated on the Naga.

Such a figure is referred to in the Chinese annals of the Liang dynasty as having been promised to the emperor by the king of Funan at the end of the fifth century, but so far no definite Funan images of this nature have been found. But the Khmer kings always trace their origin from the union of Kaundinya (which one is unspecified) with a daughter of the Naga king of the name of *Soma* (that is, 'the Moon'), and this legend brings us straight back to the Pallavā of Kānchipuram. A Pallavā inscription of the ninth century says that Açvatthaman married a Naga princess and that their offspring was Skandaçisya, who was the ancestor of the Pallavā kings; and another inscription says that Virukarcha married a Naga princess and obtained from her the insignia of royalty. There seems little doubt, therefore, that the early Khmer kings had a strong connexion with the Pallavā.

Stone inscriptions of the seventh century are relatively common. They are phrased in good Sanskrit and engraved in beautiful characters finer than those found in India itself; but those of the eighth century A.D. are few and far between, and history is more or less a blank until the coming of Jayavarman II in A.D. 802. This monarch, who reigned for nearly fifty years, established full control over the whole country, but the question of where he came from is still not definitely settled. An inscription says that he came from Java to reign in Indrapura, but afterwards founded Hariharalaya as his capital, now identified with Prah-khan in the vicinity of Angkor-Thom. He also founded two other cities, Amarendrapura (Banteai-chmar in the extreme west) and Mahendra Parvata (Beng-Meala, east of Angkor). From another inscription it seems probable that Jayavarman II was not directly related to the previous royal family of Cambodia as it says that 'he had no connexion with the soil but rose like a fresh lotus;' but whether he belonged to the Sailendra family or was an exiled Khmer prince returning to his native land, it is clear that he was inspired by the great period of temple-building in Java. And from this time dates what Parmentier calls the classic style of Khmer art, which produced some of the greatest works of man known to us today.

Before I leave Indo-China I must devote a few words to the kingdom of Champa, or Linyi as it is called by the Chinese. Aymonier says that 'Champa was well known as a name in Ancient India as the capital of the Anga kingdom now called Champa-Nagar near Bhagalpur in Bengal.' This place is not mentioned in the TIMES ATLAS and the only Champa in India proper is in the Central Provinces, due east of Bilaspur and north-east of Raipur. Champa, however, is a thoroughly Indian

name and it is clear from the buildings, statuary, and inscriptions found
in that ancient State (now occupied by Southern Annam) that the early
civilization flourishing there was due to strong influences from India.
The architecture still standing consists chiefly of isolated sanctuary-
towers akin to those found in Cambodia but rather cruder in execution,
while the Brahmanic statuary is also akin to Khmer, but the treatment
is usually, if anything, rather more vehement in character.

I must now turn to the Dutch East Indies. In Java and Bali the early
period of Indian relationship, though clear in general outline, is unfortunately just as obscure in detail as it is with the other lands already
discussed. Vogel says that in the whole literature of ancient India, both
Sanskrit and Pali, he has found only one mention of Java, which occurs
in the fourth Canto of the Ramayana. Yet that word 'Ramayana' alone
recalls the immense debt due to India by all the lands of Indonesia,
when we remember that it forms the basis of the still ever popular
shadow-plays in those countries as well as of the whole realm of ballet.
Nor does the epigraphy of India throw any light upon the contacts
made between India and the Malay archipelago. Our earliest informa-
tion comes from the rather wistful record of the Chinese Buddhist
pilgrim Fa Hsien, whose homeward-bound vessel in A.D. 414 took
refuge from a storm in a country which he calls Ye-po-ti. It is clear from
the context that this must relate either to Sumatra or to Java, and the
pilgrim laments that 'In this country heretics and Brahmans flourish
but the law of Buddha is not much known.'

Thus it appears that at this date, about A.D. 400, Indian civilization
and Brahmanism had already firmly implanted itself in the Malay
Archipelago. This fact is corroborated by inscriptions found very far
apart, first of all, oddly enough, on the east coast of Borneo in the
province of Kutei by one which tells of a State ruled over by Indian or
Indianized princes whose titles end in Varman, such as Asva-Varman,
and record in pure Sanskrit Brahmanical sacrifices offered by priests:
and, secondly, in Java, not far from Batavia, by four rock inscriptions
relating to a king named Purnavarman who ruled over the town of
Tarüma. These inscriptions can be dated in the early or middle fifth
century A.D. and are all in a South Indian character, almost identical
with the Grantha alphabet used at the time of the Pallavā dynasty, which
ruled in Southern India from A.D. 300 to 800. The earliest *dated* Brahmanic
inscriptions found in Java are much later, namely (1) at Changal of the
year A.D. 732 which describes the consecration of a *linga* by King
Sangaya of Central Java whose ancestors came from Kunjara-Kunja-

desa in Southern India; and (2) at Dinaya of the year A.D. 760, which describes the erection of an image of Agastya. In these Brahmanic inscriptions the Çaka era is used dating from A.D. 78 which is essentially a Southern Indian reckoning. The northern Vikrama era is unknown in Java.

Later on we have the testimony of I-Ching, another Chinese Buddhist pilgrim, who, during the course of a voyage to India in A.D. 671, stayed at a place he called Fo-che (now identified as Palembang, the capital of Çrivijaya in Sumatra) for six months, to acquaint himself with Sanskrit grammar. He says he found Buddhism in a flourishing condition, and the mention of Sanskrit seems to indicate that the Buddhism he found there was of the Mahayana school unless, indeed, the monks belonged to the Mulasarvastavadin sect who, although Hinayana Buddhists, had their canon in Sanskrit.

This mention of Mahayana Buddhism brings me back to the kingdom of Çrivijaya, a kingdom I may well call 'discovered' by Coedès in his essay published in 1918. By the evidence there adduced Coedès endeavoured to trace the role played in Indonesia by this Indianized kingdom, whose influence in the seventh century A.D. extended from Palembang far up both sides of the Malay Peninsula and later also over a large part of Java. From whatever part of India the influence came originally, at the end of the eighth century A.D. Çrivijaya was devoted almost solely to the practice of the Mahayana form of Buddhism, and was ruled over by a dynasty known under the name of Sailendra, though whether this dynasty had obtained its position by conquest over the former dynasty or not is still not clear.

The earliest inscription dates from A.D. 686 and was found in the island of Banka just off the east coast of Sumatra, and the two earliest found in Java are dated A.D. 778 and 782 respectively. The first of the two latter found at Kalasan records the dedication of a temple there to the goddess Tara, while the second records the consecration at Kelurak of an image of the Bodhisattva, Manjusri.

Vogel says 'epigraphical records scattered from the Coromandel coast to the heart of Java bear testimony to the zeal of the Sailendras in promoting the Good Law and raising magnificent monuments for the worship of Buddha and the Bodhisattvas.'

Everyone knows how magnificent these monuments were, from the wonder-temple of Borobodur, the only *stupa* to be found in Java (though an entirely different type of *stupa* is found in Sumatra), to its satellites, Chandi-Mendoet, Chandi-Pawon, and Chandi-Banon, as well as Chandi-Kalasan, to mention but a few of those still standing. All these may be ascribed to the eighth and ninth centuries A.D., when the Sailendra influence was most powerful in Java.

From an earlier period date those five groups of temples on the Dieng plateau, 6,500 feet above the sea, all of which are dedicated to the Brahman religion and especially to the cult of Çiva. Throughout the Indian period of Javanese history this cult prevailed in the island side by side with Mahayana Buddhism. Vogel considers that, although the Dravidian style of architecture in Southern India may show a certain affinity with the early temple style of Java, it should be remembered that the earliest surviving relics of Indo-Javanese architecture are at least three centuries later than the rock inscriptions of Western Java already mentioned, and that we should look upon the Dieng temples as the outcome of a long period of building activity of which no early specimens exist. All these temples, of which Chandi-Bima is a good example, may be said to be truly Javanese in form.

Finally, there was a complete fusion between the two religions, Brahmanism and Mahayana Buddhism. For instance, charters may be found which begin with praises to the Buddha and to Çiva at one and the same time. The whole pantheon of Çaivism became an emanation of Dhyani, or heavenly Buddhas, and monuments to Çiva were built in such a manner that they were later mistaken for Buddhist monuments.

In the island of Bali the indigenous race was addicted to ancestor-worship and the cultivation of magical practices until the coming at a still unspecified date of settlers from India, who apparently, as in Java, also practised the Çiva form of Brahmanism. By reason of their superior civilization these settlers gradually acquired ruling rights over different parts of the island, but they were careful not to interfere too much with the communal life of the village which still retained its ancient usages. Even today the three higher castes of the Hindus (for Bali has always remained Hindu) constitute only 7 per cent out of a population of over a million. The remainder call themselves 'Sudras' or servants. Very few artistic remains of the period anterior to the tenth century have been found in Bali and those surviving are closely bound up with the Indianized art of Java.

We have now reached the end of the round of visits paid to all those countries of South-Eastern Asia which derived their religion and culture from India during the first millennium of the Christian era, and it remains to sum up the evidence that we have been able to adduce. The con-

clusions reached from the evidence may be reasonably set down as
follows:

1. I see no reason to doubt the truth of the story that the first
Buddhist missionaries were sent out of India by the Mauryan Emperor
Açoka in the third century B.C. They founded the Buddhist religion in
Ceylon, and others were sent to the 'Land of Gold' which is probably
to be identified as the west part of Indonesia. No relics or traces of this
period have been found there as yet.

2. A centre for the dissemination of Hinayana Buddhism arose at
Amarāvatī on the Kistna river in the second and third centuries A.D.
The influence of this school was felt architecturally in Ceylon and in
lower Central Siam, and possibly reached as far as Sumatra in the south.
At the same time a wave of Brahmanism swept across the sea to the
Malay Peninsula, became established in Sumatra, Java and Borneo, and
reached as far as Funan and thence its vassal state (name unknown) in
the heart of Siam. The origin of this wave is not yet definitely settled,
but at present all the indications point to the kingdom of the Pallavās in
South-Eastern India which rose to power at the end of the third
century A.D.

3. In the fifth century A.D. an important school of Hinayana Buddhism
became established at Kānchipuram (Conjeeveram) on the Madras
coast, the Pallavā capital, and this period also witnessed the golden age
of Gupta Buddhist art in the north. Burma was strongly affected by
both these Buddhist centres, while the Gupta influence penetrated the
Malay Peninsula, Siam and through Siam, the ancient Funan. Throughout this period the Brahmanic wave continued and while weakening or
perhaps never very widespread in Burma or Siam, flourished in Sumatra,
Java and Cambodia.

4. The seventh to the tenth century A.D. witnessed the gradual decay
of the Brahmanic faith and the rise of Buddhism in most countries of
Indonesia. In Burma the Pyu and the Môn were always Hinayana
Buddhist and in the eleventh century A.D. the first Burmese kings out-
shone both in their devotion to that faith. In Siam the Môn again were
always Hinayana Buddhists, and, though the Khmer brought the
Brahmanic faith with them when they invaded the country, the people
at heart remained Buddhist, so much so that the Tai, or Siamese, who
came after them accepted that religion as their own. In the Malay
Peninsula, too, Brahmanism decayed with the rise of the kingdom of
Çrivijaya in Sumatra in the seventh century A.D., and under the Sailendra
kings the Mahayana Buddhist faith flourished exceedingly right up to

the twelfth century. The eighth and ninth centuries A.D. in Java, when the Sailendras were at the summit of their power, witnessed an out-pouring of splendid architecture in stone dedicated to that form of the Buddhist faith. The early art of Çrivijaya seems to have been derived from the Pallavā kingdom, but the later Sailendra certainly owes much to the early period of the Pāla kingdom of Bihar and Bengal, and Javanese art would appear to be a synthesis of Pallavā, Pāla, and indigenous influences. In French Indo-China during the period of Funan and the early centuries of Khmer rule Brahmanism was the predominant faith, though Jayavarman II (A.D. 802–49) is thought to have been a Buddhist of the Mahayana school in his early years, as many of his foundations were dedicated to Lokeçvara. This would not be at all surprising if he came from Central Java, as supposed, but as he also introduced the cult of Deva-raja, he probably subscribed to both religions. It is not until the middle of the tenth century A.D. that we find in Khmerland an inscription wholly devoted to the Buddhist faith (of the Mahayana school). From that time the two religions seem to have existed peace-fully side by side until the end of the Khmer empire in the fifteenth century A.D.

5. Finally, the last phase of Indian art to influence Indonesia is to be found in the later productions of the Pāla kingdom in the eleventh century A.D., when the early Burmese kings of Pagān opened up intimate relations with Bodhgaya and Nalandā, and introduced an entirely new form of Buddha image (i.e. new to Burma) of the Hinayana school. This form eventually found its way into the north of Siam and became the base of the Siamese national school, though this was much influenced at a later date by new forms of the Buddha image from Ceylon.

CHAPTER III

BURMA

I N spite of the efforts of Duroiselle, the late Director of Archaeology, very little has been accomplished in the field of archaeological research. In his HISTORY OF BURMA, while acknowledging his indebtedness to the help of the former, Harvey has very little to say of the early history of the country.

According to Harvey, as I stated in my general survey, the decisive factor for Burma was the rise in the fifth century A.D. of the great Hinayana Buddhist centre at Conjeeveram (the ancient Kānchipuram) near Madras under the commentator Dhammapāla.

Now I would ask you to look at the map. The land of Burma, including the Shan states, lies between longitude 10° and 28° N. and latitude 92° and 100° E. Its total length, from Victoria Point in the Malay Peninsula to the border of China, is 1,300 miles and its greatest width is 575 miles, which makes it two-thirds the length of India itself and one-third of its width from Karachi to the eastern border of Assam. Such a vast territory naturally contains a great variety of climate, scenery and races, but on the whole it has a considerable similarity to the adjoining country of Siam. That is to say, the north, east and south are mountainous regions, while the centre is occupied by an alluvial plain watered by its great rivers, the Irawadi (with its important tributary, the Chindwin) and the Salwīn. On the south-west we find the sea, while the west and north-west border on Assam, from which they are separated by a long mountain range, so high as to form a very serious land barrier between India and Burma, as the Japanese found to their cost in the late war.

In the far north are found the Naga tribes, whose predilection for human sacrifice has occasioned expeditions to stamp out this primeval practice, as well as the Kachins and the Karens and other numerous tribes, while the Shan states are naturally occupied by Shans (i.e. Tai of the same race as the Siamese), and Toungsus.

The heart of Burma is now the home of the Burmese, a Tibeto-

Burman race, who have more or less absorbed the earlier races that flourished there. But the Burmese assumption of sovereignty over Burma did not take place until the middle of the eleventh century, at almost exactly the same time as the Norman conquest of England, and it is with the earlier races living in Burma that we must deal first in considering the influences of Indian culture brought to bear upon that country. To be precise, these races were the Pyu, now extinct as an entity, and the Môn who still survive but in inconsiderable numbers, though it may be stated in passing that there is a modern movement to revive their language and literature. The Pyu are said to come from a Tibetan stock which would ally them with the Burmese and account for their later absorption by that race; while the Môn, who are now called Talaing in Burma itself, are thought to have come originally from Telingana on the east coast of India.

From the fifth century onwards we find the Pyu established in Central Burma with their capital at Old Prome (Hmawza) on the Irawadi (lat. 18.75° N., long. 95.25° E.) and the Môn in possession of Lower Burma, but split up into two kingdoms, the one centred at Thatôn just north of Moulmein, and the other at Pegu. After the fall of Thatôn and its eclipse as a religious centre in the eleventh century Pegu became the principal centre of Môn influence.

If we consider the Pyu first, the bulk of the population were peasants living in villages and then, as now, their chief crop was rice. Their standard of culture may not have been very high, as Harvey suggests, but from his own description of Hmawza it is clear that the ruling caste, which was probably Indian or semi-Indian in origin, had more than primitive conceptions of town-building.

From his account, it is the most extensive site in Burma, and the existing remains of the massive wall, more than eight miles in circumference, show that, where seven or eight villages now stand, there was once a great and powerful city. This is borne out by the chronicles of the Tang Dynasty of China (A.D. 606–918) which describe Burma as containing eighteen States and nine walled towns, all dependent on the Pyu, and also give a graphic picture of the town of Old Prome and its inhabitants.

When the Pyu king goes out in his palanquin, he lies on a couch of golden cord. For long distances he rides on an elephant. He has several hundred women to wait on him. The wall of his city, built of greenish glazed tiles, is 160 *li* in circumference, with twelve gates and pagodas at each of the four corners. They know how to make astronomical calculations. They are Buddhists and have a hundred monasteries, with bricks of glass, embellished with gold and silver. The floor is painted and covered with ornamental carpets. The King's palace is in the same style. For clothes they wear skirts made of cotton, for they hold that silk should not be worn as it involves the taking of life. On the head they wear gold flowered hats with a blue net or bag set in pearls. There is a huge white elephant image 100 ft. high. Litigants burn incense and kneel before this elephant and reflect within themselves whether they be right or wrong. When there is any disaster or plague, the King kneels down before the elephant and blames himself. The land is suited to pulse, rice, and millet-like grains. Sugar-cane grows as thick as a man's leg. There is no hemp or wheat. Gold and silver are used as money, the shape of which is crescent-like. Having no oil, they use wax and various scents for lighting. The women knot their hair on the top of their heads and ornament it with strings of pearls.

The picture drawn gives us a very clear idea of a small eastern kingdom where the people were mainly peasants, engaged in agriculture, and the royalty kept up a rather imposing state, while the priesthood occupied a key position among them.

Harvey, speaking of their burial customs, says that the writing on large urns, for the ashes of the dead, indicates at Old Prome in the early eighth century, the existence of a dynasty named Vikrama who were probably chiefs of Indian blood.

The Pyu kingdom was in close touch with the Tai kingdom of Nanchao in Southern China, and in A.D. 801 a Pyu deputation accompanied a mission from Nanchao to the imperial court of China, where they gave a performance of dancing and singing. Earlier still, in A.D. 754, the prince of Nanchao is said to have conquered Upper Burma and later to have styled himself 'Lord of the Pyu,' but it is very doubtful if he ever reached as far south as Old Prome.

One of the earliest finds, at a place called Maunggan near Hmawza, consisted, inter alia, of gold plates, containing Buddhist texts in Pali, the script of which, Professor Finot says, is like the Kadamba script of Southern India of the fifth century A.D. He cannot place them later than the sixth or seventh century A.D. From this and other finds, it seems clear that the Pyu were already practising the Hinayana canon of Buddhism by the sixth century A.D., in which case, this type of Buddhism was probably brought to Burma from Conjeeveram in Southern India. We cannot as yet go back further than the fifth century as far as Burma is concerned, but even if Açoka's missionaries in the third century B.C. found but little response to their call to the faith, I feel reasonably certain that Buddhism, and possibly Brahmanism too, had taken a hold in Burma long before the fifth century A.D. Archaeological research is still in its infancy there, and we must await the further discoveries of the excavator before we can add to our knowledge of its earliest history.

Short inscriptions in the Pyu language have been discovered and partially translated by Blagden and others, but are still not entirely decipherable. There is a beautiful stone extant from Hmawza, showing the Buddha and two worshippers, while below is an interlined inscription in (a) Pyu, and (b) an unknown language, possibly Sanskrit, in an ancient script (Fig. 1).

Of the type of man personified by the Pyu, nothing whatever was known until 1929, when a very important stela (Fig. 2) was unearthed at Halingyi in the Shwebo district, north of Mandalay (lat. 22.5° N., long. 95.75° E.)—as important a find, as Duroiselle says in his annual report, as anything discovered in Burma hitherto. The top half of the stela is broken off and only the right leg and hand of a seated person remain, but underneath this is an inscription in Pyu (almost but not quite effaced by the sharpening of their knives by cultivators) and below this again is a group of people in rows in the attitude of devotion (namaskāra mudra). Those on the right side wear crown-like head-dresses, while those on the left have their hair done in a knot with turbans round it. As the inscription is in Pyu, it may be accepted that the people portrayed are of the Pyu race, while the person seated above is obviously either the king or the Buddha, from the attitude of the attendant devotees.

The faces depicted are certainly not Burmese nor yet entirely Môn, though they bear a resemblance to those seen in Fig. 27 of my BUDDHIST ART IN SIAM. There is also a certain resemblance between both these figures and those seen on the bas-reliefs at Bharhut in India, but I do not wish to carry this analogy very far, as the length of time between them (about eight centuries) is too long to be of any great value.

This stela is unique in its depicting of the Pyu, but perhaps the most important find in Burma was made in 1926 when Duroiselle laid bare the relic-chamber of what is known as Khin Ba's mound at Hmawza. Here was, indeed, a rich discovery, and the objects found were all intact as they were reverently laid twelve hundred years ago. Two gold images of the Buddha (Fig. 3), a round silver-gilt casket in the form of a *stupa* (Fig. 4), and another square silver casket (Fig. 5), both with figures in relief and inscriptions in Pyu, two silver guardians (*Dvarapala*) (Fig. 6), as well as a number of gold-leaf manuscripts, with Buddhist texts, were all unearthed, and provide us with definite evidence of the type of Buddhist art in vogue in old Prome in the seventh and eighth centuries A.D., and of the degree of skill which went to its execution.

The large round silver relic casket, 26 inches high, shows four seated Buddhas in high relief, each with an attendant monk. The lid, which is removable, has a line of inscription round the rim in (*a*) Pyu, and (*b*) Pali in an early Telegu-Canarese script of Southern India, closely allied to the Kadambas of Vanavasi and the Pallavās of Kanchi, and is practically the same script as that seen on the plates from Maunggan already described. On the lower rim of the casket is another line of inscription, also in Pyu, and two names are mentioned in it, both ending in Varman. The figures of the Buddha are of the Hinayana school.

In the same year, at the village of Kalagangon near by, were found the remains of a *linga* 14 inches high, showing that Çaivism existed side by side with Buddhism; and in another mound at Hmawza were discovered Bodhisattvas in Pāla style, seated on the lotus throne with the right knee raised and the left leg placed on a level with the throne. These figures are somewhat later in date and are similar to those well-known from Bodhgaya in Bihar of the ninth–tenth century A.D.

Stone statues of the Buddha have also been found, undoubtedly of local make but showing Gupta influence with inscriptions in Pyu and Sanskrit. Such inscriptions, in a Gupta-like script of the seventh or eighth century A.D., might seem to point to the presence at that period of a Mahayana school of Buddhism, but it is possible that they were made by a sect called the Mulasarvastavadin who, although of the Hinayana school, had their canon in Sanskrit. This sect was spread over a vast area of Asia, including Turkestan, China, Indo-China and the East Indian Archipelago.

In addition to such finds of Buddhist objects, Brahmanical images have been discovered over a wide area of Burma, including Viṣṇu, Ganesa and Brahma at Hmawza; Vishu, Garuda and Hanuman at Mergui; and Surya, Durga and Viṣṇu in Arakan, as well as symbolical coins and terra-cotta tablets with Brahmanical objects upon them. It seems clear, then, that from the fifth to the eighth or ninth century A.D. all three types of religion were being practised in Burma, and, if one may hazard a guess, I should conjecture that the ordinary peasant folk were Hinayana Buddhists, as they are today, and that the ruling caste tolerated both Buddhism and Brahmanism alike, while small colonies of Mahayana Buddhists and Hindus existed peacefully by their side.

It is interesting to note that in India the old kingdom of the Pyu was called Çri-ksetra, which is the sacred name of the famous pilgrimage city of Puri on the Bay of Bengal.

When we come to consider the early history of the Môn or Talaing in Burma, we have even less material to build on than we have with the Pyu. Their chief centre was at Thatôn in Southern Burma, while another later centre was established at Pegu sometime after the sixth century A.D.

Thatôn was at one time evidently a seaport, as bolts, cables and other parts of foreign ships have been unearthed there, but even in the time of Anawrahta in the eleventh century A.D. she was doubtless ceasing to be a port owing to the silting up of the coast-line, and Martaban took its place early in the second millennium of our era. On the other hand Pegu, which the oldest tradition refers to as an island in a shallow sea, continued to be a seaport until about A.D. 1600, but is now far up the Pegu river and quite useless for that purpose. Its place has been naturally taken by Rangoon which was in early days also peopled by the Môn. The old Indian name for Pegu was Ussa, derived from Orissa.

Neither Thatôn nor Pegu has been systematically excavated. In fact, Sir George Scott told Prince Damrong, the venerable statesman and historian of Siam who died during the last war, that there were no signs of any extensive pagodas at Thatôn—a statement which led Prince Damrong to believe that the city conquered by Anawrahta in A.D. 1056 was not Thatôn at all but Prapatom in South-Central Siam.

In recent years the Archaeological Survey has visited the Tizaung Pagoda at Zokthok, a small village 28 miles from Thatôn by rail and thence 6 miles by road. It is a conical *stupa* with eight sides built on the remains of an older foundation. The solid base, 11 feet high, is built of laterite, resting on a plinth of laterite 3 feet high. There are four broad flights of steps, each facing a cardinal point, leading up to the summit. It is considered to be earlier than the eleventh century A.D., as laterite is unknown at Pagán.

I may mention in passing that a very similar laterite *stupa*, resting on an octagonal base, and with four flights of steps, is known at Sawan-k'alōk in central Siam. This is thought to be due to Môn influence and to date from the fourteenth century A.D. (Fig. 97 in BUDDHIST ART IN SIAM). These *stupas* of an octagonal form are found in different parts of

D

Southern Burma, the most beautiful being the well-known *Sule* Pagoda at Rangoon, and this form will be found later at Pagān.

The ancient name for the Môn kingdom of Thatôn was Rahman-nadeça or more popularly Rahman, and we really know more of this kingdom, little as it is, from discoveries made in Siam. The oldest inscription in Môn is on a pillar found at Lopburi in Central Siam and now in the Siamese National Museum, and Harvey says that the script is based on a Pallavā script of the fifth century.

Other fragments of inscriptions have been found, all of which point to a Southern Indian origin for the script, but, in spite of the researches of Blagden, Duroiselle and Halliday, our knowledge of early Môn history and language is still at a rudimentary stage. We do know, how-ever, that the people were Buddhist of the Hinayana school from early times, since in the eighth century A.D. the daughter of the Môn king of Lopburi, who was married to the king of Rahman, left her husband to proceed on a missionizing journey to Lamp'ūn in the north of Siam and founded a Môn Buddhist kingdom there, which lasted to the end of the thirteenth century.

Bronze Buddhas in the Gupta style have been found at Thatôn (Fig. 7), and there is a most interesting plaque of hard clay from the Pegu district showing musicians with a drunken dancer (Fig. 8). The style, dress and features are pure Indian. There is also a terra-cotta plaque, in an unusual style, of the Buddha with disciples from a temple in the Thatôn district. This, literally, is all I have seen of the early Môn period in Burma.

It is only when we come to the founding of Pagān and to the era of the great temple-builders that we begin to tread on firmer ground and can talk with any confidence of the history of Burma.

Not long after A.D. 800 the old kingdom of Prome began to break up owing to internal dissensions, and from that time we can date the gradual rise of Pagān to pre-eminence. Pagān itself was originally a cluster of eighteen villages near the confluence of the Irawadi and Chindwin rivers and, though now in the dry zone, was formerly fertile, since medieval inscriptions dedicate extensive rice-fields in Pagān where now no rice will grow.

An early chief of Pagān, Popa Sawrahan (A.D. 613–40), is said to be the inventor of the Burmese era beginning in March 638, which era, known as 'The Little Era,' was introduced into Siam and was still in official use as late as 1889.

Tradition also states that another prince of Pagān, Nyaung-U

(A.D. 913–64) sent to Thatôn and Prome for plans of temples, and eventually erected five temples at or near Pagān, but none of these have yet been identified. Pagān was naturally in early days a backward hinterland, but according to Harvey, Indian influences had begun to come into Central Burma not only via the coast of Arakan, as witness the Mahamuni shrine near Akyab, but also overland via Assam, bringing with them Mahayana Buddhism as early as the fifth century, as witness the lower structure of the cave-temple Kyaukku Onhmin with its great stone vault near Pagān. It is built against the precipitous side of a deep ravine, and the lower part undoubtedly dates from before the time of the Pagān kings. The two upper storeys were added by Narapatisithu, king of Pagān in 1188, but Forchhammer believed the lower structure to be similar to the Mahamuni shrine in Arakan, and to have been devoted to the Mahayana form of Buddhism.

As brought into Burma this form was of a very low order, and the *Ari* cult which held sway in Upper Burma till the eleventh century was a distinct development of Tibetan Buddhism. The *Ari* were centred at Thamahti village, a few miles south-east of Pagān and fostered a Nāga worship in which Buddha and his Çakti wives figured. The *Ari* were bearded, grew their hair four fingers long, wore robes dyed blue-black, rode horses, boxed, went into battle, drank liquor, and last, but not least, practised *le droit de Seigneur*. They had books of magic and a Mahayana canon of the scriptures in Sanskrit. It is known that Nyaung-U, who for some reason or other was called 'The Cucumber King,' followed the *Ari* teachers and set up a figure of the Nāga king instead of an image of the Buddha.

Pagān itself first became of importance as a city when its chief, Pyinbya, enclosed it with a wall in A.D. 849, of which the remains still exist at the Sarabha gate, but it does not take on the pre-eminence that it was to hold during the following 250 years until the advent of the famous king, Anawratha, in 1044. Up to this time, then, we find a very debased form of Mahayana Buddhism in Upper Burma, while in Lower Burma, in the Pyu kingdom of Prome and the Môn kingdoms of Thatôn and Pegu, the Hinayana canon flourishes, with Brahmanism of both schools living peacefully beside it, and a possible outcrop of Mahayana Buddhism at varying periods.

A brief mention must be made of another mysterious centre of Indian culture in Burma at Tagaung (the Drum Ferry) on the Irawadi just north of the Mogōk ruby-mine district. A German archaeologist, Führer, stated in 1894 that he had found there a stone slab dated A.D. 416, with a Sanskrit inscription relating how Tagaung was founded by immigrant princes from old Delhi. This was accepted in some places at the time, but the stone has never been produced and, in view of Führer's subsequent unenviable record, this evidence must be rejected now. Professor Luce states that the earliest dated inscription from Tagaung is of the year 1354, but he adds that the city was probably founded by Anawrahta, since clay tablets with Pali and Sanskrit inscriptions have been found there in some numbers with his name upon them. Anything earlier about Tagaung is at the moment gravely suspect.

King Anawrahta was the son of a pretender who had overthrown Nyaung-U. This pretender had himself been forced to retire to a monastery by Nyaung-U's two sons, and it is not until 1044 that Anawrahta, by slaying the surviving son in single combat, regained the throne which his father had won and lost again.

Sometime after his accession Anawrahta came into contact with a young Môn priest from Thatôn named Shin Arahan, who was visiting Pagán and belonged to the Theravāda, or primitive, school of Hinayana Buddhism, and was much impressed by his teaching. Professor Stewart is of the opinion that this form of Thatôn Buddhism came from Ceylon. In 1056 Anawrahta sent a courteous request to the Môn king of Thatôn for a supply of priests and scriptures to teach his people this form of Buddhism. His request was refused with contumely and, enraged at the insult, in the following year the king gathered an army together, attacked Thatôn, seized the king and carried him off to Pagán with all his priests and scriptures, the latter laden on thirty-two white elephants.

After he had captured Thatôn, Anawrahta proceeded to raze the walls of Old Prome as well; and finally stripped the temples there of their relics, which he took to Pagán to enshrine in *stupas* and temples of his own building.

Thatôn itself never recovered from this attack and its prosperity vanished; the centre of Môn culture was transferred to Pegu.

The results of the capture of Thatôn were of prime importance for religion and art in Burma. First, Hinayana Buddhism succeeded the Mahayana as the principal form of Buddhism in Upper Burma, and Pali superseded Sanskrit as the language of the scriptures. There is ground for believing that Anawrahta sent to Ceylon for scriptures and compared them with those of Thatôn. Secondly, the Burmese adopted the Môn alphabet and wrote their own language for the first time, the earliest Burmese inscription known being dated 1058. Thirdly, there was a great influx of craftsmen from Thatôn into Pagán, and Anawrahta inaugurated the great era of temple-building which lasted for more than two centuries.

At this period the kingdom of Burma was enclosed within an area 200 miles long from north to south and about 80 miles broad from east to west. The northern boundary ran with Nanchao, to the east were a host of small Tai principalities, on the west were the Arakanese, while on the south were the Môn of Pegu. Anawrahta did receive the homage of the nearer Tai chiefs, but this was largely nominal, and he had to establish outposts all along the eastern hills to prevent their raids upon his territory.

Shin Arahan, who was the son of a Thatôn Brahman converted to Buddhism, soon succeeded in driving out the debased *Ari*, and introduced a large number of Buddhist missionaries into Pagān. The *Ari*, however, did not become entirely extinct, and the Nandaminnya chapel built near Pagān as late as 1112 is covered with frescoes which are clearly of *Ari* origin. They are the best of such frescoes in Burma, and the technique is of Nepalese or North Bengal (i.e. Pāla) type.

Manuha, the king of Thatôn, was at first treated by Anawrahta with respect, and tradition says that he was allowed to build the temple of Nanpaya (Fig. 9) at the village of Myinkaba two miles south of Pagān, which he paid for by selling his great jewelled ring. This temple is one of the very few built of stone, and contains some interesting bas-reliefs among which, oddly enough, Brahmanical deities are prominent (Fig. 10).

This led Harvey to conclude that the Thatôn form of Buddhism was largely Hindu in spirit, but doubts are now being thrown upon the ascription of this temple to Manuha, and the latest researches are inclined to place the erection of this temple at the end of the twelfth century and to class it as Buddhist and not Hindu. It is certainly true that the Buddhists of Siam and Burma often include Brahmanical figures, such as especially Indra, in their fresco scenes.

Bupaya on the river bank is always pointed out as the oldest temple in Pagān, but there is nothing particular about it to show its antiquity, and the only definitely Hindu temple recognizable at Pagān is the Nat Hlaung Gyaung which is built in the form of a sanctuary-tower and is reputed to be of the early tenth century A.D. (Fig. 11). But here again Duroiselle assigns it to a later date, probably late eleventh or early twelfth century A.D., as it is built in the same form as the Bidagat Taik library which was constructed by Anawrahta for the housing of the scriptures from Thatôn. It is dedicated to Viṣṇu and is decorated with ten stone figures of his ten *avatars*, the Buddha being the ninth.

In spite of the mass of religious buildings erected at Pagān—the remains of more than 5,000 *stupas* can still be seen in or near the city covering an area of sixteen square miles—few of them can be ascribed to the hand of Anawrahta himself. Of him it can only be said that he set the movement in train (Figs. 12 and 13).

Quaritch Wales says, 'If surprise is felt that Buddhists should have adopted the Hindu form of building, it must be remembered that we have now arrived at a relatively late period, after the decay of Buddhism in India, when Pallavā and Chola ideas of building construction imported from Southern India had long since reached and been adopted in the delta region of Burma, even by people who professed Buddhism.' As a knowledge of the true arch had also arrived from Northern India, he concludes that the architecture of Pagān represented a synthesis of all these various forms, with perhaps a touch of Chinese influence added.

The latter half of the eleventh century A.D. was witnessing the closing stages of Buddhism in India, and Ceylon was being subjected to attacks as well. It is recorded that the king of Ceylon sent for assistance to the king of Burma against the Cholas of Southern India, and in A.D. 1071 asked for and obtained a deputation of monks and scriptures to strengthen the religion which had fallen on evil times. This shows that Hinayana Buddhism had already taken firm root in Pagān within fifteen years. Large numbers of devout Buddhists, fleeing from persecution in Northern India, migrated to Burma and even to Siam. Many came to Pagān, and it is from this time that we date the intimate connexion which arose between the kings of Burma and the great Buddhist centre of Bodhgaya in Bihar.

Anawrahta's chief monument in Pagān is the Shwezigon temple which he began in A.D. 1059 and which was still unfinished at the time of his death, at the hands of a wild buffalo, in A.D. 1077 This temple, which is a solid *stupa* of the type so common all over Burma, is still immensely popular owing to the fact that it was built to contain exceptionally sacred relics of the Buddha, his collar-bone, his frontlet bone and a tooth, and that it also houses the shrines of all the thirty-seven Nat spirits of Burma. It is related that when Anawrahta was asked why he allowed these barbarous images to be set up in a Buddhist shrine, he replied: 'Men will not come for the sake of the new faith. Let them come for their old gods and gradually they will be won over.'

The site for the temple was chosen by placing the tooth-relic in a jewelled shrine on the back of a white elephant and allowing the animal to roam. The spot where it finally stopped was chosen as the site. Similar instances can be quoted from the north of Siam.

Anawrahta also built the Shwesandaw *stupa* (Fig. 14) south of Pagān for other sacred relics of the Buddha, strands of hair presented by Pegu. This temple obviously shows Môn influence, having an octagonal base and closely resembling that at Zokthok near Thatôn. It is a five-terraced conical structure with a bell-shaped dome and a stone *amalaka* on the summit. Anawrahta also built a number of *stupas* in the district of Meiktila, south-east of Pagān, the other side of Mt. Popa. One of the chief features of his reign, however, was his passion for casting votive tablets. The attitude of the Buddha is the typical one of *bhumisparsa*, or 'earth-touching,' with a Nagari legend in Sanskrit and sometimes with another on the reverse in Pali. One such of the latter reads 'Mould made by King Anawrahta with his own hands in order to obtain final salvation.' Other tablets have inscriptions in Môn and Pyu, but the tablets with the Pali script are the earliest documents in that language so far recovered from Pagān. These votive tablets are found all over Upper Burma.

After a brief reign of Anawrahta's eldest son, who was a worthless creature, another son, Kyanzittha, ascended the throne in A.D. 1084. The latter had already proved his valour on many an occasion, and of him it may be truly said that he set the seal on his and his father's greatness. He was crowned by Shin Arahan who was still the primate. In A.D. 1090 he completed the building of the famous Ananda temple at Pagān (Fig. 15) which may well be called the 'Westminster Abbey' of Burma, and in which his own portrait-image, a kneeling crowned figure (Fig. 16), as well as that of Shin Arahan (Fig. 17), may still be seen. Kyanzittha's features are Indian rather than Burmese as his mother was of Indian birth. His inspiration is said to have come from eight Indian Buddhist monks who gave him glowing accounts of the great cave-temple of Ananta in the Udayagiri hills of Orissa.

Harvey says that the Ananda temple, with its dazzling garb of white and its gilt spire glittering in the morning sun, is today one of the wonders of Pagān. It is the first of the series of temples called 'caves' by the people, since the great weight of the upper storeys could only be supported by filling in the centre of the building with a solid mass of brickwork, leaving narrow galleries between the core and the outer walls.

The plan of the temple is cruciform and it is built of brick and plaster;

while the aisles and recesses, where the sun never penetrates, seem as if they had been hewn out of some deep hillside. A new feature is the curvilinear çikara, faintly resembling the Cambodian type, but ending in the familiar Burmese 'Ti,' the tapering finial which is usually copper-gilt. On the outside of the Ananda temple are fifteen hundred plaques, illustrating the Jataka stories of the Buddha's previous existences, each with an inscription in Pali or Môn; and inside the aisles are eighty niches with sculptures of the Buddha's earthly life. These are by Indian artists and, though the treatment is conventional, the detail is frequently good.

Kyanzittha also completed the Shwezigon temple of his father's time and built many other stupas and temples throughout Upper Burma, but his great claim to fame is that he restored the famous Buddhist temple at Bodhgaya in Bihar.

Two Burmese inscriptions that have been found at Bodhgaya, one of which engraved on a blackish stone is now fixed in the wall of the Mahant's residence, describe how the king of Burma sent first a Guru who was unable to finish the work, and secondly, a prince and a minister who restored the temple in its entirety including the rebuilding of the pinnacle. The work was begun in A.D. 1079 and finished in A.D. 1086, two years after the accession of Kyanzittha. There is today in Pagān a rather poor replica of the Mahabodhi temple at Bodhgaya, but this was built by Htilo-Minlo early in the thirteenth century (Fig. 18).

At the end of the eleventh century the sovereignty of the Pāla kings who had ruled in Bihar and parts of Bengal since about A.D. 750 was drawing to a close, and in the twelfth century they were ousted by the Senas. But the 350 years of their rule had seen the rise and flowering of a prolific Buddhist as well as Brahman art. In the case of Buddhism at the time I speak of, there was a distinct turning away from the Hinayana towards the Mahayana school, if we may judge from the images of the Buddha and Bodhisattvas still extant; in fact Buddhism was permeated with the Tantric view of life.

During the Pāla period, Nalandā in Bihar rose to great fame both as a university and as a mission-training centre, and there is little doubt that many of the Buddhist monk refugees in Burma came from Nalandā. This is apparent from the new type of Buddha image introduced into Burma during the early years of the Pagān period, which is clearly of Pāla origin. At a later date this type was passed on to Northern Siam, but although Mahayanism was in the ascendant in Bihar, Bodhisattvas of Pāla style are comparatively rare in Pagān, while the images of the Buddha himself were accepted eagerly and adopted as the national expression of faith. This is quite understandable as the simple peasants of Burma, having no Brahmanic teaching behind them, showed no interest in the Mahayana form of Buddhism, or any of the Tantric systems of life, but found in the simpler Hinayana form a more suitable vehicle for their devotional religion.

The type of image that found most favour in Pagān is well illustrated by an image from Bodhgaya dated from the tenth century A.D., now in the British Museum (Fig. 19). It is cut out of a black stone called *Kasti Pathar*, quarried in the Rajmahal hills in the Santal Parganas of Bengal. The Buddha is seated with the right hand raised in the attitude of dispelling fear, the left hand lying in the lap. The face is long and oval, with a small sharply-defined mouth and a highly sensitive nose, and the arched eyebrows spring from the bridge in two long upward curves. The eyes are half-closed looking downward. The robe is only lightly defined, leaving the right nipple bare, and one peculiar feature is the short upper fold of cloth which comes down over the left shoulder and ends above the left nipple in a sharp-pointed fork. The hair is composed of pronounced spiral curls, and the *uṣniṣa*, which rises knob-like from the centre of the head, is covered with similar curls. The two other especial features are (1) the throne on which the Buddha is seated is an expanded, stylized, lotus-flower, and (2) the legs are crossed with both soles of the feet uppermost.

Now let us compare this figure with a seated bronze image of the Buddha from Pagān of the eleventh or early twelfth century (Fig. 20). The execution of the figure is local, but the conception and treatment are almost identical with the one from India. The legs are crossed with both soles of the feet uppermost; the *uṣniṣa* is covered with knob-like curls ending in a full lotus-bud; the eyebrows spring from the bridge of the nose in arched curves; the body is smooth and plump above but with a very slender waist; the mouth is small and well defined, and again we see the short fold of the robe falling over the left shoulder and ending in a sharp fork above the nipple. When we look then at the lotus throne, we feel there can be no doubt as to the origin of this type of Buddha image being the sculpture of the Pāla empire of the tenth and eleventh centuries A.D.

There is another type of Buddha image illustrated in the annual report of the Archaeological Survey of India for 1926-27 (Plate 39*c*). It is clearly allied to the one just mentioned but, although it still shows a strong Indian influence, it is fast becoming Burmese. Indeed, the interest of this figure, which is probably of the thirteenth century, is that it is the forerunner of the modern Burmese type of image. The details already indicated are all present, but note that the head is just beginning to droop forward and to sink on to the shoulders, perhaps the most conspicuous feature of the modern Burmese image (Fig. 21).

Kyanzittha died in A.D., 1112 and his grandson, of royal birth, became king under the name of Alaungsithu. But Kyanzittha's only son, a love-child born in exile, set up the most important stone inscription known in Burma at the Myazedi temple south of Pagān. Its importance lies in the fact that it has four faces with the same subject-matter in four different languages, Pali, Môn, Burmese and Pyu, and also fixes the dates of the early Burmese kings which were previously doubtful.

Alaungsithu was a great builder of temples, and his chief claim to fame is that in A.D. 1144 he built the temple of Thatbyinnyu at Pagān, which, according to Harvey, dominates all the others in majesty of line (Fig. 22). It is undoubtedly built after the model of contemporary temples in Northern India: it has five storeys and represents a combination of stupa and vihara. Alaungsithu also built the Shwegu temple near by (Fig. 23), in which he was to die. The three temples, all of brick and stucco, Ananda, Thatbyinnyu and Shwegu, may be called the most distinctive Burmese types. Coomaraswamy says that there is an Indian parallel to them at Mirpur Khās in Sind, where there is a brick stupa not later than A.D. 400 with a deep square base containing within its wall mass three small shrines.

Professor Luce, however, considers that the twelfth century temples of Pagān down to about 1160 are chiefly Môn in type, with Môn writing often on the walls. There is a distinctive cast of feature and colour scheme in the frescoes, and a distinctive shape and design in the building, windows, corridors, and even in the arch itself. When the Burmese influence begins to arise and dominate with the Shwegu and Çulamani temples, all this changes, especially in the thirteenth-century temples of Minnanthu and Pwezaw near Pagān, in which Tantric and other northern influences plainly appear.

I have no doubt that the Môn must have played a great part between A.D. 1050 and 1170 in forming the Burmese taste in the construction of their temples, but I can see nothing peculiarly Môn about the buildings themselves, and I am more inclined to agree with Coomaraswamy.

Quaritch Wales says: 'These temples represent the crystallisation of a truly Burmese national tradition, but in our appreciation of these distinctively Burmese forms, we must judge them by standards fitted to the national culture they represent. Composition on the large scale is absent, incongruously the most diverse types jostle each other at Pagān while in the construction of the unit, a tendency to over-ornamentation and aspiration has already been noted.' Of the Ananda he says, 'Here we have a south Indian temple crowned by a North Indian Çikara and into the composite product has already crept a suspicion of later Burmese developments; and this tendency to produce poor copies of revered Indian buildings lasted even until the thirteenth century.' He adds that the Burmese kings strove to show their zeal for the new-found faith by the erection of buildings compounded of Indian forms whose meaning they imperfectly comprehended. Thus the best art of Pagān cannot bear comparison with classical Indo-Javanese or Khmer art, which are each the expression of a living Indian tradition.

This is a harsh criticism by Wales, and I do not think it right to call the Ananda temple 'a poor copy of a revered Indian building.' At the same time one feels there is something lacking in even the best of these temples, and that the Pagān kings wanted to build something grand and splendid without quite knowing what to build or how to build it.

Harvey is as harsh a critic as Wales: 'To stand in this ancient refuge (i.e. the lower structure of the Kyaukku Ohnmin cave-temple near Pagān) looking up at the great stone vault, is to regret the supersession of North Indian influence with its stone work and orderliness by the Talaing brick and shoddy which swamped Burma after the eleventh century.'

In the same way one may regret the passing of the Khmer dominion over Siam with its stately stone edifices, but all the same there is much of a homely charm about many of the later Burmese and Siamese temples. They breathe a very friendly, almost an intimate air, which I have experienced to the full. That the temples of Pagān are not great architecture must, I think, be admitted; but neither are they just poor copies. They represent a definite striving after something heavenly on the part of a people who have achieved an independent kingdom, but have neither the intuitive feeling for original, great architecture, nor a wide enough education to absorb it fully from outside, as the Gothic architects did in England. But theirs is no mean achievement and, though it is thirty years since I saw the Ananda temple it still remains in my mental vision as a thing of dazzling beauty.

In the latter half of the twelfth century the island of Ceylon, under Parakrama Bahu the Great, witnessed a revival of Hinayana Buddhism and from that time up to the sixteenth century, Ceylon was regarded by its brother Buddhist countries, Siam, Burma, and Cambodia, with almost as much veneration as the holy places of Buddhism in India itself, as the fountain-head of the pure Theravada doctrines.

Burma was the first of the three countries to feel the influence of the new impulse from Ceylon. Panthagu, the primate of Burma, quarrelled with the king of Pagān in A.D. 1167 and retired to Ceylon, but returned to Burma after the king's death in A.D. 1173 and resumed his high office again. He was followed by Uttarajiva who went to Ceylon in 1180 and later became known as the 'first pilgrim to Ceylon.' His companion, Chapata, who was called the 'second pilgrim,' stayed in Ceylon for ten years and, returning in A.D. 1190, brought with him four other monks including Ananda of Conjeeveram and a prince of Cambodia.

All five settled at Nyaung-U near Pagān and built the Chapata temple in the Sinhalese style (Fig. 24). Henceforth, Ceylon Buddhism was the chief influence on the religion in Burma. Chapata indeed set up a schism in the church in opposition to the disciples of Shin Arahan and the Thatôn school (known as the Môn or former order), and his sect became known eventually as the Sinhalese or latter order.

These events took place during the reign of Narapatisithu who was king from A.D. 1173 to 1210, and who built the Gawdawpalin (Fig. 25) (which Harvey calls 'superb') and Çulamani temples at Pagān, as well as the Dhammayazika which contains the first royal inscription in Burmese dating from about 1196 to 1198.

His successor, Htilo Minlo, erected a copy of the Bodh Gaya temple to which I have already referred, and the Sittana *stupa* in the Sinhalese style as well as his own particular temple which he named after himself. This was the last of the series of great temples at Pagān, though smaller ones of merit continued to be built for a generation or more.

Before I close this chapter, however, I must tell of the Mingalazedi *stupa* (Fig. 26) which was finished in 1274 by King Narathihapati, who is known as 'the king who fled from the Chinese.' The temple took six years to build, because, after it was started, a prophetic rumour spread abroad, 'the pagoda is finished and the great country ruined.' This was confirmed by soothsayers who said, 'When this pagoda is finished the Kingdom of Pagān will be shattered into dust.' The king abandoned the work but at the bidding of the primate, who upbraided him, continued it again until it was finished. It is a large *stupa* of the type familiar all over Burma and its execution is rough. But the prophecy was fulfilled. In 1287 Pagān was captured by Kublai Khan's spirited grandson and the whole of Upper Burma passed into the hands of Shan chiefs nominally owing allegiance to the emperor of China. *Sic transit gloria mundi.*

CHAPTER IV

THE MÔN PERIOD IN SIAM

FOR a clear understanding of the racial movements which have given rise to all its various schools of art, we must take a good look at a map of Siam. It will be seen that the country is divided naturally into four parts.

First, there is the north of Siam, which comprises the modern Circle of Bayab—a province larger than Ireland. Secondly, there is Central Siam, which is formed by the valley of the Menam river. Thirdly, there is North-Eastern Siam, which forms a large plateau about 800 feet high; and, fourthly, there is the Siamese portion of the Malay Peninsula. I see it stated continually that Siam is a *small* country. I always know that the writer has never traversed it on foot!

Now, as Siam is 1,200 miles long and 500 miles broad at its greatest width, and is situated in the midst of countries, whose peoples have been drawn from many different races, it follows that these four widely separated divisions have been influenced by varying types of civilization flowing into them, according to the form of culture in which each of the immigrant races was nurtured.

The north of Siam was colonized by the Môn people of Central Siam from the eighth century A.D. onwards, and was also influenced by the Indian culture and religion which penetrated the Shan states and Upper Burma at a later date. Strangely enough, although the home of the Tai (Siamese) race is in Western Yunnan, south of the Yangtsze-Kiang in China, there is little evidence of early cultural Chinese influence (if we except that of language) in the north of Siam. The temple architecture, with its sloping carpet-like roofs, which is such a feature of Siamese cities today, and which may show some Chinese influence, seems to be comparatively late in point of period. Even in the thirteenth century northern temples were still being built in the Burmese style of Pagān.

Central Siam was first of all influenced from the west, namely by the Môn of Lower Burma (and apparently at an even earlier date from Amarāvati in India direct), then from the east by the Khmer of

Cambodia, and lastly by the Tai of the north-central region of Sawank'alōk and Suk'ot'ai.

North-Eastern Siam appears at a very early period to have formed part of the Hinduized kingdom of Funan, a kingdom whose centre was in Cambodia before the rise of the Khmer, or at any rate to have been culturally under its aegis; secondly, to have fallen thoroughly under the sway of the Khmer empire, and finally to have succumbed to the Tai.

Southern Siam, on the other hand, being open to direct immigration, seems to have been directly influenced by India itself perhaps as early as the first century A.D., then by a wave of Pallavā culture from its south-eastern seaboard which resulted in the rise of the Indianized kingdom of Çrivijaya in the sixth or seventh century A.D., and lastly by another wave in the eighth to ninth century A.D. from the central-eastern sea-ports of Kalinga and Bengal. Pure Tai influence does not appear until the close of the thirteenth century, by which time a definite religious influence has been introduced from Ceylon.

If we study the physical map of Siam carefully, it is easy to see how the limits of these movements were determined.

Northern Siam is a combination of mountain, stream and jungle, with valleys between, and the foothills come down as far south as Utaradit (lat. 17½° N., long. 100° E.) before the plains begin. It forms naturally a self-contained unit of territory.

Central Siam comprises the fertile valley of the Menam Chao P'ya and the lower reaches of its tributaries, the Me Ping, the Me Yōm, the Me Wang and the Me Sǎk. It stretches from Utaradit in the north, past Lopburi to Bangkok at the head of the Gulf of Siam, and thence to Petchaburi in the south. On the west it is bounded by the range of hills which divides Siam from Burma, through which an entry is effected by the famous 'Three Pagodas' pass and also by a more northern route via Kawkareik and Myawadi; and on the east it is closed by the dense feverish forest of Dong P'ya Fai ('the Forest of the Lord of Fire') and the walls of the Korāt plateau.

North-Eastern Siam is, like the north, a self-contained unit, with the Menam valley to the west, the Mekōng to the north and east, and the Dang Rek range of hills to the south.

Finally, Southern or Peninsular Siam comprises two-thirds of the length of the Malay Peninsula, and may be said to begin about the region of the now well-known seaside resort Hua-Hin, just north of lat. 12° N., opposite to Mergui on the Burma side.

From this brief geographical survey it will be realized how complicated, and at the same time how interesting is the study of artistic remains found on Siamese soil. One conclusion from the study of the sculpture found is, however, clear and may be stated at once. All the sculptural influence brought to bear upon the peoples inhabiting Siam in historic times has come, either directly or indirectly, from India.

The most ancient objects found in or on Siamese soil came to light in August 1927 at a village called Pong Tük, about ten miles along the road to Kanburi from the station of Ban Pong, where the railway from Bangkok turns south for the peninsula and Penang. Excavations under-taken both in a banana garden and on the land of a villager near by revealed the plinth of a temple sanctuary with the steps leading up to it, and the bases of several other buildings. The temple was just over 80 feet long and 47 feet wide. The material used was mostly laterite, though in some places brick, but except for some fragments of broken pillars and stucco decoration, similar to those found at P'rapatom, no clue has yet been afforded as to the nature of the superstructures. It has been found possible, however, to propose some dates for the period of their use from the objects found in conjunction with the buildings. The earliest of these is, curious to relate, a Graeco-Roman lamp of Pompeian style, in the form of a bird's body with the erect palmette tail and head of Silenus on the cover-flap, possibly left by some unknown Greek or Roman trader as a relic of the days when China and Ta-Tsin, as the Eastern Roman empire was called, first came into contact with each other. Coedès considers the lamp as of Mediterranean make and not an Eastern copy, and places it in the second century A.D.

The next earliest object is undoubtedly a small bronze statue of the Buddha in the Amarāvati style (Fig. 27), not of such fine execution as the similar statue found at Kōrat in North-Eastern Siam and now in the National Museum (Fig. 28), but still of pleasing appearance and showing the so-called Greek influence in the folds of the drapery. These images I believe to be of Indian make, and the last figure may be compared with an equally beautiful and much larger image of the Buddha found as far east as Dong Duang in Annam (Fig. 29). In addition to the lamp and the image from Amarāvati, several bronze images of possibly local make, showing the Gupta style with stiff drapery and conventional treatment of the body, have been brought to light, which cannot be much later than the sixth century A.D. (Fig. 30). As no Khmer or Tai images or objects have been found on the site, it may be concluded that a centre of Buddhist worship existed at Pong Tük from early in the Christian era up to the sixth or seventh century A.D. at least. There is nothing surprising in this, as Pong Tük is on the Meklong river, only one day's journey distant from both the important early centre of P'rapatom to the east and Kanburi to the west. Kanburi itself is an old town on the route to the famous 'Three Pagodas' pass leading to Burma and in particular to the port of Martaban, which at lat. $16\frac{1}{2}°$ N. is in a direct line with the ancient Indian centre of Amarāvati.

As regards its style, the plinth of the sanctuary found in the banana garden is similar to the early type of platform found at Anuradhapura in Ceylon, which, according to Hocart, also owes its earliest Buddhist buildings to the great centre of Amarāvati. So it looks as if Pong Tük and Anuradhapura were subject to a common influence. Votive tablets of the Bodhgayā style, possibly of later origin but undeniably of Indian make, and pottery jars of a type hitherto unknown in Siam also formed part of the spoils of Pong Tük, which may now be seen in the National Museum at Bangkok.

These discoveries and objects indicate clearly that there must have been immigrants from India into Siam at a very early date, possibly even from before the Christian era.

Up to the present no inscriptions of the earliest, or if we may call it so, Amarāvati period have been discovered in Siam, and, apart from the finding of early Indian images, we are left guessing as to the conditions surrounding their arrival. All we can say for certain is that Buddhism of the Amarāvati school had made its way into lower Central Siam from India, probably some time during the first three centuries of the Christian era.

If we are now permitted, however, to pass over a century or two, we come to a period of Buddhist art in Siam which was certainly of local production and for the dating of which there is some archaeological evidence.

From the architectural and sculptural remains that have been brought to light during recent years, it can be said with some confidence that during the second half of the first millennium of the Christian era, and probably for some part of the first half, the dominating people inhabiting Central Siam were of the Môn race, practising the Buddhist religion of the Hinayana school. The sculpture which they have left behind is of a definite style, and is for the most part in a particular material which enables it to be readily recognized. It is entirely of a religious character.

In 1929 Coedès published his work on the early inscriptions of Siam, dealing with those connected with the ancient realms of Dvāravatī, Çrivijaya, and Lavo (Lopburi). He had already published the volume dealing with the later Tai inscriptions (Part I), in 1924. In Part II he summed up all the archaeological evidence available regarding the early history of Siam, and this has been of great value to me in the present work.

In the city of Lopburi, 80 miles due north of Bangkok, which was formerly known as Lavo and is certainly one of the oldest sites in Central Siam, the most ancient monuments standing above ground do not carry us back beyond the Khmer period, that is, before the year A.D. 1000. But in the temple of Mahā-tāt, which is in the heart of the city, and in the surrounding neighbourhood standing images of the Buddha have been discovered which are certainly of neither Khmer nor Tai workmanship and apparently belong to an earlier period of art.

One of these statues (Fig. 31) bears an inscription in Sanskrit, analogous to that seen on the most ancient inscriptions found in Cambodia, which date from a period anterior to the establishment of Angkor as the capital at the beginning of the ninth century A.D. It is 5 feet 3 inches in height. There has also been found at Lopburi an octagonal pillar with a carved cubical capital, which has definitely a Môn inscription of a peculiarly archaic type (Fig. 32). This pillar, which is now in the National Museum, is identical with several others found during the restoration of the famous temple at P'rapatom. In addition to these, there is a Hermit's cave in the Ngu hills near Rajaburi, in which an inscription containing Môn words is to be found.

A cursory examination of these images and sculptures from Lopburi and P'rapatom shows that they must belong to a school distinct both from the classical Khmer and from the Indo-Javanese school of Çrivijaya; and at the same time that they are in no way connected with Tai sculpture.

The chief features of this school of sculpture, as found in Siam, are as follows: the spiral curls of the hair and their abnormal size, the elliptical form of the face, the prominent, bulging upper eyelids, the lightly outlined eyebrows in the form of a swallow springing from the top of the nose-bridge, and the modelling of the torso, where the limbs appear from under the robe like a nude sexless body under a fine diaphanous cloth. The general appearance of these statues is very similar to that of Indian statues of the Gupta period, especially to those from Sarnath and the cave temples of Ajanta, but on the whole those locally made in Siam are more simple and austere in form. In his volume on the National Museum at Bangkok Coedès gives a large number of references in support of this kinship. For my purpose I think it sufficient to show one

E

of these references, namely, the large standing image of the Gupta
period of about the fifth century A.D., now in the British Museum
(Fig. 33). If this is compared in general outline with one of the best
preserved Môn images found at Lopburi, which is now in a niche
adorning the exterior of Wat Benchamabopit in Bangkok, a beautiful
temple built by the late King Chulalongkorn early in this century
(Fig. 34), it will, I think, be conceded that the relationship admits of
no doubt.

The material from which the figures found in Siam are carved is never
sandstone, the medium almost exclusively used during the Khmer
period, but a blackish, hard limestone which is found in the hills
situated to the east of Lopburi and to the south-west of Rajaburi, which
turns slaty-blue with age. This change of colour is one of the best safe-
guards against forgeries or imitations (which at one time were numerous),
nearly all the latter that came under my notice being distinctly blackish
in tone.

None of the statues found in Siam bears a date, but various signs
which they exhibit will allow of them being attributed to an early
period, not far removed from that of their Indian prototypes.

The statues of the Buddha which have been found, chiefly at Lopburi
and P'rapatom but also at Ayudhya and elsewhere in Central Siam, and
which are included under the term given to them of 'pre-Khmer,' may
be divided into two general types:

(A) The Buddha *standing* with his right hand raised, making the
gesture of Dispelling Fear, or occasionally with both hands raised in that
of Instruction or Argumentation. Of statues of this type there are three
in the local museum at Lopburi, four in the Ayudhya museum,
and several others at P'rapatom, besides the colossal figure now in
the Bankgok musuem, of which both forearms are unfortunately
missing.

(B) The Buddha *seated* in the so-called 'European' fashion, either
turning with his two hands the 'Wheel of the Law,' or else raising the
right hand while the left hand rests in the lap. The best specimens known
of this type are the Great Image preserved in the temple at P'rapatom
(Fig. 35) and another formerly in Wat Mahā-Tāt at Ayudhya, but now
resting in a small sanctuary attached to Wat P'ra Meru (also at Ayudhya).
The former was found in a marshy swamp near the town of P'rapatom
and is cut in five sections, which fit into sockets, from a light-coloured
quartz.

The figure with both hands raised is known in Siam as 'the Buddha

Calming the Ocean:' while that with the right hand raised is called 'the Buddha forbidding his relations to dispute.'

The statues of the Buddha sitting in the European fashion (Fig. 36), which is a position very rare if not unknown in Khmer iconography, are a realization in the round of images on early bas-reliefs representing either the first sermon at Sarnath or the Great Miracle of Srāvasti (Fig. 36). Both the statues and the bas-reliefs are akin in style to certain large rectangular votive tablets found at P'rapatom, Rajaburi and in the Malay Peninsula, all of which represent the Great Miracle at Srāvasti, and also to the great rock image of the Hermit's cave in the Ngu hills near Rajaburi. Both types (A) and (B) appear constantly in the Indian statuary of the Gupta period and are also to be seen among the rock sculptures decorating the entrance to the cave temples at Ajanta.

Now the palaeography of the characters in the well-known Buddhist formula YE DHAMMA, etc., inscribed on the votive tablets, as well as that on the rock image of the Hermit's cave, point to a period at least as early as that of the inscribed Buddhas from Lopburi. Also, it is not without interest that the sculptor of the rock image calls himself Samadhi-Gupta.

From the evidence found it is reasonable to conclude that the earliest Buddhist images of pre-Khmer style found in the region of lower Central Siam, round the head of the Gulf of Siam, must date *at the latest* from the sixth and seventh centuries A.D. It is possible, or even probable that the Gupta style of image was *introduced* even as early as the fifth century A.D., and, as the Khmer did not enter upon their rule of this part of the kingdom until the end of the tenth century A.D., this gives us therefore a range of something like five hundred years for this pre-Khmer art. Naturally, Gupta influence had ceased to come into Siam long before the tenth century, but the style may have been continued locally for several centuries after the original inspiration had ceased to influence the art, gradually becoming more and more debased, and I think this degeneration can already be detected from the material at our disposal today.

It was during the seventh and eighth centuries A.D. that the Chinese pilgrims Hsüan-Tsang (or Chuang) and I-Ching, as well as the texts of other writers, make mention in this part of the Indo-Chinese Peninsula, between Çriksetra, the ancient name for Burma (Prome) and Içanapura (Khmer-Land), of the kingdom of T'o-lo-po-ti, a name which Coedès has restored as Dvāravatī. It may be noted that the Rev. E. J. Eitel in CHINESE BUDDHISM restores T'o-lo-po-ti as 'Dvāra-pāti,' i.e. Lord of the Gate. But E. J. Thomas considers that Dvāravatī is the more likely, as this is the name of the chief place of worship of Vishnu in his *avatar* of Krishna in Kathiawar: it is known today under the name of Dwarkā. This name of Dvāravatī is one of those forming part of the official designation of the old capital of Siam, Ayudhya, which was founded as the capital in A.D. 1350 by the prince of U-t'ong. But that city was built on the site of a much older one, and was no doubt the inheritor of a much more ancient capital in the region of Supanburi, where the ancient U-t'ong was situated; and, following the immemorial custom, it had to incorporate in its own name that which preceded it, just as the present capital, Bangkok, in its full title, contains the name of Ayudhya. We are justified then in regarding the statues and inscriptions found in lower Central Siam as the products of a kingdom called Dvāravatī situated between modern Burma and Cambodia. Of this country all that can be said at present is that its predominating people were of the Môn race under the influence of an Indian civilization, that it practised the Buddhist faith and that its sculpture was based on Gupta models. Of its history we know nothing.

The Buddhist statuary of Dvāravatī is very similar to the early sculpture found in Cambodia, of which some magnificent specimens have been recently discovered near Angkor Borei in Southern Cambodia and it is not at all impossible that this style of Buddhist art was brought to ancient Cambodia, or Funan as it then was, through the intermediary of Dvāravatī.

In addition to the evidence already set forth, certain other symbols of the Buddhist Faith belonging to this period have also been discovered, chiefly at P'rapatom; the temple there I will discuss more fully in a moment. These symbols are: (1) the 'Wheel of the Law,' elaborately decorated and supported in some cases by caryatids (an unusual form), and (2) the 'Deer;' both in the same material as the images of the Buddha, namely, a hard bluish limestone. I show examples of both types from specimens in the National Museum (Figs. 37 and 38). It is not to be supposed that these symbols date from a time in the pre-Christian era before images of the Buddha were made and are contemporary with Bharhut and Sanchi in India; but they must, I think, be attributed to a reasonably early date, say the fifth or sixth century A.D. at the latest. They are probably of the same period as, and some of them possibly are prior to, the earliest images of the Dvāravatī period. I see it constantly asserted that these symbols of the Buddha, as well as certain attitudes in which he is depicted, such as 'Turning the Wheel of the Law,' are always to be attributed to the Mahayana school of Buddhism, but a great authority on Buddhism has warned me against the loose acceptance of attachment of styles to one particular form of Buddhism. Fig. 37 is just under 3 feet in height; Fig. 38 is 11 inches high and 16·4 inches long.

There must naturally still be great difficulty in dating these figures, as we do not yet know the precise limits of duration of the Môn kingdom of Dvāravatī. All that can be said at present is that none are earlier than the fifth century A.D. or later than the middle of the tenth century A.D., at the end of which the Khmer took possession of Central Siam.

There are no complete buildings of the Dvāravatī period above ground today in Siam, but I cannot omit a reference to the famous temple at P'rapatom, which stands on one of the most ancient temple sites in this country, if one may judge from the statuary and other ancient material found in its neighbourhood.

The city of P'rapatom lies about thirty miles due west of Bangkok, and is now an important station on the southern railway line. The temple, which is approached from the railway station by an avenue of trees, consists of a vast circular *p'rajedi* or *stupa* with four *vihara* grouped around it, and a terraced platform. Seidenfaden gives the height of the *stupa* as 115 metres (or 374 feet). Thus it is roughly 50 feet higher than the famous Shwe Dagon pagoda in Rangoon whose height is given by Harvey as 325 feet. According to some authorities the original form of the *stupa*, as erected by the Môn, was that of a Sinhalese *dagoba*, which was later transformed by the Khmer into a *sikhara* or Cambodian tower. The ruins of this tower were apparently still standing in the nineteenth century, though completely overgrown with jungle, and in 1860 King Mongkut decided to restore it in the form of a *p'rajedi*, as seen in the illustration shown (Fig. 39). He built four new *vihara* to replace the old ones, as well as the present circular gallery which completely encloses the *stupa*. He also placed models of the original monuments in the enclosed grounds. The entire work was not completed till the end of the reign of King Chulalongkorn, who covered the dome with the orange, glazed Chinese tiles which now add so much to its beauty. The illustration shows the temple as built by King Mongkut but before the glazed tiles were added. The model of the former *sikhara* is seen to the left.

According to the local tradition, two thousand years ago there existed on the site of the present city of P'rapatom a very ancient and flourishing city called Chaisiri or Sirichai, which was visited by Açoka's missionaries, Sona and Uttara. This is not very likely, as the present town is low-lying and the land around it was probably in early days not very fertile, consisting only of salty swamps. There are, however, the ruins of an old fortified city, Kampeng Sen, which is now entirely deserted, lying some few miles to the north-east of P'rapatom on a plateau, and here the débris of ancient *stupa* have been found, as well as Indian symbolic coins similar to those illustrated on Plate I of my COINAGE OF SIAM. But there may well have been a sanctuary at P'rapatom, lying on a kind of island and serving as a beacon for Indian immigrant settlers.

During the course of the restorations carried out in the past fifty years a large number of ancient images and other objects have been brought to light, including burnt-clay tablets bearing the well-known Buddhist *credo*, written in the Pali language and in the Grantha script, statues of the Buddha, of both Môn and Khmer origin, in all stages of repair, some singularly well preserved, others defaced almost beyond recognition, as well as many heads and other objects in stucco, both Buddhist and Brahman, and stone Wheels of the Law. Altogether, P'rapatom has been of extreme value to the archaeologist in piecing together the fragments forming the mosaic of Siam's early civilizations, and there is little doubt that more systematic digging in the neighbourhood would yield important results.

The following examples of the Dvāravatī (or Môn-Indian) school will, it is hoped, give an idea of the various styles and types found in Siam during that long period of five centuries or more.

Fig. 40, a little head of the Buddha (5 inches high without stand), in the rare quartz material, is to me singularly attractive, and has a charm all its own, with its boy-like features and its slightly snub nose. I once tested this head by asking an educated Siamese friend, but one who was not particularly interested in sculpture, whether it reminded him of anybody whom he knew. He said at once: 'No, but it is very like a Môn.' This I have always considered to be a valuable confirmation of the racial type portrayed, coming as it did from an intelligent but disinterested source.

It has been suggested to me that this quartz was probably not carved in the ordinary way with a chisel because of its tendency to chip, but was 'rubbed' with special filing instruments after it had been roughly cut to shape, just as jade is 'rubbed' today after being prepared with ruby dust. Certainly it must have been a very difficult material to handle, and it is not surprising that we find it giving way to a blackish limestone, which is found in the hills of Rajaburi and Kanburi, to the west of P'rapatom.

Next, Fig. 41 shows a large figure of the Buddha, 10 feet high or more, which has been cut in two pieces out of bluish limestone. It is now in the National Museum. Both forearms and hands are missing, but it would appear that they were originally both raised in the attitude of Argumentation. Here we have the thick, heavy, spiral curls covering both the head and the *uṣṇiṣa*, the 'swallow' type of eyebrows in one continuous line, and the body seen, as though sexless, under a thin diaphanous robe, all of which features are so characteristic of the Dvāravatī school. The pedestal is roughly carved, but obviously represents an expanded lotus-flower. There seems little doubt that this style of statue must be ascribed to a Gupta prototype.

Fig. 42, which is 10 inches high, shows a most attractive head of the Dvāravatī school in bluish limestone, the work of a Môn sculptor imbued with Indian feeling. Here the *uṣṇiṣa* is not covered with the spiral curls but rises abruptly from the centre of the head, but otherwise the features are identical with the type described and one sees clearly the fine sensitive nose, which is a marked characteristic of this school, and the fleeting smile which plays upon the lips. It is a face of ageless wisdom, which has known everything, seen everything, suffered everything. This is a masterpiece of modelling, peculiarly 'modern' in its treatment, and is the one which received from my Cambridge landlady what I referred to in Chapter I as the greatest tribute ever paid to a work of art. When one thinks of the relative remoteness in time, place, and culture, I consider this reaction of hers as literally amazing.

Fig. 43 is a mask in stucco, 6 inches high, which is also closely associated with P'rapatom, as these masks have been found there but nowhere else to my knowledge. There is no back to the head, and it was evidently intended to be stuck on to a wall or to a plaque for hanging on the wall. The specimen shown is in unusually good preservation, as the other specimens which I have seen have been badly damaged through falling from their places. All the characteristic features are prominent and we may attribute this type of mask to the sixth or seventh century A.D. It has been cut to shape after being roughly moulded and it is a wonderful piece of modelling. At an exhibition held at the Alpine Club in London in 1944 it was described by the well-known sculptress, Dora Gordine, as the finest object shown. (Frontispiece).

Fig. 44 is a terra-cotta head of Buddha partially damaged, now in the National Museum, which was discovered not long ago at P'rapatom.

It is clearly of the same period and is, like the mask in stucco, the work of a creative genius. It has been declared to be the finest work of art in the Museum, and there is much to be said for the contention.

Fig. 45 is a slab of bluish limestone, about 3 feet in height, including the socket, now in the National Museum, which shows the Buddha seated cross-legged in the attitude of *samadhi* or 'meditation,' under the seven-headed king of the Nagas, and with a small *stupa*-crown model on either side. This is the only instance so far known in the Dvāravatī period of the Buddha sitting under the Naga king, but it is interesting to note that as early as A.D. 484, when Kaundinya Jayavarman, king of Funan, sent Nagasena, the Indian priest, to the emperor of China, he promised, if his request were granted, to send the emperor, among other things, 'an image in gold (sculptured) with the seat of the King of the Dragons.' The features of this image, the spiral curls and the treatment of the robe clearly stamp it as of Môn creation, but I am inclined to agree with Coedès that it is probably 'tardive' or considerably later than the figures already shown. It was found at Prachinburi, about 60 miles east-north-east of Bangkok.

From the artistic point of view, I find the stone sculpture of Dvāravatī, especially the earlier images, entirely satisfying, though possibly to some Western eyes the treatment of the torso may appear too stiff and conventional. What is particularly noticeable in this early sculpture, to my austere taste, is the purity and economy of line, and the absence of all unnecessary decoration: moreover, it breathes the very spirit of Buddhism.

Early bronze figures of the pre-Khmer or Dvāravatī period, are, as a rule, not particularly interesting. Usually they are small and of crude manufacture, but there is one rather larger than usual (16·5 inches high). It is a standing figure with both hands raised in the gesture of Instruction (Fig. 46), but it cannot be said to possess great value as a work of art, and indeed it is clear that the art of creating bronze images was in a very elementary stage during most of this period. The feet are clumsily executed and the hands are enormous in proportion to the other features of the body. This figure always reminds me of some benevolent old country parson giving 'The Blessing.'

This clumsiness of execution raises an interesting point for discussion, namely why a people should be able to produce such astonishingly fine sculpture in a stone as hard as the bluish limestone, or in terra-cotta and stucco, and yet not be able to create anything approaching it in bronze. The same question arises with Khmer sculpture, as will be seen later, though not to the same degree. It may be that the very rarity, and consequent expense, of bronze prevented them from obtaining the same amount of practice in this art, and I am inclined to think that herein lies the probable explanation.

Stone was there ready to hand in many parts of the kingdom, to be had for the quarrying, but although there is plenty of tin in Southern Siam and a certain amount of copper to the east of Bangkok (not being worked now), it is possible that both minerals were very scarce in Dvāravatī days and only to be had in very small quantities.

The foregoing illustrations are representative of Buddhist sculpture of the Hinayana school produced in Siam before the advent of the Khmer. Many of the objects shown may have been contemporaneous with the sculpture produced in the Mahayanist kingdom which flourished in the peninsular portion of Siam between the seventh and twelfth centuries A.D. and which I propose to discuss in the next chapter. It is probable that the two schools of sculpture overlapped in the region south of Petchaburi. Of architectural remains of the Dvāravatī period in Central Siam there is practically nothing known except, as I have mentioned already, the plinth or base of a temple at Pong Tük and a few foundations found near P'rapatom, as well as certain temples in Northern Siam, to which reference will be made in the appropriate place. No doubt more systematic digging would bring to light yet other remains of the early history of Siam, and it is hoped that the present Government will not permit matters to rest where they are at present, but push energetically forward with the archaeological survey of Siam.

CHAPTER V

THE MALAY PENINSULA AND THE
KINGDOM OF ÇRIVIJAYA

IT is only within recent years that the existence of a hitherto un-
suspected Hindu kingdom in the southern or peninsular part of
Siam as well as in British Malaya has been revealed. A certain
amount of sculpture, of both Buddhist and Brahman images, has
at times been discovered in the Malay Peninsula, but there was no solid
basis on which to found any theory regarding their origin, and in the
past it has been assumed that most of these sculptures were imported by
colonists and traders from India direct.

It is only natural, however, that the Malay Peninsula, which was
known even in Ptolemy's time as the Golden Chersonese, should have
been one of the first territories of the Far East to attract colonization
from India, lying as it does 'just across the sea' from the eastern seaboard of that sub-continent, and we already find an early indirect
reference to it in the Chinese annals of the sixth century A.D. According
to the History of Liang (A.D. 500–50) among the vassal states of Funan
was one called Lang-Ya-Hsiu, which sent an embassy to China in
A.D. 515 and reported that 'Our people say that the kingdom was
founded more than 400 years ago' (i.e. in the first century A.D. and
undoubtedly from India).

This State corresponds to the Lankasuka of the Malay and Javanese
chronicles and is to be found in the region of the Malay States, Kedah
and Perak. Its existence has been corroborated by Quaritch Wales who
records that, from his recent excavations of a considerable number of
sites, the State must have been strongly Buddhist by religion. At the
base of a brick building at one of these sites on the Bujang river in
Kedah was found a remarkably fine bronze image of the Buddha,
8½ inches high (Fig. 47), which exhibits a transition from the Amarāvatī
to the Gupta school of sculpture and can safely be ascribed to the fourth
or fifth century A.D. He also found a small stone Buddha of pure Gupta
type at Wieng Sra in the Siamese portion of the peninsula, and he

relates that two bronze Buddhas of the same period had been dredged up in the tin mines of Perak. Further excavations brought to light the remains of early Buddhist *stupas* near the mouths of rivers on the Kedah coast, as well as fragments of inscriptions with Buddhist texts, in the one case in a South Indian script of the fourth century and in the other in a Sanskrit Mahayana script not later than the early sixth century A.D.

Ancient accounts of peoples in far distant lands always fascinate me and the Chinese annals give a charming description of the habits of the people of Lankasuka which certainly compare favourably with similar customs obtaining in England in the fourth or fifth century A.D.:

> All the inhabitants, both men and women, let their hair hang loose and wear garments without sleeves, made of a stuff which they call Kan-Man and which is actually of cotton material. The King and the chief nobles wear, in addition, a piece of dawn-red cloth which covers the upper part of the back between the shoulders.
>
> They girdle their loins with a golden cord and wear golden rings in their ears. Their women folk (i.e. those of high rank) cover themselves with beautiful scarves enriched with precious stones. The walls of the city, in this country, are made of brick. The houses have double-doors and pavilions with raised terraces. The king issues from his palace gate seated on an elephant, sheltered by a white canopy; he is preceded by drums and banners, and is surrounded by soldiers of very fierce aspect.

This does not read to me as an account of the customs of a savage tribe but rather of those of a civilized State. Their funeral customs are stated to be either cremation after the Buddhist fashion, where the bones are gathered and placed in a jar, or devouring by birds in the Parsee fashion, after which the bones are placed in a jar and flung out to sea.

In the fourth and fifth centuries A.D. there was another State, known to the Chinese as Tche-t'ou, in the region of Patalung on the Gulf of Siam. This was called in Sanskrit 'The Country of the Red Earth,' as witnessed by an inscription found in the northern part of Province Wellesley which contains a Buddhist stanza and a wish for the success of a voyage to be made by the captain of a junk called Buddhagupta, who belonged to the Country of the Red Earth.

Two other ancient States are known from the Chinese annals. The first is Tambralinga, which had its capital at Ligor on the east coast of the Malay Peninsula (now known as Nakon Srītammarāt). A Sanskrit inscription has been found there, dating from the sixth century A.D. at the latest, and its mention in the Pali-Buddhist Canon (*Niddesa*) in the form of Tambalingam shows that this kingdom was already in being about the second century A.D.

Another place, known to Ptolemy, was Takkola, which is also mentioned in a Buddhist text (the *Milindapanha*). This is usually sited at Tākūa Pā on the west coast of the isthmus of Kra, but it may perhaps refer to the modern port of Trang. From this port embarked the Funan embassy which was sent to India in the third century A.D.

According to the history of Liang, Funan itself received its Indianized art and culture from another ancient small State, P'an P'an, situated in the region of the Bay of Bandon, and that there was a definite cultural link between Funan, Dvāravatī and the states of the Malay Peninsula is shown by the fact that Buddhist statuary derived from a Gupta prototype has been found in all three centres. So much for the early states.

In a monograph published in 1918 Coedès put forward his evidence for the assumption that at least from the seventh to the twelfth century A.D. Southern Siam and the Malay Peninsula, from the region of Jaya on the Bay of Bandon southwards, formed part, or was under the political control, of the Sumatran kingdom of Çrivijaya with its capital at Palembang, which was a highly Indianized state, practising Buddhism of the Mahayanist school. Çrivijaya was known to the Chinese as Shihlifoshih, or more shortly, Foche.

The first time that Yi-Tsing (or I-Ching) voyaged in A.D. 671 from China to India, his first port of call, less than twenty days after his departure from Canton, was Foche (Palembang in Sumatra) which he described as having relations with both India and China, and where he remained for six months to study Sanskrit grammar. His reference to Buddhism is worth recording, showing, as it does, the high degree of culture already reached there:

> In the fortified town of Foche there are more than a thousand Buddhist monks, whose minds are set on study and good works. They examine and discuss all possible subjects exactly as in India itself: the rules and rites are identical.
>
> If a Chinese monk wishes to go to the west in order to read and study (the original Buddhist texts) he cannot do better than stay at Foche for a year or two and practise the necessary rules. He will then be in a fit condition to go on to India for further study.

After his return from India, where he spent ten years at the University of Nalandā, I-Ching paid another visit to Foche between A.D. 685 and 689. This visit lasted four years, during which he copied and translated into Chinese many Sanskrit Buddhist texts. After a brief return to Canton to obtain four colleagues to collaborate with him, he returned to Foche and wrote his two 'Memoirs,' the first on 'Distinguished Monks who have sought "the good law" in the western world,' and the second, 'The interior Law, addressed from the Southern Seas.' He finally returned to China in A.D. 695.

Coedès considers that the rise of Çrivijaya can be mainly attributed to the collapse of Funan as a sea empire, when that State was vanquished by the Khmer of Chen-La, who were essentially a continental power. A group of inscriptions found at Palembang on the heights of Batang Hari and also on the island of Banka (which lies off the coast, half-way between Java and Singapore) refer to the existence in A.D. 684–86, of a State in the region of Palembang which had just conquered Malayu (now Jambi) to the north as well as the island of Banka, and was preparing a military expedition against Java. This state was Çrivijaya, whose embassies to the imperial court of China already date from A.D. 670.

Palembang was always a necessary port of call on the voyage between India and China, and even as late as 1178 a Chinese geographer still wrote of its importance for foreign mariners, whether coming from Java, or India, or even Arabia, on their way to China.

Within a century this State had become overlord of the whole of Sumatra, the western part of Java, and the greater part of the Malay Peninsula, where an inscribed *stela*, dated A.D. 775, found at Nakon Srītammarāt (Ligor) commemorates the foundation of Buddhist monuments at the instance of the king of Çrivijaya.

As will be seen in the next chapter, in the middle of the eighth century A.D. there arises in Central Java a new dynasty of Sailendras which assumes the imperial title of 'King of the Mountain' (a title used by the later kings of Funan) and is responsible for the building of the great Buddhist *stupa* of Borobodur and many another beautiful shrine in honour of the Dhyani Buddhas, Manjusri and Lokeçvara.

These two kingdoms of Palembang and Central Java at first were on friendly terms and in the middle of the ninth century A.D. a prince came from Java to ascend the throne of Çrivijaya with the title of 'King of the Mountain.' It is from this time that the power of the Maharajah of Çrivijaya became consolidated. For Arab traders he was *the* Maharajah, sovereign lord of Zabag (Javaka), Kalah (the Kra isthmus) and Sribuza

(Çrivijaya). In A.D. 996 the Arab geographer Masudi says: 'This Empire of the Maharajah has an enormous population and innumerable armies. No one, even with a ship of the utmost speed, can go over all the isles, which are all inhabited, in less than two years. This king is in possession of more kinds of perfume and spices than any other king.'

Further references to this same State are made in the Sanskrit epigraphy of the Chola dynasty of Southern India. In the twenty-first year of the reign of Raja-raja I (A.D. 1006) mention is made of the gift of a village to the Buddhist temple at Negapatam, begun by Culamani-Varman and finished by his son, Mara-Vijayottunga Varman, who is called King of Kataha and Çrivijaya and is said to belong to the family of the 'King of the Mountain.' The two kings mentioned above can also be identified from the annals of the Sung dynasty, which relate the coming of two embassies in A.D. 1003 and 1008 respectively, and in which 'Çulamani-Varman' is rendered as 'Chu-lo-wu-ni-fo-ma' and 'Mara-vi' as 'Ma-lo-pi.'

However, these good relations with the Chola dynasty did not last very long, and in the next reign of Rajendra-Chola (A.D. 1012–42) the country of Kataha is invaded. In two inscriptions of A.D. 1024 and 1030 the story is told of a warlike expedition 'over the rolling sea,' and a list is given of the countries conquered, of which the first is Çrivijaya, the prosperous, and the last Kadara (or Kataha). Other places mentioned are Ma Nakkavara (the Nicobar Islands), Old Malaiyur, and Ilangacoga, identified with Lankasuka in the south of the modern province of Kedah, which itself is identical with the Old Kataha or Kadara.

One of the successors of Rajendra-Chola claims in A.D. 1068 to have conquered Kadara again and to have handed it back to its king, presumably because he could not hope to hold and govern it from such a distance. But some years later the tables are turned, and the embassy from San-fo-ch'i (the name given by the Chinese to this State at that period) to China then claimed that Chola was vassal to them. This is clear from a problem which arose in A.D. 1106 at the court of China as to whether the embassy from the king of Pagān in Burma (Kyanzittha), 'who was sovereign of a large kingdom,' was to be treated (as the emperor had directed) in the same way as that from Chola, which was stated to be only a vassal of San-fo-ch'i.

Quaritch Wales is not in agreement with the general presentation of the facts, as put forward by Coedès, and, while admitting the existence of a State called Çrivijaya in the seventh century A.D. in South-Eastern Sumatra, he believes that this State was supplanted in the eighth century

A.D. by a powerful kingdom called Javaka (or Zabag by the Arabs) under a Mahayanist dynasty of Sailendras, newly arrived from India, who had their capital in the Malay Peninsula. At first he thought that this capital was at Jaya on the east coast, later moved to Ligor, but he now considers it must have been in the Kinta valley in the state of Perak, which in olden days was known as Kadara or Kataha.

Wales's theory is based mainly on an interesting study of the inscriptions and other relevant data made by R. C. Majumdar, who claims that the Sailendras must have wrested the Bandon region from Çrivijaya towards the close of the eighth century A.D. and have established their authority over Java about the same time, thus bringing the greater part of Malaysia under the control of one political unit for the first time.

The introduction of a new kind of script (Nagari) from Northern India, as well as of a new type of culture, and the adoption of the name Kalinga are brought forward as conclusive evidence of the creation of this Sailendra empire. Majumdar does not commit himself as regards the site of the Sailendra capital, but holds the view that it was either in the Malay Peninsula or in Java and says that for the present the question must be left open. Krom, the famous Dutch archaeologist, has put forward the hypothesis that, while Java no doubt came under the sphere of influence of Çrivijaya, sooner or later it came to form a separate State under a member of the same dynasty which ruled over Çrivijaya. Majumdar is not inclined to concur in this, and is of the opinion that at the end of the eighth century A.D. Malaysia, including the peninsula, Sumatra and Java, formed one integral kingdom ruled over by the same Sailendra king, though by the close of the ninth century A.D. the Sailendras had lost their authority over Java.

To make his position clear, Majumdar has summarized the evidence as follows: First, the Malay Peninsula, at least the Ligor region, formed part of the realm of Çrivijaya round about A.D. 775. Secondly, shortly after this, a king of the Sailendras is found reigning in the same locality, of a different dynasty from that of Çrivijaya. Thirdly, by A.D. 782 the Sailendra dynasty had established its authority over Java. Fourthly, a powerful kingdom, with its capital in the Ligor region, is known to the Arabs in A.D. 844 under the name of Zabag. Its king is always styled 'The Maharajah.' Fifthly, the Nalandā copper-plate of Devapala's thirty-ninth year (A.D. 850) refers to three generations of Sailendras, the first called king of Javabhumi, and the third king of Suvarnadvipa. Sixthly, at first the name, Zabag, only referred to the Ligor region, but finally included the Malay Peninsula and the Archipelago, and was referred to as either Jayabhumi or Suvarnadvipa by the Indians, and as San-fo-ch'i by the Chinese. Finally, in the eleventh century A.D., although they had lost Java, the Sailendras were still ruling over Sumatra and the Malay Peninsula.

It may also be added that in later times, up to the thirteenth century A.D., this realm, at least that part in the Malay Peninsula, was referred to as Javaka, whose king, Chandrabhanu, twice invaded Ceylon, in 1236 and 1256 respectively, but was defeated on both occasions.

From the evidence at present available, I do not feel it possible to come to a definite decision on these important questions, but Wales and Majumdar have certainly put forward a case for consideration, and it is agreed by all that the finds of sculpture in the Malay Peninsula are more numerous and more important than any discovered in the region of Palembang, and are as near, if not nearer, to Indian Pāla prototypes than Sumatran or Javanese models.

We must not forget, however, that the Indianized kingdom of Çrivijaya, or Zabag, or Javaka, had no monopoly of the sculpture or inscriptions found in the Malay Peninsula. I have already related that statues of the Buddha of the Gupta type as well as numerous Brahmanic figures have also been found. Also two inscriptions are known, one in the temple of Mahā-Tāt at Srītammarāt (Ligor) written in archaic Sanskrit of possibly the fifth or sixth century A.D., and another in the temple of Maheyang in the same city written in a Sanskrit of a kind used in Cambodia in the seventh and eighth centuries A.D.

The Buddha statues of the Gupta type are akin to those of Dvāravatī, but the Brahmanic are peculiar to themselves, as will be seen from Fig. 48 which is shown as an interesting example of the type of Brahmanic image found. It is a standing image of Vishnu in limestone, now in the Siamese National Museum, and is 27 inches high. It is of rather clumsy make, but the head-dress, the ears and the decoration are astonishing in the peculiar heaviness of their style. It had originally four arms, of which the posterior left is broken off, the anterior left holds the conch-shell, the posterior right rests upon a heavy club, while the anterior right holds the discus. Similar statues to this one can still be seen *in situ* at Nakon Srītammarāt.

Brahmanic stone statues of two male and one female deities (Figs. 49 and 50) can still also be seen at the spot where they were abandoned, now protected by a huge tree which has grown over them, near the bank of the Takūa Pā river just south of Takūa Pā harbour (lat. 9° N., long. 98·5° E.). I am inclined to agree with Wales that they are fairly close to the Pallavā style of Southern India and may be dated approximately in the seventh or eighth century A.D., though it is clear that they were made locally, as they are in a slaty schist exactly similar to the stone employed in building the temple of Tung Tük on the island in Takūa Pā harbour.

There is also a statue of Vishnu, 4 feet 10 inches high, in the Bangkok Museum, which, it is stated, was found at Wieng Sra (Fig. 51) and which is undoubtedly Pallavā in style.

For prototypes in India of Pallavā images reference may be made particularly to Jouveau-Dubreuil's PALLAVA ANTIQUITIES, Vol. II, Plates 6, 7 and 8, showing Dvarapalas, Çiva, Vishnu and Brahma in the Pallavā temple at Tiruttani, and to the same author's ICONOGRAPHIE DU SUD DE L'INDE, Plates XXIb, XXXVb and XLIIIb, showing Pallavā figures attributed by him to the seventh or eighth century A.D.: also to Stella Kramrisch's INDIAN SCULPTURE, Plate XXVII, No. 73, showing two royal figures of the seventh century A.D. from the Dharmaraja Ratha at Mamallapuram.

Of the Mahayanistic or Indo-Malaysian type of Buddhist sculpture associated with the kingdom of Çrivijaya or Javaka, characteristic examples are illustrated, and anyone acquainted with the Buddhist statuary of the eighth century A.D. both of the Indian Pāla type and of that found in Java, will at once recognize their mutual affinity.

Fig. 52, which is in black bronze (or *samrit*, as it is called by the Siamese), is one of the most beautiful objects in the National Museum. It is 27 inches high as it stands now and probably represents the Bodhisattva, Lokeçvara. It was discovered by Prince Damrong at Wat P'ra Tāt at Jaya, but unfortunately the crown and the lower half of the body are missing. The beauty of the features and the proportions of the modelling bespeak a very high state of development in the art of sculpture. In his work on the National Museum, Coedès attributes this figure to the ninth or tenth century A.D., and I am inclined to think that the earlier century may be the more likely. It seems to me to be close to a true Indian prototype of the Pāla period, and, unless there was a continuous influx of new inspiration from India, I cannot think that local art of the tenth century could have produced such a masterpiece. One interesting feature is the cord running from the left shoulder down the body and reaching below the waist. This is part of the sacred thread of the 'twice-born,' of which the remainder on the back of the figure is invisible. It has no connexion with the similar thread hanging over the right shoulder. I cannot find an exact analogy to this figure in Pāla

F

sculpture, but there are certain resemblances, for instance, in Stella Kramrisch's PĀLA AND SENA SCULPTURE, to her No. 8 (ascribed to early ninth century A.D.) as to the torso, and to her No. 13 (end of ninth century A.D.) as to decoration.

Fig. 53 is again an image of the Bodhisattva, Lokeçvara, in grey-black stone, also in the National Museum. It is a fine piece of modelling, especially the face and the torso, and is clearly akin to Pāla sculpture of the same period. The sacred thread is seen falling down to the waist. There is an interesting analogy to this figure in the volume by Cunningham entitled MAHA-BODHI, THE GREAT BUDDHIST TEMPLE AT BODH-GAYA. Plate XXVI (1) shows a stone slab depicting the Buddha in the centre, with a figure on either side of him. Cunningham took this to represent the *Tri-Ratana* or Trinity of the Buddhist Faith, viz. the Buddha, the Law and the Order, of which the figure now under discussion (to the right of the Buddha) represented the Order. He stated that this was the only example of the Buddhist Trinity that he had ever seen in sculpture. But actually this figure, though inferior in execution, is identical not only in style but also in almost every detail with that found in the Malay Peninsula, and is clearly an image of Lokeçvara, as witnessed by the lotus-flower above the shoulder and by the lotus again acting as a footstool to his right foot. Cunningham thought the inscription on the slab to be as late as the twelfth century A.D., but it is difficult to assign such a late date to the figure illustrated, which seems to belong to the ninth century A.D.

In her monograph on PĀLA AND SENA SCULPTURE, Stella Kramrisch does not show any figure exactly similar to that illustrated, but her No. 28, a six-armed Lokeçvara in stone from Nalandā in South Bihar, attributed to the early ninth century, resembles it slightly, while her No. 44, which may be of later date as it is more ornate in style, is certainly analogous. No. 10, a Buddha of the time of Surapala I (A.D. 820–30) is also rather similar in the style of its architectural details in the background. R. D. Banerji, in his EASTERN INDIAN SCHOOL OF MEDIAEVAL SCULPTURE, gives an almost identical figure on Plate XIV (*a*) which he describes, however, as that of Manjusri. On the evidence of all these figures I am inclined to think that the image illustrated was probably brought from India itself.

Fig. 54 is also a figure of Lokeçvara in black bronze from the National Museum, this time in a standing posture. Here the treatment is more conventional and the general effect is not quite so pleasing as that of Fig. 52. The upper half of the figure is clearly of a higher artistic order than the lower. Once more we see the lotus, now held in the left hand; the original and attractive form of the crown, and the jewelled ornaments on the neck and arms, as well as the streamers, like strands of hair, falling on both shoulders as in Fig. 52. This figure may be a little later in date than the latter, but cannot be far removed from it in point of time. Apparently there is no sacred thread of the 'twice-born' shown on this image, since the scarf or fold of the robe across the body is seen on both the previous figures in addition to the thread. No. 13 in PĀLA AND SENA SCULPTURE has much in common with this figure.

The discovery of large bronze images in the Peninsula gives rise to an interesting thought. In Central and North-Eastern Siam, during the first millennium of the Christian era, all the bronze images known are of comparatively small dimensions and of rather rough execution, thus showing both the scarcity of metal and the inability to treat it effectively. Here in the south of Siam we have not only an abundance of metal but a highly developed technique in the sculptural art. The first may be due to the plentifulness of tin in the Malay Peninsula, as opposed to Siam proper, and the second can only be accounted for by the advent of a race from India still in the full vigour of its power and possessed of a fully developed artistic style.

But the important question that still requires an answer is—Where did the Mahayanist Sailendras who spread their art and culture throughout the whole of Malaysia originate in India?

In his popular book, TOWARDS ANGKOR, Wales believes that the original Sailendra to come to Malaya was a young prince of the Ganga dynasty of Mysore, soon after the middle of the eighth century A.D., but Majumdar suggests that they came from the country of Kalinga on the west coast of the Bay of Bengal, whose celebrated port, Paloura, was from time immemorial (according to him) the port of embarkation for the Far East. This is an over-statement in view of the importance for a similar purpose, of Tamralipti, Amarāvatī (Bezwada) and Conjeeveram (Kānchi) at different periods of Indian history. Yet we may pass it over because of two other important factors which help to shed light on the problem, namely, the introduction of the Nagari character in writing and of the name, Kalinga, to the Malay Peninsula, a name still given to the Indian immigrants who are brought to the colony as indentured labour in the rubber plantations.

Majumdar states that in the sixth and seventh centuries A.D. Kalinga was under the control of the Gánga and Sailodbhava dynasties, while in the interior, in the Vindhya region, there was also a dynasty of Saila.

The names of the Ganga kings all end in Maharajah or Mahadhirajah (as in the inscription of Ligor), and Majumdar considers that these dynasties may be considered as the origin of the name Sailendra. The Ganga family was widely spread through India, but the chief dynasties were of Kalinga and Mysore, which was their original home. Kamarnava was king of the 'Tri Kalinga' in the second half of the eighth century A.D., and Majumdar affirms that it is from this country that the Môn of Lower Burma obtained their name of 'Talaing.' It is usually accepted that the name 'Talaing' comes from Telingana which ran with Kalinga on the eastern seaboard of India, and one would only be inclined to agree with Majumdar if Telingana itself is a corruption of Tri Kalinga. The latter further suggests that Tri Kalinga conquered Lower Burma in the eighth century A.D., and that their authority gradually spread from this point southwards over the whole of the Malay Peninsula. Przyluski, in discussing the *Sailendra-vamsa*, says that the source of this Mahayanist influence must be sought in Northern India and principally among the Pālas of Bihar and Bengal. If the countries of Suvarnadvipa and Java-bhumi, referred to in it, are synonymous with the Sailendra empire in Malaysia (as seems very probable), then colour is certainly lent to the above suggestion by the Nalandā copper-plate inscription of the thirty-ninth year of Devapāla, which records the grant of five villages by Devapāla at the request of the illustrious Balaputradeva, king of Suvarnadvipa, and also significantly states that this king had built a monastery at Nalandā itself.

E. J. Thomas, the great authority on Buddhism, informs me that Sailendra, which means 'King of the Mountains,' is a name for the Himalaya Mountains, and that the Ganges river is called 'the daughter of Sailendra,' which would certainly account for a Ganga dynasty taking the name of Sailendra. He also suggests the possibility that disturbances in Eastern India and their defeat by another power in their own land may have driven the Sailendras to found a new empire overseas in the Far East.

Jouveau-Dubreuil, in his valuable ANCIENT HISTORY OF THE DECCAN, makes an attempt to unravel the complexities of all the dynasties reigning in that region and of their conquests north and south. According to him, the Gangas were the rulers over Mysore and Kalinga in the sixth century A.D., but at the beginning of the seventh a new power had arisen, and Pulakesin II, king of the Chalukyas, overthrew the Gangas, both in Mysore and Kalinga, and established a new dynasty. He became master of the Deccan and created a new kingdom of the Eastern Chalukyas. He also defeated the Pallavās of the south.

French, in his little volume on the ART OF THE PĀL EMPIRE, places the first of the Pāla kings of Bengal, Gopala, in the middle or second half of the eighth century A.D. This would leave, unless some other conqueror intervened, a period of roughly a century and a half for the rule of the Chalukyas over the eastern seaboard of India, and, if Majumdar is correct in his surmise that the Ganga-Sailendras were responsible for the colonization of the Malay Peninsula, their defeat by the Chalukyas may well be responsible for the expulsion of their power from India and their expansion overseas. Or it may be that the Chalukyas, after their conquest of Kalinga, were themselves the originators of this urge to colonize and spread their culture in the Far East. Until further evidence is forthcoming, we cannot arrive at more than a tentative conclusion, especially as some of the Mahayanistic figures found in Malaya, though they cannot as yet be exactly matched in India itself, do bear a strong resemblance, especially in their decorative motives, to the early images of Pāla sculpture, which would seem to confirm the view expressed by Przyluski, and on the whole I myself am inclined to think that the source of the Mahayanistic art found in Malaya, at any rate after the close of the eighth century A.D., is probably to be found among the Pālas of Bengal.

Fig. 55, the last one shown whose provenance is from the peninsula, is of the utmost importance as a work of art, and, moreover, presents another interesting example of the problems awaiting solution. Here we see a beautiful image of the Buddha of the Hinayana school seated on the king of the Nagas. It is about 4 feet in height and is fashioned in the highly valued black bronze (samrit) which has been gilded. It is reported to have come from Wat Hua Wiang at Jaya and is now in the National Museum at Bangkok.

The form and execution of the Naga king obviously points to a Khmer origin, but the statue itself, which is detachable from its seat, has no Khmer feature about it. From a cursory examination it might appear doubtful whether the two parts were cast at one and the same time. On the base of the Naga, which forms part with the whole statue, is an inscription in pure Cambodian, similar in language and orthography to old Khmer inscriptions. But the *script* is quite different and is nearly analogous to that of the Kawi inscriptions of Java. It reads as follows:

In 1105, year of the Hare (Rabbit), by order of the Kamraten An Maharajaçrimat, etc., etc., etc., on the 3rd day of the waxing moon of Jyestha, Wednesday, the Mahasenapati, Galanai, who governs the country of Grahi, invited Mraten Çri Nano to make this statue. The weight of the *samrit* is one *bhara*, two *tula*, and the value of the gold used for decoration is ten tamling. Erected for the faithful to venerate and worship.

Now the era is undoubtedly the *Maha-sakarat*, and the year 1105 = A.D. 1183 During the twelfth century the Khmer were masters of Central Siam, but Coedès states that there is no such king known in Khmer annals as the one named in the inscription, and that, as already shown, the title 'Maharajah' was not used by Khmer royalty. But the Sung annals of China mention, among the States bordering on Cambodia, the country of Chia-lo-hsi (Kia-lo-hi) to the south; and Chao-ju-kua, writing in A.D. 1225 says that Chia-lo-hsi was a tributary of San-fo-ch'i. It seems reasonable, therefore, to assume that Chia-lo-hsi and Grahi are one and the same country, and that Grahi is to be found in the region of Jaya and Nakon Srītammarāt, where the statue under discussion was discovered.

The use of the Khmer language in the inscription shows that Khmer influence, if not political sovereignty, was strong in the Malay Peninsula at this time. But the fact remains that the statue on the Naga king is certainly not Khmer, nor yet, I think, of true peninsular origin. It is, to my mind, closely akin to Fig. 35 in BUDDHIST ART IN SIAM, which is a late product of Môn or Dvāravatī art. I need only point to the set of the legs which are drawn inwards, to the way in which the arms and the hands are placed, the heavy folds of the robe, and the type of features with the oval face, the 'swallow' form of eyebrow and the sensitive nose, to show at once the affinity between these two figures.

The tantalizing question remains. Are the statue and the Naga of the same period?

Coedès seems to incline to the view that the image is of later date than the Naga; but if, as I believe, the image is of Môn origin, however late, one would expect it to be earlier than A.D. 1183. On the other hand, if the original Khmer statue were lost, it would be a singular occurrence to find an antique Môn figure to fit the stand exactly, as this image does. I suggest that the two figures are contemporary, and that it was an 'artist' still under Môn influence who modelled the image of Buddha, while it was a 'craftsman' under Khmer influence who cast the Naga king. According to Hodson of Cambridge, this would be in keeping with Indian traditions.

It remains to add that, towards the end of the thirteenth century A.D. the first Tai kingdom in Siam claimed dominion over the Malay Peninsula as far south as Nakon Srītammarāt, as witnessed by the stone inscription from Suk'ot'ai dated A.D. 1292. This claim was simultaneous with Javanese campaigns against Malaya and Sumatra and these double attacks put an end to the sovereignty of Çrivijaya or Javaka over the Malay Peninsula.

CHAPTER VI

JAVA AND BALI

I CANNOT pretend to the same personal knowledge of Java and Bali and of their cultural remains as I possess of the other countries treated in this book, but I have visited the enchanting isle of Bali where I found some very charming verses inscribed in the visitors' book at the hotel in which I stayed and addressed by an Englishman to the twin volcanoes, Batoer and Agoeng, which stand up close together round and smooth like a woman's breasts. It was also in Bali that I acquired by chance from an old lady the finest piece of Sawank'alōk celadon waře (about A.D. 1300 from Central Siam) that I have ever seen.

I have also travelled through the length of Java, with visits to Jogjakarta and Borobodur, from Surabaya to Batavia, where I was able to examine the great collection of Chinese and Siamese pottery and porcelain presented by Mr. Van Orsay de Flines to the Batavia Museum. I am, therefore, familiar to a certain extent with the islands and the life they contain.

The general features, both of the architecture and sculpture, although possessing a strong individuality of their own, have a definite affinity with certain of those found in the Malay Peninsula and are just as obviously derived from India as those seen in Ancient Malaya, Siam or Cambodia.

As I have already shown in my chapter on Çrivijaya, it is generally accepted now that the Sailendra dynasty, whether it came from India or not, by the middle of the eighth century A.D. had wrested the Bandon region on the east coast of the Siamese portion of the Malay Peninsula from the kingdom of Çrivijaya and that for the next hundred years the whole of Malaysia including the peninsula, Java and Sumatra, formed one integral kingdom ruled over by the same Sailendra king.

This conclusion forms a kind of nodal point on which all future research can be based, both backwards and forwards.

The four main islands of the Dutch East Indies are Java, Sumatra, Borneo and Celebes. In this chapter our chief concern is with Java, while Borneo and the Celebes come into the picture for a brief moment at a very early stage.

Java is 725 miles long and has an average breadth of about 140 miles, but in some places narrows to as little as 40 miles. Sumatra is a vast island 1,100 miles long and about 300 miles at its widest. Borneo is another enormous island about 900 miles by 700, containing, in addition to Dutch Borneo, the British colonies of Sarāwak and North Borneo. Finally, Celebes is like a huge octopus spreading its tentacles in several directions, chiefly north and east. There are many islands, such as Banka and Billiton, famous for tin production, the beautiful Bali at the tail end of Java, known as the 'Garden of Eden,' Timor, to the south, and others stretching away towards New Guinea.

The total population of these islands is about 70 millions, of which Java alone contains 40 millions. It has been stated that in Java one can never be out of sight of another person. It is essentially an island of plantations, terraced rice-fields, in which one can see the fleecy clouds reflected in the glistening water, and violent volcanoes. The famous eruption of Krakatoa in the 1880's left ships stranded on the sides of mountains, and its dust is said to have descended in Europe.

Of its modern history all that need be recorded is that the Dutch ruled Java from 1619 to 1798, and the British from 1811 to 1816 under the famous Sir Stamford Raffles, who founded Singapore in 1819. After the Napoleonic wars it was handed back to the Dutch in exchange for Ceylon, and since then the Dutch have been in command up to the recent formation of the Republic of Indonesia, with the exception of its brief occupation by the Japanese during the Second World War. To conclude, Java can certainly claim to be one of the, if not *the*, richest islands in the world, since she produces so many of the primary commodities demanded by man today, rubber, coffee, tea, tin, copra and oil.

So much for its recent history. For the beginning of my story I must go back to a period before the Christian era.

In Chapter II I have referred to the various opinions of pre-historians regarding the provenance of the Malay race, who people the islands today. In his HISTOIRE ANCIENNE I notice that Coedès, who as a philologist speaks with great authority, says: 'The criticisms of De Hevesy (who denied Schmidt's linguistic theories) cannot do away with the undeniable lexicological affinities between the Môn-Khmer languages and the Munda languages of India.'

In his latest work THE MAKING OF GREATER INDIA, basing himself on Heine-Geldern's PREHISTORIC RESEARCH IN THE NETHERLANDS INDIES, Quaritch Wales comes down heavily on the side of those who postulate a downward *Drang* from the north. He says: 'Heine-Geldern has shown that there is good reason to believe that what we may call the older Megalithic culture entered continental South-Eastern Asia from the north via the main river valleys between 2500 and 1500 B.C. as part of what he calls the Quadrangular Adze culture, i.e. the chief type of late Neolithic to reach South-East Asia.' It appears that in this region the neolithic nearly coincided with the iron age and that the bronze age was of short duration.

The chief characteristics of this older megalithic culture were the planting of rice and millet and the use of a special knife for harvesting, the brewing of beer from rice or millet, the raising of pigs, and of cattle or buffaloes for sacrificial purposes, a certain technique in pottery-making, the manufacturing of bark-cloth, the rectangular house standing on piles, the customs of head-hunting and of erecting megalithic monuments as memorials of the dead or for sacrifices. Heine-Geldern states that in Eastern and South-East Asia this older megalithic type is still alive in its pure form in Assam, the Nias islands, off the west coast of Sumatra, and, to a lesser degree, in the mountains of Annam and in the Malay Archipelago. He adds further that there are many remains of this type to which it is difficult to assign a date, and that the best known series lies in the Pasemah highlands of Sumatra, to which may be added the Central Bornean series. According to him, the monuments of this type consist of menhirs, either single or in groups, dolmen, stone seats, stone terraces and pyramids as well as various types of stone tombs.

In Java the best-preserved example lies at the height of 10,000 feet on the Yang plateau among the Argapura mountains in East Java. Sanctuary IV has three terraces faced with unworked stone, and the lower terrace is reached by a median stairway flanked by a tall menhir. A similar stairway leads up to the second terrace. At the rear of this is a walled enclosure containing two small roofless buildings. Thence another stairway leads to an altar crowned with a menhir, and on the right of the altar is a niche surrounding a sulphur spring which had miraculous properties. Although its date is uncertain, it seems hardly to have been affected by any Indian influence.

As the frontispiece to his work Wales shows a drawing of a rather remarkable temple in Cambodia, namely Wat P'u to compare with this megalithic site in Java. I have myself visited Wat P'u which lies 30 miles from the town of Bassac on the west bank of the river Mek'ŏng, and have in front of me a description which I wrote at the time and which shows, first, an artificial lake at the bottom, secondly, the base of a *vihara* of which no vestige remains of the hall itself, then a causeway flanked by a row of stone pillars on either side: in the middle of the causeway, on either side, there is a rectangular building with corridor wings. Then on again along the causeway and finally up a steep flight of steps to the temple on the summit, from which a fine view of the country all around can be obtained.

The date of the original use of the site is unknown, but the Khmer temple dates from the ninth to the tenth century and was originally Brahman, since behind it there were rich carvings of Brahma, Vishnu and Çiva; in later times it had been in use as a Buddhist temple. The great affinity between this and the Java site lay in their setting against a background of sheer rock, with cave-dwellings, and in the case of Wat P'u, of shrines with ex-votos. The temple itself is built partly of brick and partly of stone, and some of the lintels and bas-reliefs were in good repair, especially the figure of Vishnu on his three-headed elephant.

The resemblance is so striking that I think the affinity may be admitted, but whether such affinity may be taken as proof of Heine-Geldern's theory of a downward thrust of peoples from the north into South-Eastern Asia and the islands is apparently still a matter of debate among pre-historians.

In his CULTURAL HISTORY OF THE MALAYS, Winstedt goes so far as to say, 'reaching the coast these peoples (i.e. the ancestors of the Malay family) crossed to the archipelago in outrigger craft developed from bamboo outriggers still in use on many rivers of Burma and Indo-China. In their craft they voyaged as far as Easter Island and Madagascar. And early in the Christian era they colonized Polynesia.'

In the face of such a view of the movement of peoples in pre-Aryan times, one can understand the wistful comment of Thor Heyerdahl, the author, at the end of his KONTIKI EXPEDITION, that, in spite of the heroic efforts of himself and his comrades, his theory of Polynesia being colonized from Peru is still not acknowledged by the pundits!

However, so far as this book is concerned, whether the movement came southward from the north, or vice versa, we may assume that, as Coedès remarks, when the Aryan Indians reached the islands, they found not uncultured savages but organized societies, endowed with a definite form of civilization, which had certain common features with their own, if not developed to such a high degree.

A curious fact may here be interposed. As far as religion is concerned in historic times Java has been through four distinct phases: (*a*) Brahman, (*b*) Buddhist, (*c*) Moslem, and in recent times, (*d*) Christian. Of how many countries could the same be said except India itself?

It seems probable that the first contacts were made about the beginning of the Christian era, if not a little before, and that the Indians came not as an invading army, but as traders and missionaries. In Sumatra they found Malays or proto-Malays, in Java Sundanese, Javanese and Madurese, and Balinese in the enchanting isle of Bali. Judging from the present happy disposition of the island people it would not be difficult for the Indians to make the friendliest of contacts with them in the absence of any warlike preparations on their own part, and it is likely that they soon began to intermarry.

It is still not absolutely settled from what part of India the earliest settlers came. Ferguson says that Buddhism came from Gujerat and the mouths of the Indus, and Rawlinson quotes an old Gujerati proverb: 'Of those who went to Java few returned, but those who did had made their fortunes.' According to local traditions, the first colonists came from Western India in A.D. 75 under Aji Saka but had to return home owing to pestilence, and a second attempt was made in A.D. 603. The king of Gujerat was warned that his kingdom would decay so he sent his son to Java with 5,000 followers; and they reached the island and settled there.

There is another legend that, soon after the visit of the Chinese Buddhist pilgrim Fa Hsien in A.D. 414, the Javanese court was converted to Buddhism by Prince Gunavarman of Kashmir, though Fa Hsien's own comment was that 'the law of Buddha is not much known.'

Against these traditions and legends is the discovery of inscriptions, as already related in my summary, on the east coast of Borneo and in the west of Java, dating from the early and mid-fifth century A.D. respectively, written in a South Indian character almost identical with the Grantha alphabet used at the time of the Pallavā dynasty. Moreover, the earliest images of the Buddha found at Sempaga in the Celebes, in the south of the province of Jember (Eastern Java) and on the hill of Seguntang at Palembang in Sumatra are all in the Amarāvatī style of Eastern India. These must date even earlier than the inscriptions, from the second and third centuries of the Christian era, when we know that Amarāvatī became an important centre for the spread of Buddhism abroad.

In a paper on the 'Kouen-Louen' (the name given by the Chinese to the Indians who came to the islands) G. Ferrand gives an excellent description of how in his view these early Indian immigrants achieved their aims by offering suitable presents to the local chiefs, by curing the sick people brought to them and by the gift of amulets to ward off evils and dangers. In fact the stranger must assume the role of rich philanthropist, doctor and magician. His view is based on personal observation of the Moslem penetration among the Sakalaves of Madagascar, and strikes one as a much more likely explanation of early contacts than large-scale emigration from Gujerat or elsewhere in India under a reigning prince.

The early images brought by the immigrants were representatives of the Buddha Dîpankara, a great favourite among the sailors who frequented the islands of the south, and the part played by Buddhism cannot be gainsaid.

At the same time most of the kingdoms influenced by India were not slow in adopting the Çivaite conception of royalty, based on the union of the Brahman and Kshatriya (warrior) castes and represented by the cult of the *linga*.

Some considerable time appears to have elapsed before Indian customs and religions took any deep root, and it is not until the rise of the kingdom of Çrivijaya in the sixth or seventh century A.D. that we feel the islands to have become imbued with Indian culture. Even then it is agreed that the islanders still retained the essential part of their own character. Krom is emphatic on this point as regards Java and Stutterheim says of Bali: 'Hinduism has always been the cult of the upper classes and never became completely that of the general mass of the population, who were attached to their animistic cults and to the worship of their ancestors.' The same observation may be said of Burma, Siam and Cambodia, where the peasants have always remained animists at heart.

I now come to what in Javanese history may be considered as the first important remains from the art and architectural points of view.

In his MONUMENTAL JAVA published in 1912 Scheltema complains bitterly of the inertia of the Dutch Government in the last century and their complete lack of interest in taking any care of the monuments on the Dieng Plateau, and of their callous indifference at Borobodur and elsewhere. Once a lake of seething lava this plateau lies enclosed by the tops of five mountains at a height of 6,500 feet above sea-level where five Residencies meet, Samarang, Pekalongan, Banyumas, the Bagelen and the Kedu, right in the centre of the island of Java, and forms a link between the east and west chains of volcanoes, which are the vertebrae of Java's spine. Under Raffles, Lieut. Cornelius, R.E., who was sent to survey the region, reported the existence of some forty groups of monuments covered with clay and volcanic ashes. Round about 1840-45 Junghuhn made another survey and found 'more than twenty temples in a wilderness of marshy woods.' Now the woods have gone but the marshes remain, and the twenty temples have diminished to eight in recognizable shape, of which five belong to the Arjuna group at the northern end of the plateau, though the most beautiful, Chandi Bhima, stands quite isolated from the others at the southern end. Chandi means properly 'a mausoleum' but is now used to denote any monument of the Indo-Javanese period.

During the present century the slur on Dutch officialdom has been fully removed, and under modern Dutch scholars, such as Kern, Brandes, Krom, Vogel, Bosch, Schnitger, and Stutterheim the archaeological care of Java has been in excellent and enlightened hands.

In 1907-8 a complete photographic survey was carried out by Col. T. van Erp, R.E., under instructions from the Government, and strict measures were introduced for the preservation and maintenance of monuments. It was the Dutch who brought the 'anastylose' methods, now so ably copied by the French in Indo-China, to a fine art.

It is literally astounding to see thousands of blocks of stone lying scattered over a wide area, and then to behold, as at the touch of a fairy's wand, a beautiful building re-arising and standing four-square exactly as it did in its original setting.

From the seventh century Indo-Javanese civilization represents a harmonious blend between the local and Indian culture. The language used is Kawi, which is Indonesian in essence, but is full of Sanskrit words and phrases. There is no doubt that, as Krom remarks, the Indians introduced higher spiritual ideas which alone the Sanskrit language was fitted to express. In the State the king is called, first, by his own proper name which is Indonesian, and secondly, by his sacred name which is Indian, while grouped around him some of his officials bear partly Indian and partly Indonesian titles. In religious institutions the privileges of both are preserved and mingled together, while the ceremonies are performed according to Indonesian rites but invoking Indian deities. This is not to say that animistic beliefs have been completely eradicated, even by Islam, but Ancient Java recognized two religions side by side, Çivaism and Buddhism. Vishnuism, the counterpart of Çivaism in the Hindu religion, received little attention (as opposed to Cambodia) and had to occupy a back-seat. Çiva was popularly called Guru, a 'Teacher of Wisdom.'

Even so the beliefs of the early inhabitants were clearly visible in the worship of the goddess Sri, originally the goddess of glory and prosperity, but in later times of rice, the essential life-giving product.

It is perhaps a platitude to say nowadays that in the East art is bound up with religion, as it was in medieval Europe, but Java was no exception to the rule. The natural reason, forgotten in modern Europe, is that art and religion spring from the same source, the worship of beauty, truth and goodness, under whatever guise they may be found.

In Java, with rare exceptions, all the remains of Indo-Javanese art are sanctuaries and sacred statues. This art was imported, apparently, quite complete from India—but while one would look for an almost purely Indian art form, such in fact is not the case.

The earliest Indo-Javanese art, known to us now, although it is Indian in general feeling, has a special character of its own, without equivalents in India, and is usually recognizable also from other types of Indian colonial art. The reason is, of course, that those monuments in stone are of the eighth century, whereas the colonization began many centuries earlier. It is most probable that the earliest sanctuaries were made of wood, and that by the time that more durable buildings were needed, a local tradition had been formed. It is possible also that at this time new ideas and new inspirations were brought into being by the Sailendras: but, whether it was a slow evolution or a sudden change, the builders were not of pure Indian, but of mixed blood, and thus local influences were strongly at work in the execution of the plans; such influences were clearly seen in the ornamentation. The whole became a very natural result, not of two elements struggling against one another, but easily and harmoniously blended.

The plan of the temple was Indian. The principal building was placed in the centre of the group, and the subsidiary ones were set all round it, each occupying its proper place and thus forming a complete whole. The same harmony can be seen in the grouping of purely ornamental motifs and of the architectural decoration. Within certain limits there is a great variety to be found without marring the symmetry of the whole, though it is odd that the rich indigenous flora and fauna have been largely neglected.

Krom states that in this creation of decorative elements the Indonesian excelled, and in the manifold detail we can see with what spirit and boldness, as well as refinement, Indian motifs were modified to the point of total difference, in the same building. There is, moreover, a remarkable harmony and equilibrium about the monuments themselves.

There is still very little positive evidence about the origin of the buildings on the Dieng plateau. Scheltema states that the oldest inscription, now in Batavia, is dated M.S. 731, which is equivalent to A.D. 809 But the earliest dated inscription found in Java, among the ruins of the Çivaite sanctuary of Changal on the Wukir hill, south-east of Borobodur, in the central part of the island, is of A.D. 732, It is in Sanskrit, and relates the dedication by a king named Sanjaya of a *linga* in the isle of Java ('rich in grain and gold mines') in the district of Kunjara-Kunja, north-west of Malang in Eastern Java. It has been argued by some writers that this must refer to a king who fled from Southern India, where there is such a district near the frontier between Travancore and Tinevelly, and set himself up in Java. But, as Coedès points out, a true reading of the epigraph makes it clear that the sanctuary was actually set up in this district, which formed part of the Kedu plain of Central Java. This points naturally to a close affinity between these early princes of Java and the Pallavā dynasty, which ruled in Southern India from the third to the eighth century A.D. and I feel that there is a distinct relation between the two. Ferguson, the Indian archaeologist, believed that they are Chalukyan, but although it will probably never be possible to prove the exact provenance of the inspiration, I myself incline to Pallavan as the ultimate source of the Dieng buildings, which, it is stated, were all erected and dedicated to Çiva.

Here is an illustration of the Arjuna group on the Dieng plateau, at its northern end (Fig. 56), and one of Chandi Bhima, at its southern end (Fig. 57). All are built of dressed stone in the South-Indian style, with niches on the outer walls for Brahman gods which have long since disappeared. Two striking decorative features are still to be seen, first the well-known *kala-makara* motif on the lintel of the doorway of Chandi Arjuna, and secondly the monster-mask used as lintels for the niches (Fig. 58). Bronze figures of Çiva and Parvati, his spouse, also show clearly their South-Indian inspiration (Fig. 59).

At Chandi Bhima the niches in front over the entrance porch are all empty, but those at the sides and back are full of odd-looking persons who, according to Scheltema, suggest ideas further developed in the architecture on the plain of Prambanan. He adds that this sanctuary possesses peculiarities in the details of its sculpture, specially in the double lotus of the cornice, and lotus buds and diminutive Bo-trees of uncommon shapes. Architraves and mouldings festooned with foliage, flowers and seed-pods, divide the open spaces in a tasteful, sober manner. From the fact that the decoration was not completed it is inferred that the sculptors were overwhelmed by some volcanic catastrophe which depopulated the Dieng.

According to Krom, this phase of Javanese history dates from A.D. 675 to 750, when the Sailendras conquered central Javaa nd introduced a new form of art. The old kings retired to Eastern Java, there was a revolution in religious affairs, and the Mahayana form of Buddhism superseded the Hinayana form. From this time both cults, Brahmanic Çaivism and Buddhist Mahayanism, flourished together side by side, the former among the people and the latter at the court. This accounts for the fact that Buddhist sanctuaries are more prolific than Brahmanic.

The buildings of this period, which ranges from A.D. 750 to 850, are far finer and more richly decorated than the earlier ones on the Dieng plateau. There are chapels grouped round the main temples, and there are terraces, galleries and balustrades to be seen everywhere. Although the centre of the Sailendra empire was in Sumatra, the influence seen here is not necessarily Sumatran; indeed, there is only one monument of this period known in Sumatra, and that is not in any way comparable.

Coedès remarks that the name of Sailendra, which means 'King of the Mountain,' is an equivalent of Çiva in the form of Giriça, and expressed perhaps an Indian adaptation of Indonesian beliefs connected with the residence of the gods on the tops of mountains. Some authors believe that the Sailendras came direct from India and were related to the Sailobdhava of Kalinga on the east coast. There are serious objections to this, but wherever they came from, their appearance in the Southern Isles was an event of capital importance.

I have personally a strong feeling that this period in Javanese art and architecture is connected with the rise of the Pāla dynasty in Bihar and Bengal, which also dates from about A.D. 750, since there is a clear affinity between Pāla and Javanese art at this time, though the latter still retains its own distinctive character, and the Pālas were ardent Buddhists of the Mahayana school, which now becomes the compeer of Çivaism in Java. There is a soft beauty, a tenderness in their sculpture which is not to be found in any other period of Indian art, and this is clearly seen in the great masterpiece of Buddhist Java, the Borobodur (Fig. 60).

The Borobodur, which is the only *stupa* to be found in Java, was never hidden from view to the point of its existence being forgotten. Scheltema states that native chronicles of the eighteenth century

G

mention it, but he adds that it was the young engineer officer, Lieut. Cornelius, sent by Raffles to survey the Kedu plateau in 1814, who was the first to make a scientific description of it, accompanied by elaborate drawings.

Its origin and history are shrouded in mystery, since no foundation stone or relic casket has ever been unearthed or discovered, and its special purpose is unknown. As Havell points out in his HANDBOOK OF INDIAN ART, it is a remote descendant of Sanchi and Bharhut but there is nothing in India with which to compare it seriously, and Vogel does not agree with Havell when he calls it 'the Parthenon of Asia.' Such a term he says could only refer to the great temple of Angkor in Cambodia, since in the Parthenon and at Angkor it is all activity, whereas, with the Borobodur, it is all repose.

Coomaraswamy describes it admirably when he says: 'There is no nervous tension, no concentration of force, to be compared with that which so impresses the observer at Angkor. Borobodur is like a ripe fruit matured in breathless air—the fullness of its forms is an expression of static wealth rather than the volume that denotes the outward radiation of power.'

I had been to Angkor twice before I saw Borobodur, and I wished afterwards that it had been in the reverse order, since the Great Temple of Angkor dwarfs every other ancient building one is likely to see, and has no compeer for sheer magnificence and richness of decoration. But there is no doubt that Borobodur is very impressive, standing as it does on the plain with the hills in the distance all around, and he must be a very insensitive creature who is not captivated by the Buddhist scenes carved on its 'miles' of bas-reliefs.

The body of the buildings consists of six square terraces, each side relieved by a double projection and the lowest terrace is 479 feet square.

The superstructure consists of three circular platforms carrying rings of small *stupas* (Fig. 61), seventy-two in all, which are hollow and not solid. The central *stupa* on the summit is 52 feet in diameter.

The upper part of the building is completely unadorned which provides a striking contrast with the rich decoration of the lower part. This contrast is thought to be intentional and to be symbolic of the difference between the world of the senses (below) and that of the mind (above).

The terraces contain five rows of Dhyani, or Heavenly Buddhas, as evolved by the Mahayana form of Buddhism. There are ninety-two on each side; on the east, Akshobhya (Earth-touching); on the south,

Ratnasambhava (Gift-bestowing); on the west, Amitabha (Meditation); and on the north, Amoghasiddha (dispelling Fear).

The uppermost row has sixty-four, as well as seventy-two of Vairochana in perforated niches, making five hundred and four in all.

At the cardinal points of the compass there are four flights of steps with gateways (Fig. 62), and the foremost motifs of the lintels is the well-known kala-makara monster, which can be traced back to the second century B.C., where it is seen in the Lomas Rishi cave temple in Bihar.

When one ascends by the eastern flight of steps and turns left, one finds a row of 120 reliefs portraying the life of the Buddha up to the time of the 'Preaching of the First Sermon' at Benares. This followed the story told by the Lalita Vistara in Sanskrit, and deals with his childhood, youth, renunciation of the world, his period of mendicancy, and his teaching up to the time that he acquired enlightenment, i.e. Buddhahood.

The sculptors were by no means mere imitators of Indian models, but created their own distinctive form of Indo-Javanese art which, although obviously inspired by Pāla art, has a tenderness and a soft beauty all its own, comparable with the parent art itself (Fig. 63).

There are many other series of panels, covering the whole surface of the walls along the four galleries, amounting in all to thirteen hundred which, if placed side by side, would stretch a distance of three miles. These contain Jātaka stories from the Jātakamala in Sanskrit (Fig. 64)— stories of the Buddha in his previous earthly lives, which, according to the Chinese scholar, I-Ching, who studied Sanskrit at Palembang in the seventh century, were extremely popular in the islands. The basement had, it appears, one hundred and sixty more, but these are not visible owing to subsidence of the soil. Some of the panels show the marks of masons, which, according to Krom, allow of a date being allotted to the building between A.D. 750 and 800. Finally I show a typical image of the Buddha from Borobodur (Fig. 65).

Space forbids me to deal in further detail with this famous Buddhist stupa, and all who are deeply interested in its interpretation should try and obtain the 'mémoire' of Paul Mus, who may well be called the willing 'Slave of Borobodur.' This 'mémoire' was published in the JOURNAL of the French School of the Far East, Vols. XXXII–XXXV, and the leit motif is that the Borobodur was erected as a closed Cosmos, that is to say, a representation of the upper stages of the Cosmic mountain enclosed within the cupola of the sky. Quaritch Wales is right in saying that the building is Indian both in conception and architectural form, and, according to him, similar hollow *stupas* containing stones representing Mount Meru have been found in Ceylon. At this period the cult of the Deva-Raja in its Çaivite form was beginning to take second place in Java, and Schnitger goes so far as to say that, because the Javanese had their megalithic terraces before the coming of the Indians: 'It is perhaps for this reason that the Javanese appreciate Borobodur more than all their other sanctuaries. Temples with covered chambers were never popular with them, but Borobodur, boldly seated on its terraces, open to the sky, free in nature like an altar of beauty, certainly smacked of the soil.'

Three other Buddhist shrines in the neighbourhood of Borobodur deserve mention, namely Chandi Kalasan, and Chandi Mendoet, as well as Chandi Sewou, all of which were erected during the period A.D. 775–850.

In 778 A.D. the Maharajah of Panang Karau, at the instance of his spiritual mentors, founded a sanctuary dedicated to the goddess Tara, and consecrated to its service the village of Kalasa. This is the monument known as Chandi Kalasan (Fig. 66), situated to the east of the town of Jogjakarta. In A.D. 782 the ruler of a country called Gaudi (Western Bengal) named Kumaraghosha consecrated at Kelurak, not far from Kalasan, an image of the Boddhisattva Manjusri, making at one stroke a synthesis of the Buddhist Tri Ratana, the Brahman Trimurti and all the gods. The script used in both these inscriptions is North-Indian and shows the influence at this time of the University of Nalandā. Wales states that the Kalasan inscription only refers to the first of three buildings on the same site, and gives a date of mid-ninth century to the other two. This is of no great importance, as they still fall within the Sailendra period of rule.

Of Chandi Mendoet it may be said that it forms the best of introductions to the wonders of Borobodur. This latter great shrine is about twenty-five miles north-west of Jogjakarta, and on the way to it, on the left bank of the Ello river, just above its confluence with the Progo river, one finds the Chandi Mendoet. Scheltema says of it that, although much smaller, 'this temple is scarcely less nobly conceived and conscientiously executed,' and adds that although the Kedu plain is called 'the Garden of Java,' if it had nothing more to offer the visitor than the Borobodur and the Mendoet, it would reward him royally and far beyond expectation (Fig. 67).

He says that there are grounds for believing that the same prince, who began the building of the Borobodur, founded the Chandi Mendoet as a mausoleum to perpetuate his own memory, and that his ashes are deposited in it. Although he is nameless, he may be represented by two pieces of sculpture at the entrance to the inner chamber of the chapel, which represent a royal couple with a dozen children, such as we find in Western churches of the fifteen and sixteenth centuries.

In the inmost shrine-chamber may be seen one of the finest statues found in Java of the Buddha seated in the 'European fashion' (Fig. 68) between two Bodhisattvas in the attitude of preaching the law. This image, which is 14 feet high, is in a pure Gupta style and raises questions to which there seems no answer, since Scheltema says that the image was far too large to be put into the chamber, and that the latter must have been erected round it. In the triangular spaces to the right and left of the staircase which leads to the entrance are twenty-two scenes carved in stone, though very much damaged, representing fables of animals, such as the tortoise and the geese, the crow and the snakes, etc.

In point of actual area covered, Chandi Sewou, which means 'the thousand temples,' is said to be the largest of the temple groups in Java, and consists of the main building surrounded by nearly 250 subsidiary shrines in unequal rows. It may be found a short distance east of Chandi Kalasan. Scheltema says that an inscription was found near one of these, from which it may be deduced that the temple is about the same age as the Borobodur, i.e. round about A.D. 800. Quaritch Wales infers from this that Tantric Buddhism, 'of which the magic practices would be most readily acceptable by the Javanese, was by then already established in Java.' According to Krom, this is clearly shown by the Borobodur itself.

At another temple called Chandi Plaosan, north-east of Jogjakarta, is a beautiful Sailendra image of the Bodhisattva, Maitreya, in which the left leg is drawn up to rest on the throne while the right leg rests on a lion's head (Fig. 69).

At the Chandi Banon, south-east of Borobodur, is a remarkable statue of Çiva, crowned and bearded, with full protruding stomach— a very original type (Fig. 70), and the other illustrations shown in this book of the Sailendra period show a very beautiful sitting figure of the Bodhisattva Lokeçvara (Fig. 71) and a Ganeça decorated with skulls, which seems to have been very popular in Java (Fig. 72).

In the middle of the ninth century the old kings, who had retired to Eastern Java, ousted the Sailendras from Central Java and regained their power. This led to a renewal of Brahmanism in architecture, but there was no artistic reaction and it is thought by many competent judges that the majestic temple of Prambanan contains the finest sculptured panels to be found in Java. At the same time Buddhist temples of the Mahayana order continued to be built, as is witnessed by the erections of Chandi Plaosan and Chandi Sajiwan in the same neighbourhood, which shows that this form of Buddhism had taken fairly deep root.

The group of temples, called Prambanan, lie beside the main road between Jogjakarta and Surakarta, where the two Residences meet, but still in the boundaries of the former, and even in their most neglected condition, were always held in great veneration by the population. There are six buildings in two lines of three. The largest is dedicated to Çiva, and the two less important to Vishnu and Brahma respectively, and each is faced by a smaller shrine, possibly, as Wales suggests, for the appropriate *vahana* or vehicle. Krom considers the Prambanan to represent the apotheosis of Çivaism—as Borobodur does of Buddhism —and was perhaps erected as a political counterpoise to the influence of the latter. The intention was clearly to aim at something grander and more imposing than anything hitherto attempted. Certainly the sculptures are the culminating point of Indo-Javanese art in bas-reliefs.

The accompanying plan shows the position of Prambanan particularly in relation to the Buddhist Chandis of Kalasan to the south-west, and Sajiwan to the south-east and Sewou and Plaosan to the north-east. The type of image representing Çiva at Prambanan is well illustrated in the figure shown (Fig. 73) which in fact differs very little in style from the Bodhisattva at Chandi Plaosan and confirms my opinion that they cannot be separated very far in point of time.

The other two illustrations are representative examples of the Brahmanic scenes sculptured at Loro Jonggrang, the principal building, and show a liveliness in composition and execution very different from the gentle placid scenes depicted at Borobodur. It is undoubtedly this movement and activity which appeals to the European mind and eye (Figs. 74, 75 and 76).

Chinese travellers give lively pictures of the country, and one is sufficiently remarkable, curious and alarming to deserve mention. 'There are venomous young ladies on the island, and, if one has intercourse with them, one is attacked by extremely painful ulcers and dies, but the body does not in any sense decompose.' This story gives rise to many strange reflexions, on which, however, it is hardly becoming to dwell here.

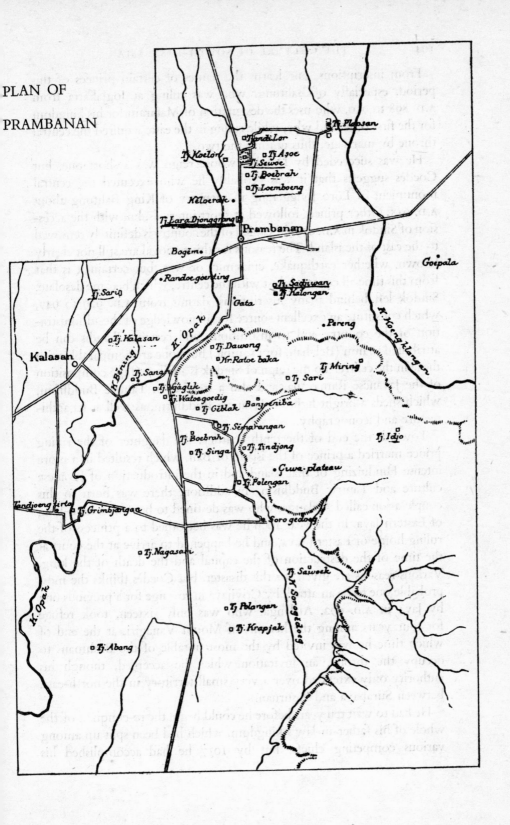

PLAN OF

PRAMBANAN

From inscriptions, one learns the names of certain princes of this period, especially of Balitung, who was ruling at Jogjakarta from A.D. 898 to 910, who uses the designation of Mataram for his kingdom for the first time, and who, while ruling in the east, acquired the central throne by marriage, thus uniting the two.

He was succeeded by Daksha, whose reign was a short one, but Coedès suggests that it was probably he who executed the central monument of Loro Jonggerang in memory of King Balitung about A.D. 915. Other princes followed at short intervals, but with the accession of Sindok in A.D. 929 the capital of the country is definitely removed to the east of the island. The reasons for this removal are still not clearly known, whether earthquake, epidemic, or war, but certain it is that from this time all contact is lost with the centre, which became desolate. Sindok left behind many inscriptions, dating from A.D. 929 to 947, which constitute an excellent source for a knowledge of the administration of the country and its institutions, and certain Chandis can be attributed to him (Belahan, for example) but none are comparable with those in the centre. To the reign of Sindok is attributed the composition of the Javanese Ramayana, and also a treatise on Tantric Buddhism, which sheds a bright light on Javanese Buddhism, as well as its architecture and iconography.

Towards the end of the tenth century, the daughter of the ruling prince married a prince of the island of Bali, which resulted in a more intense Hinduizing of that island and in the introduction of Javanese culture and Tantric Buddhism. In addition, there was born to this couple a son called Airlanga, who was destined to become a hero-king of Eastern Java. In the year 1006 he was betrothed to a princess of the ruling house of Eastern Java, and he happened to arrive at the court at the time of the destruction of the capital and the death of the king. Various reasons are given for this disaster, but Coedès thinks the most probable one to be an attack by Çrivijaya in revenge for a previous one by Java in A.D. 992. Airlanga, who was only sixteen, took refuge for four years among the hermits of Mount Vanagiri, at the end of which time he was invited by the most notable of the Brahmans to occupy the throne, an invitation which he accepted, though his authority only extended over a very small territory in the north-east, between Surabaya and Pasuruan.

He had to wait ten years before he could begin the re-conquest of the whole of his father-in-law's kingdom, which had been split up among various competing chiefs, but by 1037 he had accomplished his task and 'could take his seat on the Lion-Throne, adorned with jewels.'

Airlanga founded a number of monasteries, and the splendid image of Vishnu to be found at the Belahan Chandi (Fig. 77) is said to be a portrait of him, since he was buried there after his death in 1049. It will be seen at once that, although the origin of this image is India, the whole conception and execution have become Javanese. It is the likeness of a very handsome young Indonesian.

During his reign there was a signal outcrop of literary activity, including one of the most famous of Javanese works, the Çivaçasana, the old Javanese Code, as well as the adaptation in Javanese of three episodes from the Mahābhārata.

At his death, Airlanga divided the kingdom into two parts, to avoid a conflict between two of his sons, and these divisions were named Jangala and Panjalu.

The next hundred and fifty years remain stagnant and are practically a blank. There are no monuments of any importance known of this period, and it is not until the beginning of the thirteenth century that we can find any reflowering of Javanese architecture. About the year 1220 the kingdom, which is now called Kadiri, is captured by an adventurer of the name of Angrok, who first gained possession of Tumapel to the north-east of Malang and then revolted against the king of Kadiri and founded a new dynasty at Tumapel in Jangala. This latter State had long since been reunited with Panjalu under Kadiri, but Angrok took the credit for achieving this, as he wished to give the impression of renewing the traditions of the old Javanese State under Airlanga.

The capital of the new state was first called Kutaraja but from 1254 onwards Singhasari, and it is this latter name which gives rise to the Javanese style of sculpture seen in the two illustrations shown of Durga, the spouse of Çiva, slaying the bull (Fig. 78), and of the beautiful image of Prajnaparamita of the Mahayana canon, now in the Leyden Museum in Holland (Fig. 79). From these it will be seen how distinctive the style has become, with much freedom of movement in the one, and much grace and charm in the other. I confess to a great admiration and liking for this period, even if I find no great feeling of spirituality in the expression.

Wales is inclined to think that there was a new wave of Pāla influence from North-East India at this time, especially in the lion head and makara seen at the Chandi Singhasari, where the religion practised was

Çaivite, as opposed to the late Mahayana Buddhism seen in Chandi Djago. It seems rather late for Pāla influence to be coming from India, but there does certainly appear to be an affinity with Pāla art in the figure shown of Bhrkouti from Djago (Fig. 80) and it is possible that there was an influx of Buddhist monks from Nalandā after the final expulsion of Buddhism from India. However, in the moulding on the Chandi itself, seen in the next illustration (Fig. 81), the figures appear to be peculiarly Javanese, and to have lost touch with India; evidently the sculptors and the architect-masons were not of the same school. The animal forms, whether human or otherwise, have grown much freer and there is a humorous, even puckish, feeling about some of them. Indeed, from now onwards there is a gradual fading of the Indian influence and the rise of a purely indigenous art. It is seen, not only in architecture and sculpture, but also in Javanese literature and in the history of the Wayang, or Shadow Play, which received its form in Java at this time. Customs and manners take on a definite Indonesian tone, and thus begins that evolution of which we see the result in modern Java.

Towards the end of the thirteenth century, there were rebellions and counter-rebellions, which ended in the murder of the reigning prince and the seizure of the throne by a usurper, but in 1292 Kublai Khan sent a Chinese fleet to demand the customary tribute which had not been paid and to avenge an insult committed against his envoy; and this attack, which was in the main successful, resulted in the restoration to the throne of the rightful heir and the transfer of the capital to Majapahit (a good deal north of Singhasari and west of Surabaya) by which name the kingdom was thereafter known. It was an odd name to choose, since, according to Scheltema *Maja* is 'fruit' and *Pahit* 'bitter.'

Cordier, in his LES VOYAGES EN ASIE AU XIVᵉ SIÈCLE DU BIEN-HEUREUX FRÈRE ODORIC DE PORDENONE, relates how this Father visited Java in 1321 and gave the following interesting description of it: 'ceste isle a bien trois mille milles de tour. Li rois de ceste isle a sept rois tous couronnez. Ceste isle est moult habitée et la seconde meilleure que soit en tout le monde. . . . Le roy de ceste isle demeure en un merveil-leux palais et tres grant. . . . Le grant Caan de Cathay qui est le souverain empereur de tous les Tartres, a souvent meu guerre a ce roy cy, et souvent a lui s'est assemblés a bataille, mais cilz rois cy a tous jours vainçu et desconfit.' This would seem to be a reference to the Chinese attack of 1292, when the restored king did prevail upon the Chinese

fleet to re-embark and leave him in peace. An excellent idea of the
sculpture of this period is seen in the severely stylized figure of Harihara
(Fig. 82), now in the Batavia Museum which actually represents the
King Kritarajasa, who founded Majapahit in 1292 and who died in
1309. His mausoleum in the Çaivite form is situated at Simping. As
regards the architecture, Krom says that at this time brick was preferred
to stone, but as will be seen from the illustration, Panataran (Fig. 83),
the chief temple of the realm which still stands in the far south-east of
the island and which dates in the main about 1320–50, is built of stone.
Many later buildings were added, the last one known being dated 1454.

Of this temple Krom says that it consists of many buildings but no
cohesion, that it is in fact an incoherent mass of temples and terraces.
Even in the decoration there is the same fault; the artists were working
quite independently of one another in a haphazard kind of manner, and
the compositions and style vary throughout. This is not altogether
surprising if the buildings cover a period of 125 years. Much of it is
beautiful, but it is obviously chosen for its decorative value and has no
relation to the building which it adorns. The figures on the stone reliefs
are very similar to the Wayang cut-out figures, and there is a distinct
leaning towards impressionism (Fig. 84). Here, at long last, Çiva and
the Buddha have been united and the sentence was coined 'Buddha and
Çiva are One.' Indeed, Scheltema quoted the poet Tantular as saying
that 'Buddha is one with the Trimurti.'

Krom says of this period that the people were not inclined to
maintain their temples in good order and that, when they fell to ruin,
they made no attempt to restore them but proceeded to build new
ones. There was always the same tendency in Siam and I presume, in all
Buddhist lands; but there *was* a reason, namely, that there was no *merit*
in a son restoring his father's temple and that, to acquire merit, he must
build one of his own.

Scheltema states that there are the remains of many brick structures
in East Java and gives the names of Papoh, built in 1301, Tagal Sari in
1309, and Kali Chilik in 1349.

Basing himself on the researches of Stutterheim, Wales devotes a long
chapter to the cosmic significance of Panataran, and the religious
observances of the Majapahit period, but I do not intend to follow him
in detail in this general survey of cultural Java and will only emphasize
that throughout the whole of Javanese history there is one deity who
has always occupied a very important position, and that is the goddess
Sri, the Earth Mother and goddess of glory and fertility, especially rice,

of whom I show a beautiful illustration in bronze (Fig. 85), possibly of the tenth to twelfth century, since it has much affinity with the Pāla style, especially in the head-dress, ornaments and lotus-throne.

During the fourteenth century Western Java was allied to the kingdom of Çrivijaya, and war soon ensued between the latter and the eastern state of Majapahit for the supremacy of the archipelago. In 1377 Çrivitaya was reduced to impotence and all the islands, including even the lower half of the Malay Peninsula, recognized Majapahit as overlord.

The chief king of Majapahit during the fourteenth century was Rajasanagara who ruled from 1350 to 1389, but it seems that, although he used the temple of Panataran as his favourite place of worship, no new buildings of any importance are attributed to him. He did, however, complete the well-known bas-relief at Panataran, representing scenes from the Ramayana and Krishnayana which had been begun in 1347. He died in 1389 and from this time the power of Majapahit began to decline. First of all, there arose a civil war over the succession, and secondly Malacca was founded and began to develop as the centre for the spread of the Moslem Faith, which was not slow in penetrating the islands.

For centuries the Arabs and Indians had traded with Java and the islands. Many stayed behind, intermarried with the local women and founded Moslem communities. From the end of the thirteenth century Northern Java gradually became converted, and with the establishment of Malacca in 1402 a great impulse was given to the new creed. A certain Malik (or Maulana) Ibrahim is cited as the first apostle of Islam in Eastern Java, and the inscription on his tomb dated 1419 is, apart from an isolated one of the late eleventh century, the earliest Moslem inscription in Java. As time went on, the Hindu cults gradually took to the hills and the Javanese chronicles say that the prosperity of the island vanished.

By the end of the fifteenth century the last refuges of Hinduism were in the island of Bali, which has never been converted to Islam, and certain hilly regions of Eastern Java. I need not dwell here on the attitude of Islam towards sculpture and bas-reliefs or, indeed, any representation of the human form, and it is, therefore, fitting that at this point my tale of Javanese culture should come to an end.

CHAPTER VII

CAMBODIA—ITS INDIAN ORIGIN

To a true lover of art who has acquired a sense of world values and is free from the narrow vision given by his European training, the study of ancient Cambodian (Khmer) art is entrancing.

It is rich without being gaudy, and magnificent without being garish, and if I have to find some European parallel for comparison, the nearest I can point to is the late, rich Norman style, such as we see in deep recessed cathedral and church doorways in England, which, strangely enough, is almost contemporaneous with classical Khmer architecture at its best.

It is impossible to do full justice to my subject in the course of two chapters. It covers such a span of time—seven hundred years or more— and is so splendid, that I can only hope to awaken your interest in its glories and to incite you to study it further. My first chapter is devoted to a survey of the subject as a whole and to a consideration of the origins in India from which Khmer art and architecture gradually took shape. For my second chapter I have chosen four of the principal temples which cover a period of nearly three hundred years, and which will, I hope, substantiate the claim I have made for their richness and beauty.

Ever since the French established a protectorate over Cambodia in 1864, and the explorer, Henri Mouhot (a Channel Islander), re-discovered the temple and city of Angkor at the head of the Great Lake at about the same period, numbers of French scholars and explorers have devoted their lives to a study of Khmer art and architecture. The foundation of the French school of the Far East in 1898 gave a great fillip to those studies, and, when the whole region of Angkor was ceded by Siam to France in 1907, work on a complete survey of the wonders of Angkor began in earnest. That work, in spite of the efforts made and feats achieved during the past half-century, is still by no means finished— indeed, is still only in its youth. In 1902–7–11 Commandant Lunet de Lajonquière brought out his INVENTAIRE DESCRIPTIF DES MONU-MENTS DU CAMBOGE: in 1903 Aymonier published his three volumes on 'Le Camboge,' and during the next twenty years many long articles appeared in the BULLETIN of the French school on every phase of

Khmer art and life—until, between 1921 and 1926, George Groslier was in a position to edit an extensive work on the arts, monuments and ethnography of Cambodia, consisting of seven parts in all. Thereafter Coedès, following in Finot's footsteps, published his weighty volumes on Khmer inscriptions in Sanskrit and ancient Khmer, and in 1944 issued his comprehensive work on L'HISTOIRE ANCIENNE DES ÉTATS HINDUISÉS D'EXTRÊME-ORIENT, a work of the utmost value to all students of the culture and history of South-Eastern Asia. Quite recently, in 1947, Coedès has published an excellent little volume POUR MIEUX COMPRENDRE ANGKOR, which provides much food for thought on the beliefs of the ancient world.

In the meanwhile, in 1940, La Comtesse de Coral Rémusat produced her book on LES GRANDES ÉTAPES DE L'ÉVOLUTION DE L'ART KHMER—the first analytical work of its kind and of first-class importance to all students. I must not forget, too, that between 1929 and 1932 the French school issued seven large and beautiful volumes of photographs of the Great Temple of Angkor: and quite recently a new and up-to-date guide to Angkor by Maurice Glaize has been published in Saigon.

There are many other French scholars, Stern, Parmentier, Marchal, Goloubev, and their colleagues, who have contributed in no small measure to our knowledge of Khmer art, but they must forgive me if I do not deal specifically with their work here.

In French, therefore, there is now a mass of literary material for the study of our subject, but in England, except for a number of popular or semi-popular books, such as Ponder's CAMBODIAN GLORY and Quaritch Wales's TOWARDS ANGKOR, nothing has ever been published describing or illustrating what can be claimed, without any exaggeration, as one of the master productions of mankind, whether in architecture or sculpture.

It is true that all these monuments lie in French territory and obviously will not attract the same attention in England as those in British lands; but there are English books on the antiquities of Persia, China, Egypt, Peru and other ancient lands and civilizations: what is there about these truly magnificent remains which renders them less interesting in English eyes?

Cambodia lies to the east of Siam, between long. 102° and 108° E., and lat. 10° and 15° N., and is now one of the five States of French Indo-China. It is a protectorate and has a king, whose capital is at Pnom-Penh.

In the centre of the kingdom is a Great Lake over 100 miles long from north-west to south-east, and at the head of this lake lie the ruins of the ancient capital Angkor. Through the heart of it runs the great river Mekōng which rises in Thibet not 100 miles from the Yang-tze-Kiang and flows down to its delta round Saigon, for a length of 4,100 miles.

On the east Cambodia borders on the State of Annam which has an emperor at Hué, and to the north lie the Lao States (also with a king at Luang Prabang), and the great province of Tonkin which borders on China and contains the capital of the whole country, Hanoi. To complete the tale, the fifth state is Cochin-China, which occupies the littoral in the south, Saigon being its capital and chief port.

In the early years of the Christian era it would seem that the prehistoric migrations of Melanesian and Indonesian peoples had come to an end. In my general survey I have discussed the direction of these migrations, which is still a controversial matter, but I have no doubt in my own mind that there are strong oceanic elements in Khmer art which give it its own peculiar, individual character.

When the first contacts with India took place it is not possible to say, but it seems that sea-borne trading relations began at a much earlier date than is generally supposed, and Coedès in his HISTOIRE ANCIENNE DES ÉTATS HINDOUISÉS states that 'in many places such as Kuala Selinsing in the Malay State of Perak, and Sempaya in the Celebes Indian establishments had been installed on neolithic sites, which seamen coming from India had perhaps frequented from time immemorial.' To give but one illustration of recent puzzling finds in Indo-China—when Coedès came and lectured in London a year or so ago on 'Archaeological Research in Indo-China during the War,' the first object he showed on the screen as having been excavated in Cochin-China was a gold medallion of the Roman Emperor Antoninus Pius about the year A.D. 150. This recalls the beautiful Roman lamp which was dug up in a banana garden near Kanburi, in South-Western Siam, as I mentioned in Chapter IV.

Oddly enough the earliest records of Indianized states in South-Eastern Asia are found in the Chinese annals, which were translated by the late French scholar, Paul Pelliot, and eventually published in the JOURNAL of the French school of the Far East.

Mention is made in these annals of a State called Funan (which is thought to be a rendering of old Khmer *Bnam* = a hill, since the king of the country was called 'the King of the Mountain'). This State sent periodical embassies to the emperor of China from the third to the seventh century A.D., after which it disappears from history altogether.

There is a legend that as early as the first century A.D. a Brahman named Kaundinya journeyed to the coast of Indo-China and found a people there governed by a queen who is named 'Willow-Leaf.' The Brahman was shocked to find all these people quite naked and proceeded first to drape them in some suitable clothing and finally to marry 'Willow-Leaf' and become their king.

Something was undoubtedly known about India since in the third century A.D. one of his successors sent an embassy to India which travelled up the Ganges to visit a Murunda prince and, eventually, after four years' absence, returned with a gift of Indo-Scythian horses. In that century, too, it is recorded that Funan conquered nearly all the Malay Peninsula, viz. the Indianized states of Tambralinga, P'an P'an and others, but not the 'Golden Land of the West' which may be taken to represent Burma and Siam.

At the end of the fourth century another Brahman, also named Kaundinya, came from P'an P'an in the Malay Peninsula and was received with open arms. He Indianized the country completely and the Chinese reports declare that 'They worship the Spirits of Heaven and make images of Bronze. Those with two faces have four arms and those with four faces have eight arms.' Moreover, 'the King, when he sits, raises the right knee and lets the left knee fall.' These are obvious references to Brahmanic gods and to Indian royal customs. I published an excellent example of the sitting Khmer king in bronze in the BURLINGTON MAGAZINE for September 1944.

At the end of the fifth century A.D., it is recorded that another king of Funan, Kaundinya Jayavarman (this is the first mention of the Indian honorific suffix Varman) sent an Indian Buddhist priest, Naga-sena, to the emperor of China for help in subduing the king of Champa, his neighbour, whom he described as 'a miserable criminal.' As far as can be ascertained, no help was forthcoming and his request was 'laid on the table.' At that time Nagasena reported to the emperor that both religions, i.e. Buddhism and Brahmanism, were flourishing in Funan side by side.

In my general survey I pointed to the fact that there is a definite line to be drawn down the borders of the modern State of Annam, where India and China meet but neither overlap nor clash.

The interesting point is that, while China employed military force to conquer that portion of Indo-China which still shows her influence, India never used aggression to obtain her ends. Indeed, so far from being exterminated by their 'conquerors,' the aborigines of the various

Indianized States found, as Coedès says, 'a framework inside which their own social life and customs could merge and develop.' The Indian emigrants were either traders or missionaries, and the Indianized States of South-Eastern Asia exchanged embassies with the States of the parent land on a footing of equality, whereas all these States were treated by China as 'barbarous' and required to send embassies regularly to the imperial court to bring tribute and do homage.

The Indianization of these States is borne out by the statues of the Buddha, as well as by the splendid stone statues of Vishnu and other Brahmanic gods which have been found, not only in Cambodia and Cochin-China, but also in the Malay Peninsula and as far north as Çri-Deb in the valley of the Pa-Sak river in North-Eastern Siam. To call this statuary provincial would be to underrate it completely. It shows a breadth of conception and execution which is only given to master-sculptors and is certainly as fine as anything found on Indian soil. Some of it may be as early in date as the fifth to sixth century A.D.

First I show two magnificent images of Hari-Hara (Vishnu and Çiva combined in one) both from the southern part of Funan and now in the Museum at Pnompenh (Figs. 86 and 87), which it would be difficult to match, by any standards of form and virility, in India itself. They are both incomplete, and the second has been partially restored, but they are clearly expressions of a mature art, at once highly localized and yet showing no sign of provincialism. They are greater than life-size, and are dated in the seventh century A.D., thus belonging to the very end of the Funan, or possibly to the pre-Angkor Khmer period.

Next is a rare image of Ardhanari (Fig. 88), who symbolizes Çiva and his wife Uma united in one form. It is in sandstone, 2 feet 4 inches in height. The ears and the head-dress are very near to their Indian prototypes, and indeed the figure is an extremely rare one for Further India. Its provenance is unknown, and it was found in the Ayudhya Museum by de Lajonquière, but it undoubtedly belongs to the period of pre-Khmer art and may be confidently ascribed to the Funan period of ascendancy.

Next is an inspired image of a Yaksi in sandstone, 2 feet 4 inches in height (Fig. 89). It was found at Çri-Deb, near Petchabūn in North-Eastern Siam where other relics of an early Indian civilization have also been discovered. It is akin to the beautiful Yaksa figure in the well-known Stoclet collection in Brussels, and the hair is dressed in a form similar to that of a Yaksa found at Koh Ker, an ancient capital city of

H

Cambodia. It is one of the most beautiful works of art to be seen in the National Museum at Bangkok.

Other Brahmanic images, together with a fragmentary stone inscription in Sanskrit, have been sent down to the National Museum of Siam within the last few years by the district authorities of Çri-Deb. One of these figures (Fig. 90), together with a torso (Fig. 91) and the fragmentary inscription (Fig. 92), is shown here. The writing itself is beautiful in character but unfortunately the inscription does not give any connected sense; from its palaeography Finot places it in the fifth or sixth century A.D., and Coedès states that in his eyes 'such a period does not appear too remote for sculptures which recall so closely the Indian canon of the Gupta period.' I agree with him when he says that what especially differentiates these Brahmanic statues from the Khmer or even pre-Khmer Buddhist art in Cambodia is the triple curve of the body; I would not, however, associate these figures with Gupta art. They may be contemporary with it, but I have a feeling that the origin of all these early stone figures of Vishnu and other Brahmanic gods found in Siam must be sought in Central and Southern India, among the Pallavas, Chalukyas and Pandiyas. They are, to my eyes, the undoubted forerunners of those swaying, lissome, sinuous figures of the Chola period in the south, and pure Gupta art is too austere to introduce such sensuous feeling into its creations. In his hand-book of Indian art, Havell gives, on Plate LXI, an illustration of a fine Chalukyan relief from Aihole in the Deccan of Vishnu as king of the Nagas in the Snake world of the Cosmic Ocean, seated in the royal fashion, and surrounded by Nagas and Naginis. In actual feeling this relief shows the nearest approach to early Khmer art that I know. Havell dates it in the seventh or eighth century A.D.

The figures just mentioned are all of the Brahman religion. At the same time equally fine images of the Buddha, from the sculptural point of view, were being produced.

Two of these were found in Southern Cambodia, one standing (Fig. 93) and the other seated in what is called 'the European fashion' (Fig. 94). They have an undoubted affinity with those of the same period (sixth to eighth century A.D.) found in the neighbouring kingdom of Dvāravati (now Central Siam), from which they are probably derived, the ultimate inspiration being Gupta art from Northern India.

Some have attached the name 'Greco-Buddhist' to these figures, but I cannot find anything Hellenistic in them and look upon them as purely Eastern in spirit. If there *is* anything European about them, it must lie in the treatment of the feet.

Very little is known about the architecture of Funan, and it is probable that most of the early buildings were made of wood which has long since disintegrated and vanished. This brings me to a subject which is at once very puzzling, but, by that same token, very dear to the hearts of all scholars and antiquaries interested in the arts of Further India.

In an inspiring article published in French in ÉTUDES ASIATIQUES in 1925, and later in English in the Indian Journal, RUPĀM, in January 1929, Parmentier seeks to discover 'the common origin of Hindu architecture in India and the Far East.' He is of the opinion that the connexion is a consequence of religious dependence rather than the result of an examination of the forms. At the most he feels that there is an undefined family likeness about them, but by no means any direct relationship, although vague points of resemblance seem to establish their filiation with the monuments built in the Deccan by the Pallavas, whose relations with the countries of the Far East are an historical fact. He adds that the origin of the *sikhara*, or sanctuary-tower, has remained a mystery hitherto, and he concludes his analysis by claiming that the main forms of Indian architecture (wherever found) have their sole origin in one of the first edifices of the ancient Buddhist world, namely the venerable *sangharama* of wood of the most ancient communities. This type of building, which naturally perished in a short period of time, was taken and copied wherever Buddhism spread, and this architecture, imported at various stages of its evolution, was developed more or less independently in each country in accordance with the varying conditions obtaining there. Parmentier also states that, if we set aside Pallavā art, there is no other art in India which could serve as an origin, as the other constructed monuments are all more or less of a later date. Nevertheless, he has a strong feeling that this origin should be sought for in India itself.

I heartily subscribe to the views expressed by Parmentier and I would like to make a suggestion in regard to the *sikhara*, which seems to me likely to provide a fruitful source of further enquiry. These square towers, fascinating to the eye, which form sanctuaries in conjunction with a *mandapa* (or ante-hall), are familiar features of both Cham and Khmer art. While studying the early reports of the Archaeological Survey of India, I happened to come across an interesting description of a visit paid to the Central Provinces by J. D. Beglar, an assistant of the Archaeological Survey, in 1873–74. The two places of the greatest interest from my point of view which he visited are Sirpur and Kharod. Sirpur (lat. 21.2° N., long. 82° E.) is now a small village on the right bank of the Mahanadi river, 37 miles east by north of Raipur (Rayapura) town in Raipur district of the Central Provinces, but is reported to have been once upon a time a large and thriving town. Kharod (lat. 21.8° N., long. 82.7° E.) is three miles north-west of Seori-Narayan on the Mahanadi river in the Bilaspur district of the Central Provinces.

According to Beglar nearly all the sculpture from Sirpur had been removed to Raipur, and much of it was to be seen in the courtyard of the Brahman temple there. Beglar reported this sculpture to be Buddhistic and Jain as well as Brahmanic in form and style. At Sirpur itself he found the remains of ten temples all on cell foundations and of brick picked with stone, mostly Vaishnavic in form, but one dedicated to Indra, in which Vishnu and Buddha were both represented, and also three other temples partially destroyed but still standing, one of which is the Laksmana temple illustrated by Coomaraswamy in his HISTORY OF INDIAN AND INDONESIAN ART and by Codrington in his ANCIENT INDIA. One characteristic of them all is the fact that the roofs of the sanctuaries are formed of successively projecting courses of bricks till the latter meet. There is no second roof between the floor of the sanctum and the pyramidal tower roof (as is usual in a stone structure). The Laksmana temple is built in the same manner as the others and rises from a terrace 6 feet high above the ground. It contains a sanctum 10 feet square, an *antarala*, and a *mahamandapa*, both now roofless and in ruin. Beglar goes on to say: 'Externally the temple depended for ornament on cut brick, and the designs appear to have been executed after the bricks were put in position. The sunk false-panelled doorways with deep, delicate mouldings, and the sunshade over the doorway are features deserving of attention.'

Now it appears to me that we have been reading an almost exact description of a Khmer sanctuary tower, and indeed the sanctuary shrine at Kharod (Fig. 95) appears to be practically identical in form with, for instance, the temple of Maha Tāt, still to be seen at Lopburi in Siam (Fig. 96).

Codrington's Plate XLVII, in ANCIENT INDIA, shows in A and C the entrance doorways of the Vishnu temple at Kharod and of the Laksmana temple at Sirpur respectively, and an examination of these shows again the close affinity between them and Khmer sanctuary doorways, first, in the whole scheme of construction and most particularly in the door-jambs and lintels. Of especial interest, too, is

Beglar's noteworthy reference to the fact that in one case he found the lintel, or architrave, of the sanctuary entrance sculptured at the outer extremities with two lions' heads, the bodies being attenuated and prolonged into wavy lines ending in a *makara's* head, the design accordingly showing a lion and a *makara* with a common wavy body. These carved lintels ending in *makara* heads are a marked characteristic of Khmer art. Codrington assigns the temples at both Sirpur and Kharod to the eighth century, without giving any specific reason for doing so, but Beglar was of the sure opinion from the inscriptions found that the temples of Sirpur as a whole could not be dated later than the fifth century, although certain ones specified were clearly of a later period. In his Report for 1881–82 Sir A. Cunningham, whose pioneer work has never received the recognition that it deserves, describes briefly the inscriptions found at Sirpur, which contain the names of Chandra Gupta, Harshagupta, and Siva Gupta, and says that he has no doubt that the temple (i.e. the Laksmana temple) belongs to the same period as the inscriptions, all of which give the name of Siva Gupta, whose date he believes to be between A.D. 475 and 500. Cunningham also maintains that the carvings on the door-jambs are Gupta in style, as at Benares and Eran. He thus supports Beglar's theory.

I am not in a position to judge between these two theories, but even if we assign these temples to a date midway between the two extremes and call them both late Gupta, there is no good reason why they should not have served as models for colonial constructions overseas, and as Parmentier makes no mention either of Sirpur or Kharod in his search for a common origin, I feel that this district is sufficiently important to repay further examination, bearing in mind the aspect of immediate origins, at least, as regards the *sikhara* or sanctuary tower. Coedès refers also to Bhitargaon, where he says can be found towers with remarkable resemblance to pre-Angkorian buildings.

With reference to Beglar's remarks regarding early external temple decoration in brick, I would draw attention to a temple called Tāt Panom, on the banks of the Mekōng half-way between Nakon Panom and Mukdahan on the Siamese side, which is and has long been an object of great veneration and pilgrimage by the Tai or Siamese.

Aymonier makes scant mention of it and records little but the name and site. He points out that *Tāt* or *Dhatu* is Sanskrit, and *Panom* is Khmer = *Bnam*, or hill. He adds, however, that the pagoda is a massive pyramid built of brick, 10 metres broad at the base and 45 metres high, covered with 'moulures' and 'arabesques.'

Lunet de Lajonquière gives a more detailed account. He gives a good description of the site and temple, and then adds: 'We thought we recognized in the lower part of the edifice works in brick arranged in squares like those of a sanctuary orientated in regular fashion, which showed traces of a Cambodian hand. The sculpture on the brick to be seen there, although not of any remarkable finish, inclines to support this conjecture, for nowhere else have the Lao, who scarcely ever use any other form of ornamentation than stucco, employed this style. This original part of the work has been altered by restorations and successive retouches which have entirely modified the entire superstructure.'

In the course of an extensive tour of the north-east of Siam in January–February 1929 I visited Tāt Panon and made an inspection of the temple. The whole *stupa* was being whitewashed and was surrounded by scaffolding which made access very difficult and photography almost impossible. However, when I found that the base of the *stupa*—which fortunately had not been whitewashed at the time of my visit—was constructed of large rectangular red bricks, and that their surface was covered with spirited carving, I determined to bring away some photographic record, if this were at all possible. The results, as will be seen, if not good are sufficiently clear to show the nature of the carving, part of which at least to my eye is undeniably of Khmer handiwork, but the other part is much more Indian in type.

The scenes depicted on this sculptured brick in a progressive series are as remarkable in execution as they are lively in composition. They are 'alive' to an unusual degree, even for early Khmer work. First, we have the Buddha himself seated in the attitude of 'Turning the Wheel of the Law' or 'Preaching the First Sermon' (Fig. 97), attended by an *apsaras* on each side above and devotees below. The Buddha appears to be seated on a lotus-throne, but it is hard to see whether his legs are crossed or not; I am inclined to think that they are. The sculpture is undoubtedly a link with the *Amarāvatī* school. Next follow scenes of animal and court life that may be by a different hand but show a vigour and a sense of proportion which would do credit to any artist. Look at the two elephants. In the one (Fig. 98), how urgently vehement is the animal's tread as he strides along with his rider standing on his back in his eagerness to advance—and in the other (Fig. 99), how measured and stately is his tread, with the rider now seated as if in some royal procession. Look again at the horseman with left arm raised and his steed with legs outstretched galloping along at the fullest speed (Fig. 100). This is the only example of the 'flying gallop' known to me in Siam, but it has of course been known in China from Han times at least. Notice also the intricate carving of the leafy detail in which the scenes are set. Whoever were the authors of this sculpture, this is no 'primitive' art—the detail alone would rule out such a suggestion—but an art which is clearly in the vigour of its prime.

In the absence of other similar sculptures which could be put alongside for comparison, it is difficult to ascribe a date to this frieze, but we know that the earliest buildings in the Khmer period were built of brick and not of sandstone, and I am left wondering whether we have not at Tāt Panom some of the earliest Khmer sculptures still in existence. On the other hand, the Buddhist figure at the beginning of the series shows a clear relationship to early Indian forms, and I suggest that the whole frieze of sculpture may be attributed to an early date, the sixth or seventh century A.D. at the latest. What is remarkable is to find a Buddhist structure at this early date in the heart of Indo-China.

The kingdom of Funan was in the habit, like all the other States of South-Eastern Asia, of sending embassies with tribute to the court of China, but in the Sui-shu (History of the Sui, A.D. 589–618) a new State, Chên-la is mentioned for the first time as following this admirable custom. In the Chinese annals it is stated that Chên-la, from which the first embassy came to China in A.D. 616–17, lay south-west of Champa (which occupied then the coast of Annam) and was originally a vassal state of Funan. The dynastic name of the king was Kshatriya and the personal name Chitrasena. This king is said to have conquered Funan, and his son, Içanasena, who succeeded him, lived at Içanapura. It is clear from this that Chên-la represents the Khmer kingdom. It must, however, be borne in mind that when Chên-la first conquered Funan, it was split up into two parts, Chên-la of the water (i.e. the Great Lake and the lower reaches of the Mekōng), and Chên-la of the earth (i.e. the Lao states to the west of Annam). It was not until the eighth century A.D. that the northern part obtained control over the whole of Cambodia.

The capital of the kingdom of Funan was situated between Pnompenh and Chaudoc to the south of it, and the earliest Khmer kings, after conquering Funan, established themselves at Vyadhapura or Angkor Borei, about lat. 11° N. and long. 105° E. According to a Sanskrit inscription from Cambodia dated A.D. 665, Kaundinya Jayavarman of Funan died in A.D. 514. His eldest son, born of a concubine, killed the legitimate heir and reigned as Rudravarman. This is the last king of Funan to be mentioned in Chinese annals.

The Chinese annals quote Chitrasena (Mahendravarman after his accession) as the conqueror of Funan, but Pelliot thinks it was probably his elder brother, Bhavavarman, who performed this feat in the second half of the sixth century A.D., and this is the view generally accepted now. Inscriptions describe him as ruling from Stung-Treng on the Mekōng (lat. $13\frac{1}{2}°$ N., long 103° E.), and as far south as the present province of Treang (Cochin-China). The father of Bhavavarman and Chitrasena was Viravarman, but it is known that he did *not* reign. Texts which celebrate the successes of Bhavavarman attach him to the race of the Sun, but are silent about his predecessors. It is also not clear whether Bhavavarman was related to Rudravarman. Perhaps the former was a vassal ruling in the north—for there were then two parts of the kingdom —and on the death of Rudravarman seized the major throne. We do not know for certain, but whoever was the founder, it may be confidently accepted that the beginnings of the Khmer empire date from the second half of the sixth century A.D.

From a study of six interesting maps prepared by Parmentier, one can follow the gradual expansion of the Khmer empire as shown by the stone inscriptions found in various centres.

From the second half of the sixth century A.D. down to the reign of Jayavarman II, who came to the throne in A.D. 802, practically all the inscriptions found are in the southern and eastern portions of Cambodia and Cochin-China. There are, however, a few scattered about above lat. 14° N., namely in the regions of Korāt and Surin in Siam, at Wat P'u on the Mekōng just south of Bassac, and one as far north as Chan Nakon—at the junction of the Mekōng and Mūn rivers: and, though these show that the Khmer had at an early date penetrated the Korāt plateau, the great bulk of the inscriptions found indicate that, when the Khmer of Chên-la had overthrown the kingdom of Funan, they naturally confined their main attentions at first to the centre of that kingdom.

In the early years of the ninth century A.D., Jayavarman II established the supremacy of the north over the south and was the first king to remove the capital to Angkor in the north-western region of the Great Lake. Towards the end of that century one of his successors, Yaço-varman, built the original city of Angkor T'om. Early in the tenth century A.D. Jayavarman IV temporarily removed the capital to Koh Ker, just south of the mountain temple of P'ra Vihāra on the northern border. Of this period inscriptions are still fairly frequent in the south, but hitherto no inscriptions at all have been found in North-Eastern Siam.

The Funan dynasty always claimed to be a lunar one, based on the marriage of a very early king with a daughter of the moon. As just stated, the earliest Khmer texts attach the conqueror of Funan, Bhava-varman, to the race of the sun, but this custom died out, and later Khmer kings were very anxious to trace their ancestry from the dynasty of Funan—presumably to give them a more legal claim to the throne.

It is interesting to note that the Pallavā dynasty, which ruled in Southern India from the third to the eighth century A.D. is also a lunar one, deriving from a marriage between the founder of the dynasty and a Naga princess, and that Kānchipuram (Conjeeveram near Madras), the capital of the Pallavā kingdom, is the only place in India so far discovered as being mentioned in early Khmer inscriptions.

The eighth century in Khmer history is almost a complete blank and was evidently a period of great unrest and confusion, and towards the end, of foreign invasions. It is not until the early ninth century that the whole country comes under the control of a single king, Jayavarman II, who reigned for over fifty years from A.D. 802 to 854. One inscription tells us that he came from Java to reign in Indrapura, and another says that he had no connexion with the soil but rose like a fresh lotus. It is still sometimes debated whether this Java is the Java we know today, but it is certain that he introduced into Cambodia the cult of the Deva Raja (the king-god) which had its special sanctuary and a priestly hierarchy to conduct its ritual. This ritual was drawn up so that Kambuja-Deça (Khmer-land) might no longer be dependent on Java, but have its own paramount monarch. As this special cult obtained both in Champa and Central Java, it seems most likely that he did come from modern Java, and this for another reason. The latter half of the eighth century was the heyday of Indian influences in Central Java, when the Sailendras were in power and the great temple of Borobodur was being built; and certainly Jayavarman II was inspired by the great period of temple-building in Java, since it is from his time that we date the classic style of Khmer art, which produced some of the greatest and most beautiful works of man known today.

Until the advent of Jayavarman II the capital of Southern Chên-la had been at Sambhor on the Mekōng river due east of the Great Lake. Here are found the earliest types of Khmer temples, or rather sanctuaries, all dedicated to the Brahman religion. Parmentier says that 'out of sixty-five early temples of which remains still exist in Cambodia, forty-five consist of single isolated sanctuaries [Fig. 101], but at Sambhor there is a triple temple, each sanctuary separate from the others. Of this type eight are known. These early temples are built of brick and more often rectangular than square. The cell within, intended to receive the image of the god, usually had only a single doorway and the roof-vault consisted of a pyramidal tower formed of bricks overlapping until they met: there was no true arch.'

In her work the Comtesse de Coral traces very clearly the evolution which took place in Khmer architecture, beginning with these isolated sanctuaries in the Gupta style in the sixth or seventh century and culminating in the twelfth century in that colossal masterpiece, the Great Temple of Angkor.

According to the Comtesse, during the seventh, eighth and ninth centuries it was chiefly brick that was used for the construction of monuments; that even in the tenth century it is still seen in some of the larger buildings and that it is not until the eleventh century that it is finally displaced by sandstone. It is rare that the towers are entirely composed of brick. Almost always the framework of the doors is in schist, whilst the lintel and the small columns are in sandstone.

Sandstone is not very plentiful in Cambodia and is only found in certain definite regions: laterite, on the other hand, is abundant in the sub-soil and is very largely used for the interior of pyramids, minor buildings, annexes and outer walls.

The development of the Khmer temple was to a large degree conditioned by the problem of the vault. As is well known, there are two kinds of vault; that formed by a keystone, which represents the true arch, and that formed by successive, projecting courses of stone, or brick, placed one upon the other until they meet at the summit. This type of vaulting only permits of spanning a relatively small space. The true arch has been used in the West from Roman times at least, whereas those civilizations dependent upon India for their inspiration have only known the 'pyramidal' type of arch, and thus their use of it has been very much restricted.

The building is generally square, or slightly rectangular at times, and usually consists of a central tower which shelters the god and forms the sanctuary. Sometimes there are lesser towers grouped round the central one, and these are enclosed in concentric galleries.

As time went on, these groups of towers were raised on platforms, representing mountains.

At Damrei Krap in the region of the Kulen hills, we already find at the beginning of the ninth century three brick towers arranged side by side on a common platform. At Prah Ko (dated A.D. 879 (Fig. 102)) and Lolei (A.D. 893), there are six and four towers respectively on a single platform.

At Bakong, where Indravarman built his sanctuary for the god-king in 881, eight brick towers are arranged symmetrically round the mountain platform in stone. At Phnom Bakheng (c. A.D. 900), the centre of the first city of Angkor, this new style begins to develop. Five sandstone towers, of normal size, are built on the uppermost storey of the pyramid, while other smaller towers are erected on the lower graded platforms.

At Koh Ker, to which the capital was removed between 928 and 944, the mountain-temple is entirely artificial and is a graded pyramid much less squat than that at Bakong. Apparently it supported a single sanctuary tower of which only a few ruins remain; but at the foot of the pyramid there is an important series of towers and galleries erected on the ground, to which the name Prasat Thom was given.

There is a similar single brick tower of great charm of about the same period as Koh Ker in the Angkor group of temples called Baksei Chamkrong.

The temple of Eastern Mebon (A.D. 952) marks a step forward. Here we have a pyramid entirely in stone, on the top of which are five large brick towers. In addition, on the first storey are built long halls, which thereafter pursue a long line of development, but evidently the architects were a little afraid of their hardihood, since they made the whole edifice very squat.

This was followed by Pre Rup (A.D. 961) and Ta Keo (c. A.D. 1000) (Fig. 103), where the towers are higher and the pyramid, too; and the gallery on the second storey is covered with bricks and not with perishable materials as hitherto.

A little later on, at Phimeanakas in the second rebuilt city of Angkor there is yet another advance in that the gallery has a stone vaulting and is carried right round the upper terrace.

Thus the stage was gradually set for the building of the Great Temple of Angkor in the reign of Suriyavarman II (A.D. 1110–50), which shows us a Khmer temple at its apogee of construction after five hundred years of steady and continuous development.

CHAPTER VIII

THE CLASSIC PERIOD IN CAMBODIA

IN a book of travel entitled ESCAPE WITH ME, Sir Osbert Sitwell is the first Englishman of literary repute to describe Angkor adequately in terms understandable by the general reader.

He is not deeply concerned with the history of the ancient Khmer, but he can recognize grandeur and beauty when he sees it, and this is what he says: 'Let it be said immediately that Angkor, as it stands, ranks as chief wonder of the world today, one of the summits to which human genius has aspired in stone, infinitely more impressive, lovely and, as well, romantic, than anything that can be seen in China, than even the Great Wall or the Ming tombs.' And again later on: 'The only artistic influence ever to be detected in Angkor is Indian' (though he remarks on an analogy with Mayan art of Central America). 'Certainly this influence and this resemblance both exist: but, as certainly, the Cambodians were a people of the finest aesthetic perceptions, and no Mexican, Javanese, Siamese or Indian temple or work of art can compare with their productions. Their genius permeates every piece of sculpture in the ruins.'

As I have said elsewhere, I would substitute 'Polynesian' for 'Mayan,' but otherwise I agree with every word Sir Osbert says.

I cannot undertake to present a complete survey of Khmer art and architecture in this book, but, to illustrate the theme which I developed in my previous chapter, I have, after careful consideration, chosen four Khmer temples, all of which I have visited personally, and which not only vary in date and style, but also possess many characteristics attractive in themselves. These are, in order of date:

1. Banteai Srei, an exquisite temple in miniature, about 15 miles north-east of Angkor.

2. P'ra Vihara, a mountain-temple on the borders of Cambodia and north-eastern Siam.

3. The Great Temple of Angkor; and

4. The Bayon, the temple in the centre of the second city of Angkor Thom.

Here, perhaps, is the place to say something about the methods of restoration employed today by the French school of the Far East. It is some years, twenty to twenty-five, since I visited these temples, and since then I believe that all four, except perhaps P'ra Vihara, have undergone very careful restoration on modern lines of treatment.

The new system now adopted was evolved by the Dutch in Java, following precedents created in Greece, and in the issue proved so successful that the French school sent a special mission to Java to study it, with results which have been equally successful in French Indo-China, the first temple to be reconstructed being Banteai Srei.

I have recently translated, for publication in the JOURNAL of the Royal India, Pakistan and Ceylon Society, a lecture given in London by M. Glaize of the French school, in which he describes this method in detail. The keynote of the system is that, wherever necessary, the whole building is taken to pieces, and reconstructed, stone by stone, exactly as it stood originally, and reinforced by modern methods, as it never was before.

I never quite realized how insular we still are, here in England, until some years ago I attended, as a delegate of the Royal Asiatic Society, a great gathering of archaeologists at their headquarters in Regent's Park, to study the future of archaeology. The Far East was never mentioned at all, and nobody seemed in any sense aware of the work done by the Dutch and French schools in Java and Indo-China respectively, or of the modern methods they employed.

The vastness of the problem confronting the French school at Angkor alone is well expressed by Glaize in his lecture on the temples there. After saying that a few years ago Angkor appeared to the general public as (1) the quincunx of towers of the Great Temple, (2) the many sanctuaries with four faces of the Bayon, and (3) certain statues of the Leper King, everybody today knows that it is not a question of a single building but of a mass of buildings, a succession of temples covering an area of about 10,000 acres (three-quarters of the surface of Paris) in which are to be found twenty monuments of major importance. These monuments are found at intervals, on the inside of a 25-kilometre circuit called 'The Grand Circuit,' and cover the reigns of more than twenty kings, from the ninth to the thirteenth century A.D. The city of Angkor Thom alone covers 2,200 acres, and the Great Temple outside it, including its moat basins, at least 500 acres. A plan of the Angkor group of temples is shown.

Before I begin with Banteai Srei I must not omit mention of the

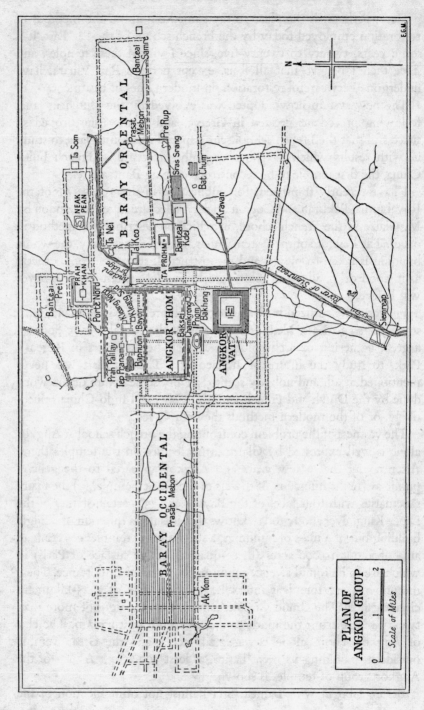

PLAN OF
ANGKOR GROUP

Scale of Miles

central sanctuary on the summit of Phnom Bakheng at Angkor (Fig. 104). For a long time it was supposed that the walls of the present city of Angkor Thom were the original ones and could be dated back to the second half of the ninth century, when it was known that Yaçovarman built the first capital city there after Jayavarman II had experimented with various sites in the neighbourhood. But it is now certain that Phnom Bakheng was the centre of the original city, which overlaps the second city built by Jayavarman VII at the end of the twelfth century, of which the Bayon is the central mountain-temple. The sactuary on Phnom Bakheng is thus of considerable importance as representing the earliest home, at Angkor, of the Deva Raja or Royal God, a cult brought from Java by Jayavarman II, intimately connected with the worship of the *linga*, and dates from about A.D. 890. I will refer to this again later.

Now I begin with Banteai Srei.

This is the name given to an exquisite temple—in miniature compared with the Great Temple of Angkor—which lies in the jungle about 15 miles north-east of the city of Angkor (Fig. 105). The name is described by Glaize as meaning 'The Women's Citadel,' an appropriate name, and the temple, which forms part of an area called in olden times 'Içvarapura,' was dedicated to Çiva. The ruins lay entirely unknown until January 1914 when they were discovered by Lieut. Marec of the Geographical Service, who brought away with him two pieces of sculpture. Two years later, in 1916, Parmentier embarked on the first study of the temple, the substance of which appeared in 1919 under the title, ART OF INDRAVARMAN, where he wrote: 'The smallness of the sandstone buildings was well compensated by the intrinsic interest of the sculpture and the absolute perfection and beauty of its execution.' In spite of this, for some years nothing could be done in the way of conservation owing to the existing commitments of the French school elsewhere. In November 1923, however, a band of robbers visited the temple and broke off several of the Apsaras or Heavenly Dancers adorning the walls of the southern sanctuary. Fortunately they were tracked down and arrested, and their trial gave rise to a minute examination of the temple.

This examination, which was made by Parmentier and Goloubev, led to the discovery of a number of sculptures and inscriptions and to the publication of the first volume of MÉMOIRES ARCHÉOLOGIQUES in 1926. This sumptuous volume, which has forty-eight plates of architecture and sculpture, eleven plates of inscriptions, and twelve architectural plans, contains a full account of (*a*) the temple itself, (*b*) the images found there, and (*c*) the inscriptions, by Parmentier, Goloubev and Finot respectively.

I paid visits myself to Banteai Srei in January 1927 and December 1932 when a certain amount of restoration had been carried out, as will be seen from the illustrations, but I believe that the whole temple has now been restored in its original setting and forms a miniature master-piece of Khmer architecture. I can indeed testify to the skill in execution and the beauty of the setting (Fig. 106).

From certain inscriptions which he deciphered, Finot, who was then Director of the French school, came to the conclusion that, although the temple was partly built in the reigns of Rajendra- and Jayavarman V in the tenth century A.D., the bulk of the buildings and sculpture must be dated early in the fourteenth century A.D. This has since been proved an erroneous conclusion by Coedès, who succeeded Finot as Director, and it may be accepted as certain that the beautiful sculpture which I am illustrating belongs to the second half of the tenth century A.D. when classical Khmer art was beginning to come into full flower.

In this respect it seems to me a pity that the volume in question was published as early as 1926, before the temple had been completely restored and all the multifarious and difficult questions and problems connected with it had been satisfactorily answered and resolved. From the very beginning the chronology of Khmer temple architecture has given rise to long and serious misunderstandings and disputes, and it is only now that any sort of agreement has been reached. When I first read the volume on Banteai Srei, I was very puzzled to find the most beautiful of the sculptures ascribed to the early years of the fourteenth century A.D.—but Finot's name carried great weight and I accepted his dictum—only to find at a later date that his chronology had been rightly rejected and the original date of tenth century restored. It certainly seemed to me as nothing short of extraordinary that, at a time when the Khmer empire was definitely on the wane, it should suddenly, after a hundred years of gradual decadence, produce its most beautiful and artistic sculpture.

I will say at once that the chief glory of Banteai Srei lies in its pediments, and it is not too much to claim that the one shown is one of the most beautiful pieces of sculpture in the world (Fig. 107). The lacy setting is superbly executed, and the balanced rhythm and harmony of the scene itself cannot be surpassed in any work of man.

The scene depicted is a very human story taken from the Mahābhārata, and shows the Apsaras, Tilottama, between the two demons Bhima and Duryadhana. Apparently these two demons were causing such havoc in the world that the great gods became extremely anxious as to the damge they might do. As the result of much deliberation it was finally decided to create the beautiful Apsaras, Tilottama, and send her down to earth as a distraction. When the demons beheld her, each desired her for himself, and so heated grew their passion that eventually they fought for her and killed one another. Thus was the world saved.

The actual fight is seen on another pediment (Fig. 108), and there is yet another remarkable pediment, showing the demon king Ravana shaking the cosmic mountain Kailasa on which sits Çiva with his Sakti, Parvati (Fig. 109).

The temple is laid out in two distinct parts. The main part is an enclosure roughly 40 metres square, containing two main entrances (gopuras) of considerable size on the eastern and western sides, two inner entrances with the same orientation, three separate sanctuaries in the heart of the enclosure, all facing east, the centre one being much longer than the two side buildings, two so-called 'libraries' in the eastern half, and six detached and oblong galleries running round the whole. This enclosure lies within a much larger one, nearly 100 metres square, in which, however, there are no buildings except the entrance porches facing west and east, that facing east being on a much larger scale than the other.

Outside this eastern gopura is the second part. This consists of two buildings, facing north and south, and from here stretches away a gallery about 70 metres long and 17 metres broad with a large gopura at the eastern end. North of this gallery is one isolated building about half-way along it, and to the south are three similar buildings, all parallel and equidistant from the main gallery.

Thus the whole conception is of a square mirror with a long decorated handle. The three separate sanctuaries in the heart of the main enclosure are guarded by stone monkeys, as well as by lions on pedestals, and the buildings themselves, as well as the gopuras, are decorated with standing apsaras in niches, and other beautiful stone sculpture (Fig. 110).

In her work on THE PRINCIPAL STAGES IN THE EVOLUTION OF KHMER ART, the Comtesse de Coral Rémusat considers that Banteai Srei corresponds to one of the periods when Khmer art took on a new lease of life: when the sculptors invented new forms and sought for new sources of inspiration in both past and foreign styles. In any event, it is clear that the architecture of Banteai Srei, together with that of the

I

transitional groups of Eastern Mebon and Pre Rup, which are dated A.D. 952 and 961 respectively, marks a definite advance over anything that had gone before. Indeed, one may say that it represents the first conception of considerable magnitude or complicated design. All the earlier forms were of a much simpler pattern.

I should like to linger over Banteai Srei, since it captured my imagination completely, but space forbids and I can only hope that, in this short description, I have imparted some of the beauty which it possesses.

From Banteai Srei we pass to P'ra Vihara, which, from the stand-points of its location and the labour involved in constructing it, is perhaps the most remarkable of all Khmer monuments and certainly the most romantic.

The temple of P'ra Vihara is situated on the map, about $14\frac{1}{2}°$ N. by 104° E. The north-eastern railway of Siam runs from Bangkok to Ubon, a distance of 575 kilometres, or 360 miles. About 40 miles from Ubon is the station of Srisaket, and from this town one has to travel just 65 miles almost due south, until one comes to the foot of the Dangrek range of hills, the eastern end of which forms the boundary between Siam and the French territory of (what is called on the Siamese side) Lower Cambodia. These 65 miles have hitherto been the stumbling-block in the way of travellers, for the region is very sparsely populated by jungle tribes of Sui and ancient Khmer stock, and the way leads in many parts through thick jungle which holds a very dangerous foe, for the whole district has a bad reputation for malaria. One or two Siamese officials, hardier spirits than their fellows, have in the past made the trip, but have returned home only to die of fever, and the people say that it is the wrath of the gods descended upon them for disturbing their sleep.

But by leaving Srisaket at half-past six in the morning in a lorry, we managed to arrive at the foot-hills at three in the afternoon, having covered the distance inside nine hours. I still shudder when I think of that lorry and its leaking radiator which had to be filled every quarter of an hour with green slime from stagnant pools!

From the foot of the hills we had a good two hours' climb, in many places over extensive outcrops of sandstone, to which I will refer again, and finally reached our camp on a ridge of the hill at the foot of the temple at half-past five in the evening. Imagine yourself on a jungle hillside about 1,500 feet above sea-level, with thick forest on one side and open outcrops of rock on the other. No sign of habitation or life within miles. You suddenly dive down a path, cross the rocky bed of a tiny stream and clamber up the other side, to see in front of you, going up the hillside, an imposing staircase consisting of 160 broad stone steps, each a foot in height and at least 30 feet wide. You can just see the ruins of some kind of building on the top, but it is too far away to discern with any certainty what is before you. In some places the natural rock has been cut to take the place of a step, but by far the greater part of this staircase is composed of great slabs of sandstone cut out of the hills near by (Fig. 111).

When you have arrived at the end of your toilsome climb, you see before you another short stairway with a balustrade on either side down which come two magnificent guardian 'Nagas' rearing their heads 10 feet into the air. On the top of the stairway is a *gopura*, or entrance, in reality a small temple in itself, but now almost a complete ruin, formed of solid sandstone blocks and monoliths (Fig. 112). Passing through, you continue your pilgrimage up a long, paved causeway until you reach another short flight of steps, and, crowning them, another *gopura*, rather larger than the first one, but constructed in much the same form. On your left, as you climb up, you pass a tank or reservoir, now a delightfully shady spot, with overhanging trees and tiers of sandstone steps, cut out of the rock all round, leading down to the empty tank. On the right-hand side, at a short distance from the causeway, there is a raised road which seems to have been specially made for hauling up the blocks of stone, and one can see clearly many places at hand where the stone was quarried. I actually thought I saw marks of the instruments used on the face of the hewn rock. Looking back at the second gateway you see a beautifully carved lintel over the door (Fig. 113).

Passing through the second gateway you continue to climb, as in a fairy-tale, up another long causeway, now an avenue of trees, lined on either side with stone ornaments somewhat in the shape of a *linga*, until you reach a third short flight of steps, and on the top, not this time a *gopura*, but a large rectangular temple (Fig. 114) with two subsidiary buildings containing long galleries, one on either side of the main building. At the left of the steps there is a *stupa*, in fairly good preservation, evidently a memorial to some long-dead warrior or king. Passing through the central building you come to another short flight of steps with broken Nagas on either side, and near by the bases (all that is now left) of two smallish buildings, also one on either side. Then on you go again up the third causeway, and finally you climb a short stairway and reach the *gopura* of the last and largest temple on the summit of the hill. Keeping outside to the right of this temple, you pass behind it and, crossing the intervening space of some forty yards, you come to a rocky prominence, from the edge of which you see the whole panorama of the country stretched out before you, and at your feet a sheer drop of 2,300 feet (Fig. 115). Here is a bird's-eye view of the whole temple (Fig. 116).

The main building on the summit is in the shape of a double temple with a wall (pierced by a gateway) between the two halves. The inner courtyards contain galleries and a number of buildings, some still in good condition, some in utter ruin, but it would take too much space to describe them in detail here. Outside the main building there is a subsidiary building both to right and left, that on the left containing four baths sunk into the floor. From the first step of the grand staircase to the brink of the precipice is exactly half a mile.

It is difficult for me to describe to you the magnitude or the simple grandeur of this work, or to attempt to inspire you with the glorious feeling of mastery that the creator of it must have experienced in the achievement of his conception. One can almost see the priest-king stretching out his arms to the four winds as he stands on the cliff's edge. Well might one cry, *in excelsis gloria!*

The utter stillness now—even the birds seem to have forsaken the spot. The thick jungle but a few yards away on either side. The haunting air of mystery, as if one were indeed prying into another's secrets, and hidden eyes were watching you.

There this monument has stood defying the elements for nearly a thousand years and, if it has been compelled to succumb in part, enough is still left to fire the imagination of the sensitive soul.

According to the Comtesse de Coral this temple, which was constructed in the second quarter of the eleventh century (c. 1040 A.D.), represents a transition between two distinct styles, and shows certain new features in the development of Khmer architecture. The pediments, although still decorated with foliage, end simply in Nagas without any intervention of the Kala-head. For this reason the arc of the pediment seems to represent the body of the serpent. Also here are found triangular pediments which disappear during succeeding periods, when vaulted galleries came into use.

It was obviously a Brahmanic temple as there was no sign of Buddhist influence to be seen anywhere, except, oddly enough, in the *stupa* near the top. Only one statue was seen, a broken, headless, kneeling figure, possibly in the form of the famous so-called 'Leper King' at Angkor. Also there was a lion at the foot of the staircase, and two others at the entrance doorway to the second temple.

Before we leave P'ra Vihara I must unburden myself of an incident that occurred during my visit to that temple, which has nothing to do with Khmer architecture but which has weighed on my mind for over twenty years.

I have referred to the rocky fields we crossed in climbing the hillside. In the middle of one of these, about fifty yards square, I suddenly came across the *single* imprint of a human foot sunk, in parts at least, an inch deep in the rock. I took off my boot and put my own stockinged foot inside it, and it fitted very well, except that the big toe of this imprint was much splayed out, showing that the person was bare-footed. Search as I might, I could not find another human foot print on that rocky platform.

What is the meaning of that footprint? It would be interesting to know if any similar imprint is known elsewhere in the world, and if so, what is the most feasible explanation of its occurrence.

Now we come, in point of time, to the Great Temple of Angkor.

To sing the praises of this superb work of art to their fullest height would require the knowledge of a skilled architect, the imagination of a poet, the flair of a born artist, and the fluent pen of a master prose-writer.

When he first brought it to the knowledge of the modern Western world in 1860, the explorer, Henri Mouhot, said of it, quite simply, 'This architectural work perhaps has not, and perhaps never has had, its equal on the face of the globe.' And since Mouhot's day every sensitive being who has seen it has stood in awe and wonder at a building which, in its highest form, embodies that time-honoured reverential saying, 'Majesty, might, dominion, power': and to these I would add 'harmony and beauty' as well. It is, indeed, a marvel that at a time, eight hundred years ago, in a place remote from the centre of the civilized life of the day, and among a people whom we should look upon as 'ignorant barbarians' there should have arisen such a conception in the minds of even the highest among them, and not only that, but a capacity to execute that conception by the building of a temple in honour of Vishnu which would stand unattended, with the jungle growing up around it, for two hundred years at least and still not crumble away or even lose any of its architectural form. To me it still seems incredible (Fig. 117).

It is an historical fact that the Khmer empire collapsed about A.D. 1440 after a disastrous hundred years' war with the Siamese, and that from that time the capital was withdrawn from Angkor to its present site, Pnompenh. During the succeeding hundred years or more there is a blank as regards the state of the Great Temple, but towards the close of the sixteenth century Portuguese or Spanish missionaries who travelled through Cambodia reported that they had found an ancient city buried in the jungle, which was undoubtedly Angkor.

Now it is probable that, with the accession of Jayavarman VII in A.D. 1181, the worship of Vishnu ceased, and the Great Temple was devoted to Buddhist worship of the Mahayanist order: and when the new wave of Buddhism came from Ceylon via Siam in the fourteenth century, this would be changed to that of the Hinayanist order. Numbers of images of the Buddha have been found in the temple, and it would appear, from certain late inscriptions found there, that it became the object of a much frequented pilgrimage from about A.D. 1550 onwards, with a Buddhist monastery attached to it. One of these inscriptions, dated A.D. 1577, states that the reigning king restored the Great Temple and put it in the same condition as it had been originally: and another, dated 1579, informs us that the king repaired the great towers of the temple, and placed his young son under the protection of the Buddha. In 1666 a French missionary reported that the priesthood of Angkor had acquired the same authority as the Pope at Rome, and their dicta on doctrine were accepted by all the Buddhist countries surrounding Cambodia, viz. Burma, Siam, Tenasserim and the rest.

But, from 1700 to 1907, when that part of Cambodia containing Angkor was ceded to France by Siam, it is clear that the building itself received very little maintenance or attention, and the official report of the French Far Eastern school states that it took three years, from January 1908 to May 1911, to clear the building free of vegetation, and to make it presentable for the public to visit. There was, however, no constructional work of a major kind found necessary and evidently the ancient masons, however empirical their knowledge of architecture, knew how to distribute the mass and the stresses derived from it (Fig. 118).

Now let us for a moment consider its size. The temple-building itself is almost an exact square, each side being 220 yards long, and thus it covers an area of some 48,000 square yards. According to the guide-books our noble cathedral of Canterbury is 500 feet long and 85 feet wide, covering an area of 42,500 square feet or 4,700 square yards: and so, by a simple calculation, we can see that the temple of Angkor could contain that great and beautiful cathedral no less than *ten* times!

I have paid two visits to Angkor myself, each of a week's duration, with six years between them, and whenever I think of it now, it seems so vast and awe-inspiring that, if I attempt to describe it, I hardly know where to begin. And yet, like the (by comparison) diminutive Taj Mahal, which I have also seen and photographed at sunrise, it *is* a whole—a superbly artistic and majestic whole.

The building of the temple began early in the twelfth century, and the duration of time required to complete it is still debatable, within limits.

Groslier, in an article on Angkor which appeared in 1924, considers that a period of fifty years may be put down as the maximum, and Coedès, in his POUR MIEUX COMPRENDRE ANGKOR, is inclined to cut this down still further to thirty or forty years, in fact to the duration of the reign of Suriyavarman II (A.D. 1113–50) by whom it was conceived and dedicated to Vishnu. In his chapter on 'Personal Cults,' which were introduced by that great monarch Jayavarman II about A.D. 800, Coedès makes it clear that the Vishnu venerated in Angkor Wat was not the ancient Hindu god, nor even one of his traditional *avatars*, but the King Suriyavarman II, identified with Vishnu after his death, consubstantial with him and living in his mausoleum decorated with numbers of beautiful figures of *apsaras* (i.e. heavenly dancers) just like Vishnu himself in his heavenly palace. The image of the king may, indeed, be seen on the bas-reliefs of the south gallery where he is twice represented, once seated in the midst of his court, and the other time standing erect on his war elephant.

Obviously this great massive building, with a topmost tower of 220 feet above the ground and others set at each of the four corners (Fig. 119), must, as far as the main physical toil was involved, have been erected by slave labour—but no slave labour could have drawn the plans or calculated the stresses to which the different parts of the temple would be subjected: nor could a mere slave have begun to execute one single piece of the sculpture to be found on its pillars or pediments.

Whether any elaborate architectural plans ever existed will never be known now, and it is more than likely that the architect-masons worked on their store of knowledge gained by tradition from their forefathers by empirical, rather than scientific methods.

As I have already said, they did not know how to construct a true arch, and it was fortunate for them that a temple dedicated to a Brahman god does not demand large vaulted spaces for the meeting of congregations, since the god himself is enshrined in a sanctuary only to be approached by the priest, while the worshippers perambulate round the gallery outside. Thus, no great halls of worship are necessary, as in Christian or Buddhist churches, and the building consists of different *étages* or storeys with a gallery running round the outside and containing the whole, and a series of sunken courtyards with pillared cloisters surrounding them (Fig. 120).

The building is constructed entirely of sandstone with no morticing or mortar, and if any wood was used, it has long since perished. As far as I am aware, none of the tools used for preparing the stone have ever been discovered. The Khmer certainly made use of bronze, and I was lucky enough to find in Bangkok a most beautiful large ring and a hook for use on a palanquin, which have now been acquired by the British Museum. These were illustrated in an article in the BURLINGTON MAGAZINE in October 1941, on 'Ornamental Khmer Bronzes,' together with finials for chariot-poles now in the National Museum at Bangkok. I have also seen a bronze lion and bronze images of the Buddha and various Brahmanic gods, but all such objects are mostly small and of considerable rarity, and, in any event, it is doubtful whether bronze tools could be made sufficiently hard and sharp-edged to work on the stone, even though the stone used was sandstone, which is softer than many other stones used in building.

I may mention here a point of interest for the engineer. I do not remember noticing them in the Great Temple itself, but at the Bayon and many another Khmer temple I have examined the square pillars carefully and they are almost always covered, *on one side only*, with a series of holes, about an inch deep. These may form an oblong, square or triangular pattern, but they are uniformly equidistant and obviously made with some object in view. If they were sunk for the insertion of clamps for dragging purposes, why are they only on one side of the pillar? I have consulted many people on this subject, but no one has yet provided a satisfactory answer.

To anyone conversant with Indian forms, it is clear that the original inspiration must have come from India, though there is no comparable building in that land itself, and when we examine the mass of decorative carving, the subjects are obviously derived in the main from Indian literary sources.

But they have been transformed almost beyond recognition by the indigenous influences at work and, although I cannot point to any definite similarity of form, I seem to feel that there must be a strong Malayo-Polynesian or oceanic force mingling with the Indian. It is almost certain that there was *not* a continuous supply of fresh Indian craftsmen from Southern India into Cambodia, and quite possibly no supply at all after the sixth or seventh century A.D. But whether this is true or not, all must agree that the final result is startlingly real, alive and beautiful.

The outer gallery running round the whole building contains just half a mile of bas-relief on the back wall (Fig. 121); and there are no less than 1,750 life-size figures of *apsaras* contained in the exterior decoration, almost every one of them with a different form of magnificent head-dress (Figs. 122 and 123). Added to this, all the pediments, lintels, false doors, and many of the pillars are carved with intricate and delicate scenes and patterns in almost bewildering confusion (Fig. 124).

Although, of necessity, I can only illustrate the temple and its decoration fragmentarily, yet I hope I have chosen enough to fill you with some slight idea of its majesty and beauty.

Finally we reach the Bayon.

The temple called the Bayon stands in the centre of the second or later city of Angkor Thom, built at the end of the twelfth century A.D., at the point where the four roads leading inwards from the four principal gates of the city meet. It is called 'The Mysterious Temple,' and indeed, it has always been surrounded by mystery (Fig. 125).

When Pierre Loti first saw it, it was enveloped in jungle, and he writes: 'I raise my eyes towards these towers which stretch far above me, covered with vegetation—and suddenly I shudder with an unknown fear as I see a broad, fixed smile on the face which looks down upon me from on high—and then another smile from another tower—then three more, then five, then ten—they are everywhere and I feel myself secretly overlooked from every quarter of the temple' (Fig. 126). Even Henri Parmentier, the archaeologist, who was in daily contact with Khmer monuments, could not escape this sense of haunting mystery. He says: 'The Bayon was, before we started work on it, an incomprehensible, even dangerous maze; yet, on the other hand, it gripped one's imagination and exercised an extraordinary and romantic effect upon one's senses.'

When I first saw it myself in 1927, the vegetation had disappeared—

the site of the temple had been cleared by Commaille between 1912 and 1914—and it was just one vast mass of sandstone blocks, and looked, for all the world, rather like one of the Rocky Mountains!

But even so there were towers everywhere and from them the huge faces of Brahma or Çiva (as they were then called), gazing out in every direction, looked down upon me with that enigmatic sleepy smile, creating such an air of mystery that one felt oneself to be just a minute, crawling insect, useless and purposeless (Fig. 126). Why is it that the East, wherever one may go, always has some immaterial food to offer, and the West so seldom? This, to me, is the greatest mystery of all. I think that here, at Angkor, although the buildings are not of any great antiquity, I realized the age and wisdom of Asia more than I had ever done before.

For many years the Bayon was considered to belong to the ninth century A.D., and to have been erected by Yaçovarman when he built the first city of Angkor about A.D. 890. But in 1927 what the Comtesse de Coral calls 'The mirage of the Bayon's antiquity' was shattered by Philippe Stern of the Musée Guimet, who made a profound study of Khmer sculpture and, having divided it into two very distinctive styles, proved clearly that the ornamental sculptures of the Bayon and of the gates of the city of Angkor Thom, which were definitely allied to one another, belonged to the second or later style. This led to a prolonged discussion from which two important questions emerged: (1) What was the actual date of the Bayon, and (2) Where was the true central mount of Yaçovarman's original city?

All doubts on these two problems have now been fully resolved, the first by Coedès in 1928, and the second by Goloubev, who conducted an intensive research during the years 1931-34; and it was in the latter year that he came to London and I heard him give a most illuminating lecture on his discoveries.

By means of his researches and aerial photographs he was able to show that, as I have already stated, Phnom Bakheng was the central mountain of the original city of Yaçovarman, from which radiated a well regulated system of causeways and basins. Moreover, broken sculptures, ceramic sherds, and the remains of bridges and stairways proved that at one time a considerable population was housed around the central mountain.

In the meantime Coedès had in 1928 discovered epigraphic material in the shape of *stelae* erected by Jayavarman VII at the four angles of the present Angkor Thom, in which he found a passage where this monarch takes pride in having built a *jayagiri* and dug a *jayasindhu*, which terms clearly indicate the walls and moats of Angkor Thom. Thus it can now be taken as practically certain that the Bayon was built at the end of the twelfth century A.D. and is a Buddhist shrine of the Mahayana school dedicated to Lokeçvara, the compassionate future Buddha.

The city of Angkor Thom lies about a mile from the Great Temple along a direct road which passes Phnom Bakheng on the way, and one enters by the southern gate (Fig. 127).

Leading up to the 'Porte Nord' is a most attractive causeway (Fig. 128) lined with gods on the one side (Fig. 129), and demons on the other (Fig. 130), both of gigantic size, 20 feet high and apparently engaged in a tug-of-war for the domination of the world. The demons look to be a 'tough lot,' but I seem to sense a feeling of quiet, confident, determination on the faces of the godlike crew, which is most reassuring to one who, while suffering from no illusions and in spite of all evidence to the contrary, still remains an optimist. Yet I think we are all aware that it *is* going to be a tough fight all the same, if mankind is going to find any true impulse in life beyond materialism.

How I wish that the West could absorb one hundredth part of the spiritual life engendered and bred by the East, without falling into its easy, slothful ways of living! Then, indeed, it would have a full life to offer the world: yet my purpose here is not that of a moralist but only that of an interpreter.

Of the Bayon itself it appears that at some stage of its building there was an alteration in the plans. Parmentier says of it: "In its present state the monument produces an odd feeling of 'piling up' and 'pressing together': the towers crowd against one another, the various buildings press against one another without any free circulation and the courts are just wells without air or light."

This feeling is particularly apparent between the second storey galleries and the 'massif central,' where there remain nothing but dark, damp sinister trenches. Without going into details it seems clear that the original plan did not envisage the colossal mountain now called the 'massif central' but in its place, according to Parmentier, a complex series of buildings on the same system as at Ta Prohm and Banteay Kdei, two other temples, both of which lie to the east of the city at some distance, and which form a transition between the architecture of the Great Temple and that of the Bayon.

It is a little difficult to follow exactly what did take place, or why, but according to Parmentier, before the work of restoration began, the courtyard which separated the inner and outer galleries was choked by an accumulated mass of stone blocks among which it was practically impossible to move.

When this confusion was finally sorted out it was found that sixteen halls, with a vestibule at either end, divided the courtyard into sixteen tiny little courts. From inscriptions engraved on the uprights of the doors of the outer gallery it was learnt that these halls served as chapels, and that each contained several statues, reproducing the features of celebrated images venerated in various provincial sanctuaries. It now appears that these halls were built *after* the outer galleries, but *before* their decoration with bas-reliefs, and that they were wantonly destroyed at an unspecified later date, since the whole courtyard was ruthlessly levelled and the doors, which pierced the wall of the inner gallery to allow of approach, were carefully walled up.

During the restoration one interesting fact emerged. At a depth of about 11 feet below the present floor of the court which separates the inner and outer galleries appeared another floor or paving in laterite which acted as the foundation to a building older than the present Bayon, whose centre was a little to the south-east of the actual centre today. What form this older building took we shall never know, but it seems doubtful if it was ever completed, and it is certain that it did not allow of the present outer galleries whose foundations only go down one metre below the present surface.

Coming now to the decoration of the monument we have to deal principally with the bas-reliefs on the walls of the inner and outer galleries. First, however, I show what for me have a peculiar charm, namely, the dancing *devas* on the pillars (Fig. 131). The balance and harmony, as well as the lively movement of the figures, seems to me a notable achievement in stone, especially at such a late period. They have an obvious affinity with Indian figures of the Pāla period, and yet they are essentially different. For one thing, they are much more lively, and secondly there is a complete absence of eroticism. This latter comment applies to all Khmer art.

Of the bas-reliefs, of which I illustrate some remarkable examples, it is clear that those in the outer galleries are radically different from those in the inner, and, as Coedès remarks, belong to two different worlds. Those in the outer galleries show us the world of men and of historic events: those in the inner galleries the world of gods, of legends and of epic stories (Fig. 132). In the absence of any epigraphic evidence, it is not possible even to guess the subjects depicted in the latter. But the former to a large degree explain themselves, and one can readily absorb the daily life and manners so admirably drawn in stone. I never cease to marvel at the extraordinary skill and sureness of hand portrayed, not only in these scenes, but in practically all scenes in classical Khmer art, no matter where the temple or sanctuary may be found.

In talking of the Great Temple, I mentioned the fact that no tools for dressing the stone had ever been discovered. I have recently been discussing with an artist friend the problem of the decoration and of how it was carried out almost faultlessly, in every temple or other building. He suggested, as a possible solution of this mystery, that the masons did not use metal tools for carving purposes but stone implements with which they 'rubbed' the blocks of stone when these had been set in position, much in the same way as one 'rubs' jade with ruby dust. This is an interesting suggestion and may account for the complete absence of metal tools. However they may have been carved, they certainly show an amazing vitality. Look at the procession of warriors, elephants and horses (Fig. 133), with that magnificent drum-major in the centre, wielding his baton as forcefully as I saw the W.R.A.F. drum-major 'do her stuff' at the Royal Military Tournament last year. Again see the warriors with raised spears and looking so odd in their pagoda-shaped hats being rowed across the river by that superb gang of galley-slaves, of whom every face is a portrait, clear-cut and individual (Fig. 134).

Now we come to more homely domestic scenes on the banks of the river. Can you imagine a more graphic or lively scene than that of the baking of cakes or loaves and their carriage by porters (Fig. 135)? Look at the little fellow kneeling down on the left—his job is obviously to keep the oven-fire burning (Fig. 135). Or again at the woman tending her children on the left, and the lady (I think) who appears to be having her hair washed. What the dwarf-like figure is receiving from the person turning towards him is difficult to say (Fig. 136). Lastly, there is an ideal scene of porters carrying loads, exactly as I have seen them do a thousand times and more. The setting, the harmony, the poise of these figures are perfect (Fig. 137).

CHAPTER IX

THE CAMBODIAN PERIOD IN SIAM

B Y the Cambodian, or Khmer, period in Siam, in Siamese archaeological circles, is generally understood the period of Khmer dominion over Central Siam, i.e. the valley of the Menam river, with its chief centre at Lopburi, or Lavō, as it was then called: and Khmer sculpture found on Siamese soil is generally attributed to 'The school of Lopburi.' This begins to date, roughly speaking, from the year A.D. 1000, i.e. from the reign of Suriyavarman I, whose father, coming from Nakon Sritammarāt in the south, had seized the throne of Lopburi from the reigning Môn king towards the end of the tenth century A.D. In A.D. 1002 his son, Suriyavarman, proceeded to capture the throne of Cambodia itself at Angkor, and by this means brought the whole of Central and Southern Siam within the Khmer dominions.

But the Khmer dominions once embraced almost the whole of North-Eastern Siam, and especially the valley of the Mūn river, and in any survey of Khmer art in Siam, we have to take both regions into consideration. It may be stated in passing that at a later date, when the Tai had finally smashed the Khmer power in the middle of the fifteenth century A.D., Cambodia became a vassal state of Siam. Right up to modern times Angkor itself was in Siamese territory until it was ceded to France as lately as 1907.

This is why Siamese and Cambodian customs, dress, music and dancing are today so much akin, in spite of the fact that the two languages, which are allied in script, have remained separate in speech. Indeed, though I have been able to converse freely in Siamese with old Siamese-born residents of Angkor, who were bilingual, I could scarcely understand a word of the Cambodian tongue.

The Cambodians, or Khmer, began to penetrate the north-east of Siam at an early date, in the seventh and eighth centuries A.D. Now it is true that certain examples of Dvaravati (Môn) images of the Buddha, usually small bronze figures, have also been found in North-Eastern

Siam, but it is not likely that the Khmer had the same forceful competition to meet there, in the cultural world, as they found later on at Lopburi in Central Siam. It will be interesting, therefore, at this point to give illustrations of two images of the Buddha, both made in Siam, and both products of Khmer art, the one from the garrison town of Pimai near Kōrat, and the other from Wat Mahā-Tāt at Lopburi (Figs. 138 and 139).

These two will, I think, exactly illustrate the differences which I wish to demonstrate. Let us take the Pimai image first (Fig. 138). Notice the slight downward tilt of the head, as well as the downward cast of the eyes; also the manner in which the hair is treated, and the uṣṇiṣa. There is little doubt that the Pimai image is the work of a pure Khmer artist carrying on the traditions of the metropolis, as seen in those typical twelfth-century images from Angkor. Now look at the Lopburi figure (Fig. 139). The uṣṇiṣa and the hair treatment, which are entirely different in the Pimai figure, are characteristic of Khmer figures created in Central Siam. The eyebrows are slightly curved and the half-closed eyes look straight ahead. What is very noticeable is the broad fold of cloth hanging from the left shoulder; and this brings me to the main point of my contention, which is that in Lopburi the artists were following in the Môn tradition of sculpture, and that Môn influence which was entirely absent at that time in Angkor, has, as one would expect, its part to play in fashioning the Khmer figures of Central Siam.

To buttress my contention and advance it one stage further, I now show a bronze image of the Buddha about 15 inches high, which also comes from the Lopburi region (Fig. 140). At a casual glance this image might easily be ascribed to the Lopburi school of Khmer sculpture, and there is a noticeably strong Khmer influence in it. But actually it represents a perfect example of the transition from Môn to Khmer in Central Siam. The square head, the long mouth and the straight forehead are typically Khmer, but the treatment of the hair and uṣṇiṣa, the inward curve formed by the legs, the broad fold of the robe, and the peculiar raised fold of cloth showing round the waist are equally typical of late Môn sculpture. One has only to compare this image with Fig. 35 in BUDDHIST ART IN SIAM, which is clearly not Khmer, to realize the affinity between the two.

In his work on the National Museum at Bangkok, Coedès says that 'even if certain images from Lopburi possess all the characteristics of statues originating from Cambodia itself, the greater number of those found show peculiar features which mark a period of decadence or, more precisely, of transition. It is from the school of Lopburi, rather than from the classic art of Cambodia, that Siamese art has borrowed a portion of its traditions.'

I accept this statement as regards the influence of the Khmer on the Tai who came later, but it does not give any weight to the transition period at the other end, or indicate how the Khmer themselves inherited the Môn traditions at Lopburi and thereby produced a sculpture which, while showing its Khmer origin, was yet different from the parent art in Cambodia itself. As for 'decadence,' it may be said of Khmer sculpture at Lopburi that it ranges from the sublime to the ridiculous. It has produced masterpieces of sculpture such as the reddish sandstone head in my own collection (Fig. 141) and at the same time specimens of the crudest provincial art, such as may be seen today in the local museum at Lopburi. This is not to be wondered at, seeing that Lopburi, after all, was only a provincial centre of Khmer rule.

An interesting point made by Coedès deals with the proportions of the statues from Cambodia itself and those of a later date from Lopburi. Cambodian seated figures are cut, so to speak, to the square, that is to say, the width from one knee to another corresponds to the height of the figure, and this is the case in the two statues from Pimai and Lopburi just illustrated, both of which may be dated as pre-thirteenth century. In Khmer statues from Lopburi of a later date the width is appreciably less than the height.

A survey of all the sculptural art from Lopburi reveals the astonishing fact that the school of Lopburi, used in its broadest sense and not to denote the particular Khmer period, must have been in existence for over a thousand years, always changing in style with the predominating race but remaining unbroken until the seventeenth century A.D. There cannot be many schools of art of which the same can be said, and one reason why the study of art in Siam is such a fascinating one is because one can follow therefrom all the racial changes that have taken place in that kingdom.

From the historical evidence, it is clear that Khmer monuments will be commoner in north-Eastern than in Central Siam. This region took its place in the natural expansion of the Khmer empire, and parts of it probably belonged to the ancient kingdom of Funan or its vassal state, Chen-la. Central Siam, on the other hand, was always an outlying province.

In an interesting article on the temple of K'ao Panom Rung, which lies 42 miles south-east of Pimai, Seidenfaden discusses a strong local tradition of a Khmer king who left Angkor to found settlements elsewhere in his kingdom. He followed the course of the ancient highway, 140 miles long, which connected Angkor with Pimai, and of which the remains can still be traced today. Finot, in his DHARMAÇALAS AU CAMBODGE, gives a plan of the road and states his opinion that the numerous rest-houses for pilgrims, still found (in ruins) along that road, were built by Jayavarman II who came to the throne in A.D. 802.

Now the oldest Khmer inscriptions in Siam are those written in Sanskrit found at T'am Pet Tong (cave of the Golden Duck), 15 miles south of Nang Rong near Panom Rung, at Pāk Mūn (mouth of the Mūn river), at Tam Prasāt near by, and at Surin, all dating from the time of Chitrasena (Mahendravarman) early in the seventh century A.D. There are also others, in both Khmer and Sanskrit, dating from the seventh century A.D. which have been found at Ban Hin K'on, 8 miles south-east of Pāk Tung Chai, and at Bo Ika, just north-west of Sung Nern, all in the Korāt region.

Seidenfaden concludes, therefore, that the region south and west of Korāt already at that early period formed part of the Khmer kingdom: in which case it might possibly be Chitrasena who built the road between Angkor and Pimai. On the other hand, during the reign of Chitrasena Angkor was not yet the capital of ancient Cambodia and, unless it were already a military fort, there seems to be no good reason why he should choose Angkor as the starting-point for his road. On the whole, it seems more likely to have been Jayavarman II who constructed it and who is the king of the Panom Rung tradition, seeing that it was he who removed the capital to the north-western region of the Great Lake, and who was one of the most important kings in the whole of Khmer history. The probability is, then, that Chitrasena carried out certain military expeditions into the region of the Korāt plateau and left behind him stone inscriptions to commemorate those explorations, but that it was not until two centuries later that the task of bringing these outlying portions of the empire into close contact with the capital was completed.

Strange to tell, there appear to be no inscriptions of Jayavarman II himself in the region of Korāt and Pimai. The earliest inscriptions from the temple of Panom Wan near Korāt date from the eleventh century A.D. and continue up to A.D. 1187, while the only one found at Panom Rung dates from A.D. 1113.

There are still today remains of extensive Khmer temples at Pimai

K

and Panom Wan near Korāt, and also at Panom Rung and Müang Tam on the road from Pimai to Angkor. The temple of Pimai was built during the reign of Jayavarman V (A.D. 968–1002), that of Panom Wan during the time of his successor, the usurper, Suriyavarman I (A.D. 1002–49).

Now, as is known from the Lopburi inscription of A.D. 1022, Khmer kings appear at different times to have tolerated and even patronized all forms of Indian religion, whether Mahayana or Hinayana Buddhism, or Brahmanism, or pure Yogism. They themselves sometimes inclined to the one, sometimes to the other, and in all probability Buddhism and Brahmanism often flourished together, the people following the Buddhist Faith and the royal court surrounded by Brahman rites and ceremonies. For instance, although Suriyavarman I is described as being born of the Sun (Suriya is the Brahmanic Sun-god), and possessing the grace of Vishnu, it is probable that he was a Buddhist by faith, as his posthumous name was Nirvāna Pada.

The temples at Panom Rung and Müang Tam are clearly Brahmanic in character. But at Panom Rung, in addition to much Brahmanic sculpture, there is one peculiar scene portrayed on a large square *stela*, which is possibly of a Buddhist nature and recalls reliefs from Bharhut, Sanchi, and Mathura (Fig. 68 in BUDDHIST ART IN SIAM). On the right is the figure of a woman in typical Cambodian dress, i.e. nude as to the upper part of the body but with a folded skirt concealing the lower part, with her left arm raised and her left hand grasping, above her head, a tall stem ending in an animal's head. Her right hand rests on a pillar. It is difficult to imagine what this stem is intended to represent. To her right are two figures of men. One, standing upright, is a Brahman with a long beard who is holding some object, which is not distinguishable but is possibly a conch-shell, in both hands which are raised. The other figure, who is not bearded, is kneeling at her side and appears to be offering something in his folded hands.

Seidenfaden inclines to believe that this represents a figure of Queen Maya giving birth to the Buddha in the Lumbini garden; but there is no sign of the child and, although the figure of the woman is strangely reminiscent of ancient Indian reliefs, I cannot see any particular reason for drawing this conclusion; the kneeling figure looks rather like a slave. In addition to Seidenfaden, both Aymonier and Lunet de Lajonquière have described the temple of Panom Rung. A comparison of these two accounts is of interest, as it shows how difficult it is to accept the account of one author alone, however conscientious and careful he may be. According to Aymonier, in the sculptures, which are of a good quality, 'one sees neither gods nor men, but only rosettes, lianas and acanthus leaves.' He thinks that the temple was probably devoted to Buddhist worship and goes back to Suriyavarman I in the eleventh century A.D.; but adds that also a Sanskrit *stela* of Suriyavarman II of the twelfth century came from Panom Rung.

Lunet de Lajonquière says of the building which is situated on a hill, 500 feet above the surrounding plain, that although it is much in ruins now, still enough can be seen to show that, in execution and decoration, it is one of the most perfect of its kind. All the best means of Khmer ornamental art are employed here. He cannot understand Aymonier's remark that no gods or men are to be seen in the sculptures (and neither can I), since there are many lintels and other pieces which are decorated with figures of Brahman gods. There is nothing to show that it was a Buddhist shrine; in fact, all the evidence is against it, and the building is similar to many others in Cambodia which have nothing Buddhist about them. He concludes: 'In spite of certain differences, this building presents the general characteristics of those which we have called "Palaces," and it must be classed in this category. In this case the second palace is missing. There should have been one, and a more important one, on the other side of the causeway in front of the first.' I give illustrations of the group of buildings and of the main sanctuary inside (Figs. 142 and 143).

The temple at Pimai, on the other hand, appears to be Buddhistic, though probably of the Mahayanistic order, judging from the carved lintels over the doors of the main sanctuary, two of which are shown (Figs. 144 and 145).

This temple, of which considerable remains are still standing, is enclosed within a rectangular wall, but it is not yet clear whether it served as a temple purely and simply or was designed as a guardian-fortress. Seidenfaden states, from reports given him by the late Siamese Lord-Lieutenant of the Province, that there are the remains of a much larger enceinte near by, which the latter considered to have been the main town of Pimai in Khmer days. It will remain for future archaeological research to determine the character of this site, and whether perhaps the older site was the work of Jayavarman II in the ninth century A.D.

Fig. 146 gives a clear indication of the type of moulding found at Pimai, which is admirably decorative, and I would draw particular attention to the 'ball-flower,' which is in general use there and which strongly resembles the ball-flower used in Gothic architecture in England of the Decorated period in the first half of the fourteenth century A.D. The only difference is that the globular flower has four petals at Pimai against three in England. A coincidence, no doubt, but a striking one.

From Pimai to Lopburi is a distance of about 125 miles, or a little less than that from Angkor to Pimai. The road would pass through the present town of Korāt (Nakon Rajasima), and debouch from the plateau on to the plains through a pass adjacent to the town of Prabāt, which has been a centre of religious pilgrimage for many centuries past owing to the presence there of a famous 'footprint' of the Buddha.

In Central Siam Lunet de Lajonquière only records eight monuments and six inscriptions of Khmer origin. Of these monuments two of the principal ones are situated at Lopburi. Another, Wat Maha-Tāt, is at Sawank'alōk, and another, Wat Çulamani, is at Pitsanulōk, but this latter is very largely a ruin today.

Lopburi, which was a centre of Môn culture from very early times and which was afterwards a summer residence of the Tai kings of Siam after the capital had been established at Ayudhya, was probably the seat of a Khmer viceroy for Central Siam from the time of the accession of Suriyavarman I in 1002. It now wears a most venerable aspect, and its ancient sites are invested with all the charm of an old world city. It also possesses two rarities of the animal kingdom, said locally to be peculiar to itself, namely, a white squirrel and a blue chameleon. I can testify to their presence there as I have seen them both myself, though I cannot affirm that they are peculiar to Lopburi.

The two main Khmer temples still standing are Wat Maha-Tāt and P'ra Prāng Sām Yot (The Temple of the Three *Stupas*). Both these temples have recently been restored by the Royal Institute of Siam and a considerable amount of sculpture has been discovered in the débris.

Wat Maha-Tāt (Fig. 147) presents, to my eyes, a particularly imposing effect, and its affinity to the architecture of Angkor is obvious. It is on the usual plan of a sanctuary-tower with a *mandapa* attached, the whole in a walled enclosure, and it seems to carry the eye with it as it soars upward to heaven. All the images found here are of the Buddha, and there is little doubt that, in spite of its likeness to a Brahman sanctuary, it seems to have been always used for Buddhist worship. From the fact that Môn images of the Buddha of the Dvāravatī period have also been excavated here, it is almost certain that the Khmer temple was erected on the site of a more ancient one.

P'ra Prāng Sām Yot (Fig. 148), which stands on rising ground, presents a more difficult problem. When I first visited it a good many years ago, the temple was full of sandstone images of the Buddha seated on the Naga king (now mostly removed to the Lopburi Museum), as seen in the illustration (Fig. 149), which was taken at the time *in situ*, thus showing that it must have been used for a long period as a Buddhist temple. But the design is certainly not Buddhist, and the three towers ranged alongside one another inevitably bring to the mind the Hindu Trinity of Brahma, Çiva and Vishnu. Non-Buddhist figures, too, have been found on the towers—bearded figures with their hands resting on clubs—which also points to an originally Brahman construction. As far as I know, however, no images of Brahmanic gods have ever been found on this site, and, whatever the original intention may have been, this temple may be looked upon as a Buddhist one for our purpose.

The French archaeologist, Claeys, attributes the building of this temple to, probably, Tai 'main d'œuvre.' I cannot understand this. It may be late in date and if he simply means that Tai workmen were employed in erecting it, I have no wish to gainsay him since I do not know, but there is absolutely nothing Tai about the building itself—which is, indeed, quite foreign to Tai ideas. If one looks at the shape of the towers, at the figures of the *Rishis* on the door-jambs, at the figures on the antefixes, and at some of the faces moulded in stucco on the exterior (which recall contemporary grotesque Norman faces on some capitals of pillars in English cathedrals), to say nothing of the style of vaulting and framing of the doorways, one must surely admit that they are all typically Khmer and have nothing in common with Tai architecture.

Most of the images of the Buddha formerly in this temple are covered with black lacquer and gilt, though much of the lacquer and gilding has now disappeared. At one time I formed the opinion that these images must be Tai copies of Khmer originals, as the lacquer face in every figure is obviously Tai in form and expression. But, quite recently, since the removal of the images to the local museum, the lacquer has been removed from the faces of several images by the authorities, and when once this with the cement filling had vanished, an easily Khmer face emerged from beneath, glad to see the light of day once more after wearing a mask for so many centuries! It seems, then, that apparently in the seventeenth century the Tai worshippers became dissatisfied with the Khmer presentment of the Founder of their common Faith and decided to transform him into a real Tai Buddha. Figs. 150 and 151 illustrate an example of a Buddha from which the lacquer has been removed. It is 29 inches high and the proportions are excellent, while the look of meditation bespeaks the very spirit of Buddhism. This figure is from my own collection now on loan at Oxford.

The folds, hood and tail of the Naga are also remarkably well executed, and there has been a good deal of discussion regarding the design which appears on the centre of the hood. It is thought by some to represent the 'Wheel of the Law,' but I personally agree with those who look upon it as a stylized lotus-flower, as often seen depicted on the open hand or foot-sole of the Buddha in Siam.

The question of the different materials used by sculptors of different nationalities in Siam is of great interest. As has been shown, there are still extant early figures of the Buddha in a light-coloured quartz, but this material is obviously too liable to chip for general or extensive use, and as a rule the Môn sculptors worked in a blackish limestone which is quarried in the hills of Kanburi and Rajaburi, and which is a singularly attractive, though rather hard material for modelling. Apparently the Khmer tried their hand on the limestone, for I have seen several images, of Khmer inspiration, of this material in the Lopburi Museum. But they are clumsy in make and some of them are unfinished; and it looks as if the Khmer in their turn found the limestone too hard and abandoned it at an early date for the softer sandstone, in the handling of which they showed such remarkable skill. I have also seen two Khmer heads carved out of rhyolite, but this is very exceptional. There is still a firm tradition in Lopburi, Korāt and elsewhere in the old Khmer regions of Siam that none of the sandstone figures of the Buddha were genuinely sculptured by the Khmer artists, but that they were all moulded out of crushed sandstone mixed with a sugary glue. One ancient official in Korāt assured me that he had actually seen it done, but a long time ago, and that the art was now lost. How this legend arose one cannot say, and it is, moreover, possible that attempts were made in the past to mould figures out of crushed sandstone. One has only to look, however, at the illustrations I give, to rest content that the Khmer was also an accomplished sculptor.

Fig. 152 is the head of a Bodhisattva, 10½ inches high, with the Dhyani Buddha in front of the *usnisa* in reddish sandstone from the Lopburi region, and is an example of what may be called the classical style as found in Siam. The head is square and the forehead is straight.

The jaw is square and firm. The eyebrows are almost straight, the nose is rather flattened, and the mouth is long with full lips. The eyes look downward and seem almost closed. The hair is no longer formed of spiral curls but seems like scales divided by partition lines. The whole gives the appearance of a strong, ruthless Being, which, if satisfying artistically, is too human to fulfil the conditions necessary for the representation of a Buddha or a Bodhisattva. There is here little conception of an ideal. It is the portrait of some individual character. Fig. 141, however, 12 inches high, already mentioned, from which emanates a mysterious feeling of beauty as well as of dominant strength, is more akin to the Angkor type than is usually found at Lopburi. The face is more oval and the jaw not so pronounced. The eyes look down and seem almost closed, while the mouth is long and the lips are very full. This is a masterpiece of modelling and a work of the very highest order. This head and other Khmer, as well as Môn and Siamese, sculpture from the author's collection, may be seen in the new Eastern Museum (a branch of the Ashmolean) at the Indian Institute, Oxford.

Fig. 153, 15½ inches high, now in the Victoria and Albert Museum, is an unusual type of Khmer head found in Siam. Sculpturally it is not quite of the same high quality as the preceding one, but there is a nobility of expression and sensitiveness in execution that are very pleasing.

The question of treatment, from both an artistic and a religious point of view, is important. The Môn-Indian art of Siam was based on Gupta prototypes, and the sculptors of that school did succeed in evolving, in their images of the Buddha, their conception of the form of some ideal Being far superior to themselves, as did also the sculptors from Çrivijaya in the Malay Peninsula. With the coming of the Khmer to Siam we see this abstract form giving way to a truly human form which we can judge by human standards, and this is probably why Khmer figures always make such a strong appeal to the Western mind with its intense individuality of expression and its close attachment to Mother Earth. Later, with the expulsion of the Khmer by the Tai, we see the human form once more displaced by symbolism and the abstract conception of an ideal Being: and there is, therefore, a much truer spiritual affinity between the Môn and Tai schools than there is between the Môn and Khmer, or the Khmer and the Tai.

The Khmer at Lopburi, though in most cases using their beloved sandstone for the creation of large images for temple worship, did not neglect bronze in the making of smaller images for private household use, and on the whole they reached a reasonably high standard in this respect, though in no way comparable with their execution in stone. Large bronze images of the Lopburi school are exceedingly rare (though occasionally good forgeries are met with), but there is one of exceptional size and quality now preserved in a niche behind the *bōt* of Wat Benchamabopit at Bangkok (Fig. 154). By some this figure is considered to show already some signs of Tai influence, and indeed it may, I think, be attributed to the end of the Khmer dominion over Central Siam. The smaller seated bronze figures are sometimes particularly pleasing and show a variety of decoration, especially in the stands and frames for the image, which is surprising. They are sufficiently rare and are much prized in Siam. I show a characteristic figure of the Buddha seated on the Naga king which is a good example of their skill in bronze.

Fig. 155, which is 6 inches high (without the wooden stand which is modern), shows the Buddha seated in the attitude of *samadhi* or Meditation under the shade of the Naga king. The features are typically Khmer, as are also the crown on the head, the jewelled collar round the neck, and the still existing portion of the original bronze seat. The ears touch the shoulders. But even here we still see the Môn influence in the treatment of the legs, which are drawn inwards forming a curve in the centre. The proportions are good, and the slender-waisted little figure wears a calm and dignified air.

The standing images are not so interesting. They sometimes reach a height of 2–3 feet, but the treatment is usually much clumsier, especially in the hands and feet and lower part of the body, which are modelled on purely conventional lines. Neither the Khmer nor the Tai seem to have worried themselves unduly about the treatment of hands and feet—to us essential features—but to have lavished all their care and art on the head and torso of the image. Considering the degree of skill which they bring to the modelling of this part of the body, it is hard to believe that they were incapable of showing equal skill in the treatment of the former, had they chosen to do so.

I show one other figure (Fig. 156). This is the figure of an ordinary Cambodian young woman in her ancient dress, or undress. Its interest is twofold: first, it is the only such figure in bronze or stone known to me; and, secondly, it shows in a remarkable manner the ancient Khmer mode of 'doing the hair.' Presumably the spike at the top is a hair-pin!

The Khmer remained in possession of Central Siam for, roughly three centuries, and during the course of that period, penetrated as far north as Pitsanulōk and the region of Sawank'alōk-Suk'ot'ai, where Khmer temple ruins are still to be seen. From a study of the remains there it would seem, however, that the Khmer never annexed what is now the north of Siam. As far as the historical evidence goes, this latter region was occupied from the ninth century onwards by Tai tribes, who took up their abode peacefully in the valleys between the ranges of hills without any violent disturbance of the aboriginal tribes of Lawā. During succeeding centuries these Tai settlements, growing stronger, gradually pressed farther and farther south, and I have no doubt that, during the Khmer occupation, there were considerable bodies of Tai living in the Sawank'alōk and Pitsanulōk areas. Probably they had reached as far south as Kampengp'et on the Me Ping river, and some even to Lopburi. But it was not until the Mongol invasion of China had broken up the original home of the Tai in Nan Chao south of the Yangtsze-Kiang, and thereby caused an important further emigration of the Tai southwards, that the latter became powerful enough to contest dominion over Central Siam with the Khmer, as well as to establish a Tai dominion over the Lawā in the north. This fresh emigration, which pressed on the Tai already established in the Shan states, happened to coincide with the waning power of the Khmer empire which had already lasted for close on seven centuries and resulted in the establishment of the first Tai kingdom at Suk'ot'ai and Sawank'alōk about the middle of the thirteenth century A.D.

CHAPTER X

THE ARRIVAL OF THE TAI IN SIAM

THE coming of the Tai, or Siamese as they are called by Europeans, and the cultural influences which they brought with them offer a problem, the solution of which is still by no means clear.

The Tai are a Mongoloid race with a tonal speech akin to Chinese (though much influenced later by Sanskrit), and their original habitat is believed to have been in Southern China, south of the Yangtsze-Kiang; but what religion, if any, they held when they first came to Siam is not clearly established, nor yet what cultural influences had been affecting them during their journeys southward.

According to Credner, a German geologist, the Tai were always a people who preferred rice cultivation in a tropical climate to living on hill-tops, and concludes therefrom that their home must be sought in the tropical lowlands of the river plains and coastal regions of Southern China, in the provinces of Kwang-Si and Kwang-Tung.

This theory is opposed to all previous ones and has not yet found general acceptance, but, wherever the Tai came from originally, it is certain that at the time of the rise of the T'ang dynasty of China (A.D. 618–906), the province of Yunnan was divided into six Tai principalities, and that about A.D. 650 Meng Hua became the chief of these principalities under a prince called Hsi-Nu-Lo.

This prince's great-grandson, P'i-Lo-Ko, who reigned from A.D. 729 to 748, made himself master of the whole of Western Yunnan and set up his capital at T'ai-Ho (Tali-Fu) at the south-west corner of the great Lake Erh-Hai. His kingdom was called Nan-Chao or 'The Southern Lord,' by the Chinese. Credner has explored the site of this ancient city and found the remains of a fortress as well as portions of brick- and earth-built walls. Pi-Lo-Ko had cordial relations with the Chinese emperor, who honoured him with a grand title, but his son, Ko-Lo-Feng, who succeeded him, allied himself with Tibet and waged war against China, the former's mortal enemy, on account of alleged

insulting treatment which he had received from the Chinese governors
of the bordering provinces. In T'ai-Ho may still be seen the *stela* which
Ko-Lo-Feng set up in A.D. 766 to commemorate his victories over
China, for which he was given the title of 'Emperor of the East' by
the Tibetans. The inscription on this *stela* is in Chinese.

Ko-Lo-Feng is stated, in the annals of the T'ang dynasty, to have
conquered P'iao, or the land of the Pyu, i.e. a great part of Burma,
and also Sian-Chuan, which I am told lay between Myitkina on the
Northern Burmese border and Southern Szechuan. The conquest of
Lower Burma was evidently only temporary as the Shan or Tai Yai
did not take possession of the plains until the twelfth century.

Chavannes quotes the T'ang annals as saying that 'the barbarians
(i.e. the Tai) worship the spirits and those who preside at the sacrifices
offered to them are called "sorcerers".' This would tend to show that
in early T'ang times the Tai were still animists, pure and simple, and
that Buddhism had not yet reached them. On the other hand, the *stela*
records that Ko-Lo-Feng opened the door to all three religions of
China—Confucianism, Taoism, and Buddhism. This is the first mention
of Buddhism in the kingdom of Nan-Chao, and it must be borne in
mind that the Buddhism here referred to means the *Mahayana* or
Greater Vehicle, and not the *Hinayana* or Lesser Vehicle adopted by
their Tai descendants both in Burma and Siam.

It is certain that Nan-Chao had a profound affinity with China, to
whom she owed all her intellectual culture. The native tongue, probably
an idiom of Tai, had no script, and Chinese was the only language
written, as in Korea, Japan, and Annam. A Chinese, named Cheng Hui,
composed the text of the *stela*, and an old Chinese family of Tuan
presided at its erection as counsellors of state. Indeed, at a later date, a
descendant of Cheng Hui destroyed the last of the Nan-Chao Tai
royal family about A.D. 900, and in A.D. 938 a member of the Tuan
family founded the realm of Tali on the ruins of Nan-Chao.

In the tenth century Buddhism apparently enjoyed much favour in
Nan-Chao and magnificent temples were built at a place called San-
T'a-T'zu. The Mahayanistic form of Buddhism was evidently being
practised as Rocher found a bronze headless statue of Kuan-Yin two
metres in height.

Wood, in his HISTORY OF SIAM, states that the Tai kingdom of
Nan-Chao was a highly organized State and that the Tai, although
labelled as such by the Chinese, were no more 'barbarians' than the
Chinese themselves. There were ministers of state, censors, generals,

record officers, chamberlains, judges, treasurers and so forth, while the administration was divided among different departments called *Shwang* which is probably the same word as the modern Siamese word *Krasuang*, for a 'ministry.' Military service was compulsory, as in modern Siam, for all able-bodied men, lots being drawn for each levy; while land was apportioned to each family according to rank, a system still surviving in Siam in the nominal *sakdina* grade conferred upon officials, which originally signified the number of fields granted by the king to a noble.

With regard to the religion of the Tai, Wood gives it as his opinion that Northern Buddhism was probably known to the Tai of Nan-Chao for several centuries before many of them migrated south and some of the inhabitants may have been Buddhists, but that the bulk of the people were almost certainly animists and those coming to Siam did not adopt Buddhism until their arrival there, since these have always been adherents of the Southern or Hinayana school of Buddhism which has flourished in Siam from the earliest times.

While one may agree with Wood's opinion as a general statement, I feel that, before coming to a definite conclusion, more light needs to be shed upon the cultural environment of the Tai who, according to the *Pongsawadan Yonaka*, set up the first Tai principality in the north of Siam in the second half of the ninth century A.D.

Prince Damrong states that, at a time when the Tai were still powerful in Nan-Chao, members of this race had set up an independent State in the valley of the Salwin river and that, owing to the pressure of population, a number of them migrated farther westward and settled in Burma, while others went east and south to Tonkin and the region of Lūang Prabāng. From that time they continued to found colonies in the south until about A.D. 860 a Tai prince called Brahma crossed the Mekōng river and founded the first Tai settlement in what is now Siam at Chai Prakā in the district of Chiengrai. Those who settled in Burma and the valley of the Salwin became known as Tai Yai (Great Tai), now called Shan, and those who settled in the Lao states and Siam were called Tai Noi (Little Tai), now the Siamese. These epithets apply to the stature, not to the qualities of the race.

It seems then that the Tai first made their appearance in Siam at a time when the Tai kingdom of Nan-Chao was within sight of its close. The question, then, which requires an answer is—What relations, if any, had the Tai who came south with their kinsmen whom they had left behind in Nan-Chao? I myself incline to the view that, although they were of the same original stock, the intimate links which had bound the two branches together had weakened to a considerable extent and that, having long been subjected to foreign influences from the west and south, the emigrants to Siam brought influences much more closely connected with India (through Burma) than with China.

Today the two branches of emigrants, the Shan and the Siamese, are easily distinguishable, both physically as to features and dress and culturally as to language, showing that the process of differentiation from the parent stock must have begun many centuries ago.

In Northern Siam it is difficult to find traces of an *early* Chinese influence (except in the use of the cyclical calendar of years) either in customs, dress, literature, art or religion; and the many quasi-Chinese tribes, such as the Yao and Miao, who inhabit the hilly regions of Northern Siam, keep themselves strictly apart and do not mix with the local population.

The only obvious relationship between China and Siam today lies in the temple architecture, where the tiers of roofs so commonly seen in Siamese temples are certainly akin to Chinese forms. It is not yet known when this style of roofing was first introduced into Siam, or by whom, but it must have been some time after the arrival of the Tai, since even their early temples in Siam are in the form of Pagān buildings. Fig. 157 shows a temple in the district of Müang Hai in the Chinese province of Yunnan (lat. 22·2° N., long. 100·2° E.), which has certain obvious affinities with the architecture of Northern Siam as seen in Fig. 158, which is the well-known Wat Sing at Chiengmai. In the Chinese temple there is a kind of Yamen entrance court, which is lacking in the Siamese building, and the eaves come down rather closer to the ground, though similar low eaves are also to be found in Northern Siam, especially where there are no side-walls. The serpent gable-ends seen on the roofs of Wat Sing are a distinctive feature of Siamese architecture, though I understand they are also to be found in Norway. They are not seen in China, or, I believe, in Burma.

We must now turn to consider the cultural and religious conditions as they existed in the north of Siam at the time of the arrival of the Tai. The indigenous inhabitants, the Lawā, were apparently animists, pure and simple, and their culture was of a very primitive form.

The earliest cultural centre of which we have any certain knowledge was Haripūnjaya, the ancient name for the modern Lamp'ūn, 17 miles south-east of Chiengmai, on the river Me K'uang, a tributary of the Me Ping. There has always been a strong Siamese tradition that this town was founded and the district around it colonized by a Khmer princess, Chām T'ewi (Chama Devi), who came north from the Khmer city of Lavo (Lopburi) in the second half of the seventh century, with a large following including 500 priests learned in the scriptures. This theory has now been exploded, and Coedès has shown conclusively that the culture and religion which was brought to the north by Chām T'ewi was Môn in origin. Strong natural confirmation of this lies in the fact that there are no signs of Khmer dominion anywhere in the north of Siam, while the Môn tradition is still very strong in certain parts of the country, especially in the districts round Lamp'ūn, Lampāng and P're, which latter town lies 60 miles east of Lampāng. This influence is still often seen today in the use of the *Hamsa* bird, the emblem of Môn sovereignty, to adorn the summits of the 'flag'-poles of monasteries.

The earliest epigraphical evidence so far discovered only takes us back to the beginning of the thirteenth century, but the seven inscriptions found at different temples in Lamp'ūn are all in the Môn language, and the script is identical with that of the Môn inscriptions of Pagān. Three of these inscriptions are dated A.D. 1213, 1217 and 1219 respectively. But in addition to these, much further evidence has been obtained from two chronicles, recently translated and annotated by Coedès, namely the *Camadevivamsa* (The History of Chama Devi) written by the monk Bodhiramsi about the beginning of the fifteenth century either at Chiengmai or Lamp'ūn, and the *Jinakalamalini* ('The Garland of the Times of the Buddha') by the monk Ratanapanna of the Rattanavana Mahavihara monastery at Chiengmai in A.D. 1516. Both are translations from Pali manuscripts in the National Library at Bangkok.

Ratanapanna was a monk of the Hinayana sect which, having been established in the Lao country about 1375, received a fresh impetus from Ceylon in the fifteenth century and expanded its influence under the name of Sihalagana. His narrative, as relating to history, is concise, even dry, but he gives the essential facts in a form which is worthy of every credence. Bodhiramsi is more discursive in his style, and much of his narrative is legendary, but he is of considerable use as a check on the *Jinakalamalini*.

According to the latter, Chām T'ewi was a daughter of the king of Lavo who married the king of Ramannanagara (i.e. the Môn country of Lower Burma), but left her husband in A.D. 663 to lead the missionary expedition to the north of Siam. She was already pregnant at the time and, soon after her arrival at Lamp'ūn, gave birth to two sons, one of whom became king of Lamp'ūn, and the other king of a new city, Lampāng (K'elāng).

The statuary of the Dvāravatī kingdom, the finding of the Môn-inscribed pillar of the seventh century at Lopburi and Chām T'ewi's alliance with a Môn king of Ramanna point clearly to the conclusion that the ruling class in the south was of Môn descent, and that the people who went with Chām T'ewi to the north of Siam, if not pure Môn themselves, were probably Môn-speaking and imbued with Môn customs and religion. The c.d.v. says that Chām T'ewi founded five monasteries in Lamp'ūn, among others, the Mahayana to the west of the city. There is still a temple of that name near the west gate of Lamp'ūn, and one of the Môn inscriptions was found there. Chām T'ewi is also credited with the foundation of another city at Alam-banganapuri (Lampāng Lūang), 10 miles south-west of Lampāng, where she built a temple and retired after her second son became king of K'elāng (Lampāng); though she went back to Haripūnjaya to die. The memory of Chām T'ewi is still preserved at Lampāng Lūang, especially in connexion with a well which gave forth water at the queen's entreaty. To the temple at Lampāng Lūang, which is one of the most beautiful in all Siam, I will refer again later.

Coedès is inclined to put the arrival of Chām T'ewi in the eighth and not the seventh century, but this is of minor importance, as there is no vestige of remains in the north today, either architectural or sculptural, which can be attributed to her period, and in both chronicles we have from that time nothing but a list of names of kings until we reach the end of the tenth century. The only possible relics of the first millennium are certain coins resembling bracelets or crescents from the north of Siam which appear to be allied to coinage types of the Pyu of Lower Burma. The j.k.m. records that in the reign of Trabaka, which Coedès places towards the end of the tenth century, this king of Lamp'ūn made an attack by river on the king of Lavo, whose name is given as Ucchitta-Cakkavatti. When the latter went forth to meet his rival, another king, Jivaka of Siridhammanagara (Ligor in the Malay Peninsula), siezed the opportunity to capture Lavo: whereupon both the other kings fled towards Lamp'ūn, but the king of Lavo arriving before Trabaka, the latter was forced to return to his original attack on Lavo. From the evidence of subsequent history, it is clear that this assault was in vain, and he vanishes from the picture. The j.k.m. further records that, after this event, the king of Lavo came north to attack Lamp'ūn but was heavily repulsed. From the fact that Ucchitta was welcomed in Lamp'ūn and reigned there as king, it would seem probable that the dynasties of Lavo and Lamp'ūn were still of the same race.

The theory of Môn dominion over Northern Siam is again reinforced by a passage from the c.d.v. which records that in the middle of the eleventh century A.D. the people of Lamp'ūn fled *en masse* from the city and district to escape a severe epidemic of cholera. They went first to Thatôn, north-west of Moulmein, but being harassed by the king of Pagān, went on to Hongsāwadi (Pegu), where they were welcomed by their brethren, because 'their speech was identical, without showing the least difference.' There is no reason to doubt the accuracy of this record, and it is perhaps the most conclusive evidence of the identity of the settlers in Northern Siam with the Môn people of their home-land. The c.d.v., indeed, in recounting the fights that took place between the realms of Lamp'ūn and Lavo always refers to the people of Lamp'ūn as Ramanna, the name given to Lower Burma, and when it refers to a village of Tai boatmen, it calls it Deyyagama (i.e. Pali for Tai).

From the point of view of our present study, this flight of the people of Lamp'ūn to Burma is of the first importance. The reference to the king of Pagān harassing them at Thatôn is to King Anuruddha (or Anawrahta, as he is called in Burma), the first Burmese king of Pagān, who attacked Manuha, the Môn king of Thatôn, in A.D. 1057, sacked the city and carried off the king and all the monks and sacred scriptures to Pagān, as I have related in Chapter III.

In Anuruddha's time the centre of culture in Northern Siam was still at Haripūnjaya (Lamp'ūn), and the *Pongsāwadān Yonaka* records that, when the people came back from Pegu after the epidemic of cholera had run its course, many of their Burma brethren came with them and introduced the Môn style of writing. This may well be true as the modern Lao form of script is very similar to the Môn and Burmese (and not at all like modern Siamese), and the Môn inscriptions of the early thirteenth century found at Lamp'ūn are almost identical with Môn inscriptions from Burma of the same period. It is also suggested that the Lamp'ūn people taught the Môn of Pegu, and thence the people of Pagān, the art of lacquer-work when the former migrated to Burma in A.D. 1057.

There are no remains as yet identified of the time of Chām T'ewī, and the earliest temple building standing at Lamp'ūn is Wat Kukut in the village of Sān Mahapol, about half a mile west-north-west from the west gate of the city (Fig. 159). It is said to have been erected by the Môn king, Dittaraja, A.D. 1120–50, to commemorate his victory over the army of Lavo which came north to attack him. It is a square monument in brick with five storeys rising from a plinth and surmounted by a ringed, or terraced pinnacle. There is a smaller leaning *stupa* beside it. On each side of the main *stupa* are fifteen niches in five rows of three, with a standing image of the Buddha in each, making sixty images in all. It is very similar to the Sat Mahal Prasada at Polonnaruwa in Ceylon, which dates from the end of the twelfth century A.D. and there is also an analogous temple, of later date, called Wat Si Liem (the Square Temple) near the site of Wieng Kūm-Kām, Nang Hoi, on the Lamp'ūn road, which was the actual site of the first city built by Meng Rai, the Tai conqueror of the north in the second half of the thirteenth century A.D. (Fig. 160). At the temple of Wat Kukut Coedès found two Môn inscriptions of the early thirteenth century, and Dupont, in an interesting article draws attention to the figures of the Buddha in the niches, in which he sees a distinct affinity, if of late date, to the art of Dvāravati. With this I agree, and indeed, it is not in any way surprising when we consider that the city was still in the hands of the Môn who were responsible for the art of Dvāravatī at an earlier period in the south.

The origin of this type of structure has still to be determined. In Ceylon itself it is of a most exceptional style and was pronounced by Bell to be of Cambodian origin; but without further ocular demonstration, I cannot accept this attribution, and if, as seems likely, the temple of Kukut is anterior in date to that at Polonnaruwa, one is inclined to think that it was the result of an original conception on the part of the Môn king of Lamp'ūn, from which the Ceylon temple was copied, unless, indeed, we have here the one remaining example in Siam of the architectural style of Dvāravati, a possibility which is not by any means without the bounds of reason.

The Môn king of Lamp'ūn who followed Dittaraja is known as Adittaraja, and is famed in history as the builder of the Great *Stupa* at Lamp'ūn between the years A.D. 1150–75 (Fig. 161). The present *stupa* is not the original one, but as it appeared after its restoration and enlargement in the Tai style in A.D. 1447 by Tilokaraja, the valiant king of Lānnatai, as the northern kingdom was then called. The original temple is said to have been connected with the miraculous appearance of a golden casket of Açoka's reign containing a relic of the Buddha. The relic emitted six different colours, and, having been duly worshipped, then disappeared into the ground. Adittaraja promptly built a *stupa* over the spot to mark the celebrated occasion. This took place about A.D. 1163.

In the eleventh and twelfth centuries A.D. wars with the Khmer kings of Lavo were frequent owing, no doubt, to the Khmer desire to incorporate the north within their empire, but, although their attacks came to nothing, a relic of the contact with Lopburi is still to be seen at the Great *Stupa* in the shape of an image of the Buddha which is called 'P'ra Lavo.' The present image is of fairly recent date but is doubtless a copy of an ancient image.

Evidence of the actual relations between the north of Siam and Pagān during the great period of that kingdom, between A.D. 1050 and 1250, is at present scanty in the extreme. Harvey relates that in Anuruddha's reign a party of Lao Shans (Tai) from the Chiengmai district raided Pegu, and that Kyanzittha, his successor, drove them off and by his feat became a hero to the Môn of Pegu. The Lao chronicles make no mention of this raid. Harvey also records that, when he became king, Kyanzittha called in a wizard of Hti Laing, by name Shin Popa, who had studied at Chiengmai and was probably an Ari. At the end of the eleventh century A.D. Chiengmai had not yet been built, but if the term is merely used to refer to the north of Siam generally, it opens up a problem of the introduction of Ari Mahayanism which requires further investigation. Possibly the small Tai principalities of the far north of Siam were not sufficiently important to warrant any court relations between the two countries, and the connexion was formed by the natural coming and going of wandering priests and travelling traders.

But, as I have related in Chapter III, it is now clear that during the early part of the Pagān period a new form of the Buddha image was introduced into Burma from India, and passed on by the Burmese to the Tai of Northern Siam, who were gradually rising to power in that region.

The latter half of the eleventh century A.D. was witnessing the closing stages of Buddhism in India, and Ceylon was being subjected to attacks as well. It is recorded that the king of Ceylon, Vijaya Bahu I, A.D. 1065–1120, sent for assistance to King Anuruddha against the Cholas of Southern India, and in A.D. 1071 asked for and obtained a deputation of monks with scriptures to strengthen the religion which had fallen on evil times. At this time Pagān became an important religious centre and pilgrims came from far and wide, even from India itself, to worship at its magnificent shrines.

As in Burma, so in Northern Siam, the people preferred the Hinayana form of Buddhism. It must not be forgotten that to the vast majority of Siamese (and Burmese) peasants Buddhism is, and always has been, what I call 'The Decoration of Life,' and the people themselves have remained at heart animists. Their lives fall into two parts. They pay their devotions and give their offerings to the Lord Buddha, so that their merit may increase and their Karma may enrich them in future lives, but in the present life there are a host of '*p'ī*,' or spirits, to be propitiated if evil is not to befall them, and the latter are, therefore, continually courted and feasted to this end.

As an outstanding example I have in my possession a small silver elephant, with trunk upraised, which was clearly used as a mascot against bullets and swords, as it was dug up on a battlefield and has a tiny hole drilled through the trunk for attaching to a cord. It is dated B.E. 2146 (A.D. 1603). One side is covered with cabalistic signs, while on the other side one can still see the outline of the Buddha, who expressly forbade the use of the former. But, evidently, the soldier was leaving nothing to chance !

I give an illustration of a bronze image of the Buddha from Northern Siam (Fig. 162). It is representative of what is called the Chiengsen or pre-Suk'ot'ai period, and is probably the earliest form of Tai Buddha image to be found in Siam. There is a subtle change in the physiognomy as rendered by the Tai artist. The face is more oval in shape; the nose is more pronounced, but the mouth is even smaller, and the eyebrows are more rounded and do not meet at the top of the bridge. Were it not for this definitely local expression of racial form, this image would be hardly distinguishable from the images described in Chapter III, so closely has the artist adhered to the formula laid down for throne, body, legs, clothfold and *uṣṇiṣa*.

With this evidence before me, I feel on safe ground in agreeing that the ultimate origin of the northern school of Tai art must be sought among the Pālas of Bihar. The student will find further examples of that school, bearing out this type which came to Burma and Siam, in Banerji's book on Eastern Indian Sculpture—two particularly clear and happy examples—and also in Stella Kramrisch's work on 'Pāla and Sena Sculpture.' I show one more example (Fig. 163) 15 inches high, which is already taking on a more local Tai expression of feeling, and is perhaps the most beautiful example of the Chiengsen school known. There are some fine life-size images of this early period at Wat Benchamabopit in Bangkok.

Having thus shown the affinity between the Pāla style of image and that introduced into the Chiengsen area of the north of Siam through the intermediary of Burma, it will be of interest to record that one direct connexion, at least, can be traced between the north of Siam and the Pāla school of sculpture. At Wat Chiengmān in Chiengmai is still preserved a much venerated image of the Buddha known as *P'ra Sila* (which simply means 'the Stone Buddha,' Fig. 164). To show how local traditions are formed, this image is said by the legendary histories to have been made by Ajatasatru at Rajagriha after the death of the Lord Buddha, and to contain relics of him: to have been taken to Ceylon by three monks and thence brought to Chiengmai via Suk'ot'ai and Lampāng. It is now firmly connected with 'prayers for rain,' and it is confidently believed that, if water is poured upon the image with due ceremony and ritual, rain will certainly fall and the crops be assured.

The image itself, which is in a blackish stone (later gilded over) with a wooden stand and frame, is a representative example of a type which seems to have been a favourite one at Bodhgaya in the ninth and tenth centuries A.D. The scene, which is common to both schools of Buddhism, is that of the Buddha taming the fierce elephant, Nalagiri, which was sent to kill him by Ajatasatru, and the small figure to his right, holding the fan, is his chief disciple, Ananda. The treatment of the torso and drapery still carries on the Gupta tradition, with the diaphanous robes and suggestion of a sexless nude, but there is already a much more sensuous feeling creeping into the artist's conception, foreign to Gupta art, in the swaying hips and rhythmic movement of the arms and hands.

Another style of image which has found favour in the north of Siam is seen in Fig. 165, now in the British Museum, which represents a Bodhisattva seated in the earth-touching attitude. The image, which is in the same grey-black stone as Fig. 19, is of about the tenth century A.D. and the three peculiarities of the Pāla school are again seen, namely the lotus-throne, the short fold of the robe over the left shoulder, and the crossed legs with both soles uppermost. But the presence of the crown and diadem, the neck collar, the bracelets on the arms and the elaborate ear decorations stamp this figure clearly as belonging to the Mahayana school.

We may compare the above with the illustration (Fig. 166) which depicts a type very popular in Northern Siam, especially among the Lü tribe, where it is known as *P'ra Song Krüang*, or 'the decorated

Buddha.' In Burma it is apparently not common. This particular image, which is in bronze, may be as late as the sixteenth century, but if so, it has retained very faithfully the chief peculiarities of its prototype. Especially noticeable are the ear decorations. The attitude in this case is that of *samadhi* or Meditation. I do not think that it is necessary to assume from this form of image that Mahayanism was prevalent among a certain sect of Northern Tai or Lü, but rather that the type appealed to them as being beautiful, and consequently they rejoiced in fashioning it. In much the same way we find bronze statues of Vishnu, Çiva, and Lakshmi made by the Tai in the fifteenth and sixteenth centuries, but we must not conclude from this that the Tai nobility were turning from Buddhism to Brahmanism.

A third type, which has always enjoyed great favour in the north of Siam, indeed, throughout Siam, is seen in Fig. 167, also in the British Museum, which represents the *Maha-Parinirvana* of Gautama, the Lord Buddha, with disciples mourning below. A novel and amusing feature is introduced into the *stela* in the heavenly hands and arms beating the drum and clashing the cymbals seen above. The relief is in blackish basalt, and here again we see the fidelity to type in the treatment of the *uṣṇiṣa* and the short fold of the robe. I know of no reclining images of the Buddha in the north of Siam early enough in period to be strictly analogous to the Pāla style, but the scene depicted in this type of image is so common in Siam that there seems little doubt as to its origin, if we take it in conjunction with the other styles introduced. R. D. Banerji, who also gives illustrations of the *Maha-Parinirvana* from examples of Pāla sculpture, remarks: 'In the Bengal school we find a class of image bas-reliefs, representing the death of Buddha, which are very rare in Indian sculpture.' This statement is a strong confirmation of the theory of a Pāla derivation for the type found in Siam.

Before leaving the subject of the origin of the Chiengsen school, I must refer to an interesting suggestion made by Dupont in this regard. In his monograph on Siamese Art he remarks that 'the curious stylisation of the arcaded eyebrows in particular, which already appears in Indo-Greek Buddhas from Afghanistan, must come from China of the Wei period (Tien Lung Shan) after passing through Central Asia.' He then quotes me as indicating the existence from the ninth century onwards of images in the style of Chiengsen but adds 'he has not published these, nor has he given any reasons for proposing this date.'

I must admit that for a long time I was inclined to Dupont's theory myself, although I could never find any support for it among other

savants, and even now there is still a kind of lingering belief in my mind
that the Tai must have brought with them some small portion of the
Chinese spirit which would appear in their earliest images. But the
Wei period is much too far removed in point of time, and the evidence
here produced (especially Fig. 19) is, I fear, too strong to allow me to
retain the theory of conscious adaptation any longer, and, except that
the local Tai expression of the Pāla school may instinctively show some
affinity with China from which the Tai came, one must definitely
attribute the origin of the style to India. It may be that Dupont has
been influenced to some extent by my indication of a Chiengsen style
from the ninth century onwards: if so, I hasten to correct it. In the
Table of Schools of Sculpture in Siam, annexed to my article in
INDIAN ART AND LETTERS, published in 1930, the print is so faint
that possibly the question-mark preceding the words 'Ninth to Twelfth
century A.D., Chieng Rai,' was not noticed by him. The fact is that
I was for a long time puzzled by the find of a stone image of a saint
fast embedded in a limestone cave some distance from Chiengrai, of
which I was able to recover the head, as it had been broken off and was
lying on the floor of the cave. This head presents unusual features,
since in profile it has not only a sharply ridged, straight, sensitive nose,
but an exceptionally firm mouth and chin, almost Graeco-Roman in
type; and I wondered if this might not be an early expression of Tai
art in the north of Siam. I am, however, satisfied now that it must be
an example, though an unusual one, of Ayudhyan art of the fifteenth
century. I must therefore withdraw my suggestion of the possibility of
an early Tai school of stone sculpture in Northern Siam.

In considering the introduction of the Chiengsen school I agree with
Dupont's suggestion that the artistic development of the Tai did not
necessarily correspond with the period of their independence. It is
quite possible, in fact probable, that the earliest examples of the Chiengsen school in the north of Siam date from the twelfth century A.D.
What is likely to have happened is that after the Tai had settled in
Siam, they first found contact with Buddhism of the Môn type, which
by this time was artistically decadent, and that, when the new impulse
of the Nalandā school was introduced into Burma and thence into
Siam, they eagerly adopted it.

CHAPTER XI

THE RISE OF THE TAI AND THE KINGDOM
OF SUK'OT'AI

URING the eleventh and twelfth centuries A.D. the Tai
were, in ever greater numbers, penetrating Northern and
North-Central Siam and gradually consolidating their
position there. At the end of the twelfth century the Môn
element in Siam, since the conquest of their parent kingdom of Thatôn
by Anuruddha, had gradually lost their source of power and were being
assimilated with the Tai, with whom they had more spiritual if not
more racial affinity than with their conquerors, the Khmer. The time
was becoming ripe for a revolution in political, religious and artistic
thought, and about the middle of the thirteenth century A.D. certain
events happened which brought this revolution to a head. Once again
the old saying proved true that 'the hour produces the man'—in this
case, 'the men.'

First of all, the kingdom of Nan-Chao in Southern China was
conquered by the all-powerful Kublai Khan, thereby causing a further
pressure of Tai southwards into the Shan states, Burma proper and the
no-man's-land bordering Siam, and though I do not think that this
event exercised any artistic influence, still it probably played its part in
the rise of the Tai to power in Siam. Also about the same time two male
children were born, Meng Rai and Rām K'amheng, who were each
destined to bring part of the territory of Siam under Tai sovereignty
for the first time, the one in the north and the other in the centre and
south. Let us deal with the northerner, Meng Rai, first.

Meng Rai, who was born in A.D. 1239, is always regarded by the Tai
as a Tai, but was actually the son by a Tai mother of the last Lawā
chief of Chiengsen. He succeeded his father as chief of Chiengsen in
A.D. 1259, founded Chiengrai (to which city he gave his name) in
A.D. 1262, and after a long series of campaigns finally in A.D. 1292
captured Lamp'ūn, the Môn capital, thereby making himself master of
practically the whole of the north of Siam. In 1290 Meng Rai paid

a visit to Pagān, which was then under nominal Chinese suzerainty but in reality in the hands of Shan (Tai) chiefs, and brought back with him artists and artisans. In A.D. 1296, with the help and guidance of his brother chief, Rām K'amheng, and also of the chief of P'ayao, he founded his new capital city, Chiengmai, which from that time onwards became the most important town in Northern Siam. In the meantime another Tai Shan, Makato or Wareru, had founded a new kingdom of Martaban, which included Thatôn and Pegu, and Meng Rai came to blows with him in A.D. 1287 over the frontiers of their respective realms. In the end Wareru presented one of his daughters to Meng Rai together with a town on the river Me Niam as a dowry, and peace was concluded.

Meng Rai was evidently a devout Buddhist and, as a result of his visit to Pagān, had already founded in A.D. 1292 the temple of Chieng-mān, whose remains still stand in the most northern part of the old palace-fort of the city of Chiengmai, though the present *stupa* is probably not the original one but as restored by the later Tai king, Tilokaraja, in A.D. 1471 (Fig. 168). This is the oldest foundation inside the city of Chiengmai, and is clearly in the Pagān style, though in the original construction there were possibly none of the stucco elephants which now adorn the base.

There is, also, another temple on the outskirts of Chiengmai near the Chang Kien stream of Doi Sut'ep which may well be attributed to Meng Rai, namely Wat Chet Yôt, or the Seven-spired Temple. This temple is obviously a copy of the Mahabodhi temple at Pagān, which was built early in the thirteenth century A.D. by Htilo-Minlo, the last of the Burmese builder-kings, and which itself is an imitation of the famous temple at Bodhgaya in Bihar (Fig. 169). Meng Rai is the only king of Northern Siam known to have visited Pagān, and, although there is no record of its foundation, it was already considered an ancient monument when discovered by Tilokaraja in A.D. 1453. The latter founded an *aram* there and planted a sacred *ficus*. Later he built a *vihara* and in A.D. 1487 his successor rebuilt the *stupa*; and it is probably from his time that the seated figures adorning the outer walls date, as they are typically Tai in style (Fig. 170).

When Kublai Khan's grandson conquered Pagān in A.D. 1287 and put an end to the Burmese line that had ruled there since the days of Anuruddha, Meng Rai seems to have escaped his attentions and to have preserved his independence, possibly because he had already acknow-ledged the Mongol emperor as overlord and had agreed to pay tribute,

like all the other princelings and chiefs of Eastern Asia, but in A.D. 1303
he rebelled and refused to send the tribute, and once again in A.D. 1312
On both occasions expeditions were sent against him, but they appear
to have been only half-hearted and peace was eventually restored. The
J.K.M. gives the date of Meng Rai's death as A.D. 1311 at the age of
seventy-two, but the HISTORY OF THE NORTH is probably more
correct in its statement that he died (was struck dead by lightning) in
A.D. 1317, having reigned as Chief of Chiengsen and Chiengrai from
A.D. 1259 to 1292 and as king of practically the whole of the north
from A.D. 1292 to 1317.

And now to turn to his brother king, Rām K'amheng, who may
justly be called the first Tai king of Siam. In the middle of the thirteenth
century A.D., Suk'ot'ai and Sawank'alōk were under the control of
a Khmer governor, while somewhere in the vicinity were two uniden-
tified petty states, Müang Rat and Müang Bang Yang, ruled over by
two Tai chiefs under Khmer sovereignty. The origin of the rising is
still obscure, but suddenly these two Tai chiefs, having joined forces,
simultaneously attacked both Suk'ot'ai and Sachanalai (the name formerly given to old Sawank'alōk). But little resistance was offered, and,
Suk'ot'ai once occupied, the chief of Bang Yang was crowned king by
his friend and ally, under the title of Çri Indrapat-Indraditya, usually
shortened to Indraditya and sometimes referred to as Rocaraja. Thus
was founded the Tai state of Suk'ot'ai, which was destined, within
fifty years, to achieve sovereignty over the whole of Central Siam but
which, within a hundred years, was to give way to the new Tai
dynasty that established its capital at Ayudhya, 150 miles farther south.
Indraditya has, however, since been immortalized by the Tai under the
name of P'ra Ruang, their national hero.

Indraditya had three sons, of whom Rām K'amheng was the youngest.
The eldest died young, while the second only reigned for a few years;
and about the year 1273 we find Rām K'amheng ruling over his
father's State. Before his death he claimed to have established dominion
over most of modern Siam (except the north), as far north-east as
Lūang Prabāng on the Mekōng, as far south as Nakon Sritammarāt on
the east side and Mergui on the west side of the Malay Peninsula, and
as far west as Raheng and Mesöt on the Burma border. Even Pegu and
Martaban acknowledged him as overlord. Indeed, he has more real
claim, in spite of his father's successful rebellion against the Khmer, to
be considered the national hero of Siam.

Relations between Suk'ot'ai and the court of China were of a cordial nature, and the annals record that Rām K'amheng paid two visits to the emperor, the first in A.D. 1294 while Kublai Khan was still alive, and the second in A.D. 1300. On the latter occasion he is said to have married a Chinese princess, and to have brought back with him a number of Chinese potters, who established the kilns of Suk'ot'ai, where a coarse type of Tz'ū-Chou black and white ware was produced, and later took over the Tai kilns at Sawank'alōk, where they introduced the traditional Celadon and most of the other Sung-like wares of the period. For those interested in ceramics I have described these wares fully in the BURLINGTON MAGAZINE for October and November 1933. Those visits were probably the result of the arrival of Chinese embassies at the court of Rām K'amheng in A.D. 1293 and 1295 (or 1296) to announce imperial orders. In A.D. 1299 the king of Hsien (as the kingdom of Suk'ot'ai was called by the Chinese in contradistinction to Lohu, the name for Lopburi or Lavo) petitioned the emperor for white horses with saddles and bridles and gold-thread garments, as given to his father. But the emperor was advised not to accede to this request (as Hsien was only a small kingdom) and in the end only gold-thread garments were given. But although Rām K'amheng maintained such excellent relations with the imperial court and sent tribute regularly up to the time of his death, there is no indication that he was ever influenced by the Chinese form of Buddhism or introduced any Chinese form of the Buddha. On the contrary, he himself, in his famous *stela* of A.D. 1292, gives the clue to the problem of how the great change which now occurred in the iconography of Siam came about. In North-Central Siam in the regions of Suk'ot'ai, Sawank'alōk, Pitsanulōk and Kampengp'et the Khmer style of Buddha image disappears entirely, and its place is taken by a totally different conception of the Founder of the Faith; in other words, there is an artistic revolution, a complete break with Khmer art. Instead of the square, strong, ruthless man's head and face we find an idealized conception of a Higher Being almost feminine in feeling. Indeed, Europeans often mistake this form for one of a feminine divinity, so fully developed is the upper part of the body. The face becomes long and oval, the eyebrows highly arched, the nose long and hooked; the lips are pressed together and the mouth is small, while the chin is represented by a single incised curve. The eyes look downwards with a half-closed mystic expression, and the eyelids are formed of wavy lines rising upwards towards the outer corners. The treatment of the hair is entirely different from the Khmer style, being composed of large shell-like spiral knobs circling from left to right, and a long, pointed flame-like emblem (which the Siamese call *ketumala*) rises erect from the *uṣṇiṣa*. In seated figures the legs are never crossed but rest one above the other, and the fold of the robe-cloth comes down as far as the hips. The hands sometimes rest together in the lap in the attitude of meditation, or one hand rests on the right knee in that of the Conquest of Mara or 'Earth-touching,' while the other rests in the lap (Fig. 171). The standing figures are more often than not depicted in the act of walking, with the right (or sometimes the left) hand raised in the attitude of preaching, where the thumb and forefinger are seen to be touching. In the earlier forms the body is represented as particularly lissom and supple and the movement is very free (Fig. 172), but in later images the treatment becomes stiffer and more conventional, while still maintaining all the traditional features.

Now where did this new conception of an idealized Super-Being in the minds of the Suk'ot'ai folk originate? No single, direct answer can be given to this question, but it seems clear that Burma, through its intermediary Chiengsen, played a certain part, while the new impetus of Hinayana Buddhism from Ceylon, which at this time penetrated the heart of Siam, duly left its impress on the new forms now to be modelled. It is only reasonable to suppose that the Chiengsen type of Buddha image had been well known among the Tai of the Suk'ot'ai region for many years past, and I feel satisfied that in the main the Suk'ot'ai style is a natural evolution from the former school. Pierre Dupont inclines to think that the chief influences that went to form the Chiengsen school came from China, but though for a long time I held the same opinion myself and should still like to think so, I cannot now sustain that conclusion. Still, accepting the Chiengsen type as the base of the Suk'ot'ai school, there are obviously other influences at work, and there is no doubt that the origin of these must be sought in Ceylon. The true Suk'ot'ai type is thus a blend of Chiengsen and Ceylon.

That island, after undergoing many vicissitudes in the realm of religion, in the eleventh century A.D., under Vijaya Bahu I, witnessed a revival of Hinayana Buddhism, and Parakrama Bahu (A.D. 1164–97), who deserves his title of 'Great' and who is called 'The incomparable Champion of the Faith,' brought about a reunion of the Church and the triumph of the Hinayanist school. From this time onwards up to the beginning of the sixteenth century A.D. it is true to say that Ceylon was regarded by its brother Buddhist countries, Siam, Burma and Cambodia, with almost as much veneration as the Holy Places of

Buddhism in India itself, as the fountain-head of the pure Theravada doctrines.

It is not absolutely certain when Sinhalese Buddhism first came to the Malay Peninsula, but it was probably at the close of the twelfth or the beginning of the thirteenth century A.D. The Ceylon chronicles record that during the reign of Parakrama Bahu II the king of Javaka twice unsuccessfully invaded Ceylon, in A.D. 1230 and 1256, and it has been suggested with some plausibility that these attacks were primarily made to gain possession of a miraculous image of the Buddha, the famous P'ra Sihing, whose renown had reached Siam. This fact in itself is strong evidence that peninsular Siam was by this time throwing off its allegiance to the Mahayana school and was ready to receive the new, purified Hinayana doctrine from Ceylon.

The history of the P'ra Sihing (or the Sinhalese Buddha) is important, as it is closely bound up with the new style of image which appeared in Siam, and was the cause of many struggles for its possession in that country. In the middle of the thirteenth century A.D. the Tai king of Suk'ot'ai was paying a visit to the king of Nakon Sritammarāt and heard glowing accounts from the latter of a wonderful Sinhalese image of the Buddha. He at once desired its possession, but was dissuaded from going himself to secure it by the latter, who told him that Ceylon was protected by four powerful divinities. This evidently refers to his own unsuccessful attacks. Thereupon the two kings sent an envoy to the king of Ceylon earnestly entreating that the image might be presented to them, and the Sinhalese king was pleased to accede to this request and solemnly handed it over to the envoy for safe conveyance to Nakon Sritammarāt. On the way back the envoy's ship was unfortunately wrecked on a reef, and the image went floating away to sea resting on a ship's plank. Through the power of the Naga king, however, it was borne in the direction of Nakon Sritammarāt and the king of this city, having been apprised of its arrival in a dream, recovered it from the sea and brought it home in triumph and paid due homage to it. But it was not to remain with him for long, for, as soon as Rocaraja heard of its arrival, he came south post-haste, and, claiming it as his own, carried it off to Suk'ot'ai. To provide it with a suitable setting, Rocaraja built at Sachanalai (Sawank'alōk) a magnificent *stupa* in brick and stone, covered with white stucco, and a *mandapa* of gilded copper. The image remained at Sawank'alōk for a hundred years, but it would take too much space to recount its adventures during the succeeding fifty years, between A.D. 1350 and 1400, when it became the 'sport' of all the local chiefs and kings to try and gain its possession. Suffice it to say that it was taken successively to Chaināt, Ayudhya, Kampengp'et, then to Tāk (Raheng), thence to Chiengmai, Chiengrai, Chiengsen, back to Chiengrai, and finally came to rest at the end of the fourteenth century A.D. at Chiengmai in the temple named after it, Wat P'ra Sihing (or Sing), where it remained in peace until the capture of the town in A.D. 1662 by King Naraiyana, who carried it off to Ayudhya. When Ayudhya fell and was sacked by the Burmese in A.D. 1767 the image was restored to Chiengmai, but in A.D. 1795 was brought to Bangkok, where it has been ever since. It now rests in the chapel of the erstwhile second king's palace, which forms part of the National Museum.

There are, however, two other images of the Buddha in Siam which claim to be the image of the legend, one at Nakon Sritammarāt and another at Chiengmai which exhibits all the normal characteristics of the school of Chiengsen. Coedès thinks that the image now in Bangkok has the best claim to be considered the genuine image for which the Tai principalities fought in the fourteenth century, as it possesses all the qualities which distinguish the school of Suk'ot'ai from that of Chiengsen, and presents a fair example of what must have been the first type of image made at Suk'ot'ai in the middle of the thirteenth century A.D. He adds: 'Without any doubt it is the one which reproduces most faithfully the features of the renowned P'ra Sihing, the Sihalapatimā, that is, the Sinhalese image of the legend.'

Wherever the image, now so much venerated in Siam, was made, one thing is clear: it was not made in Ceylon, as will be apparent from a comparison of the renowned statue itself with a typical Sinhalese image of the thirteenth century (Figs. 173 and 174). And yet this comparison is interesting, for it shows a close connexion between the two. The P'ra Sihing image of Siam, which is 26 inches high, is seated on a lotus-throne, the head is lifted more off the shoulders, the hair is formed of more pointed and sharply defined spirals, and the lyre-like emblem on the top of the head has taken on a more flame-like form, but the position of the hands and legs, the wide-spreading knees, and the whole conception of the body are so akin in both images that there can be little doubt whence the P'ra Sihing derived its inspiration.

Its attachment to the Chiengsen school is, however, still shown both by the lotus-throne and by the face, which is round and has not yet assumed the oval form which later became so characteristic of the Suk'ot'ai school. As for the statue now at Chiengmai, it may well be the copy referred to in the J.K.M. as having been made by the Chief of Chiengrai of an alloy of gold, silver, copper and tin, while the famous image remained in his possession.

The use of the *ketumala*, or flame-like emblem, raises an interesting problem as to its symbolic meaning. The word itself is both Sanskrit and Pali, of which *ketu* means 'sign' or 'mark,' and *mala* 'a garland.' This does not help us very much, but Childers in his DICTIONARY OF SINHALESE PALI says that it is an emblem of the Buddha equivalent to the halo of Christianity; and a former well-known missionary in Ceylon has supplemented this to me with the interesting suggestion that it represents the 'aura,' or emanation of light, which proceeds from the Buddha.

In Ceylon the emblem takes the form of a lyre-like instrument, but in Siam it assumes much more the likeness of a flame, and I have noticed that in many Siamese images the central portion has the form of the *urna*, which is a definite mark of the Buddha. In Sanskrit the *urna* is the tuft of hair growing between the eyebrows from which emanate rays of the six colours of the Buddhist Faith lighting up the world. Thus the *urna* may well be said to be the 'aura' of the Buddha, and it is indeed sometimes, though not often, actually seen on the forehead of a Siamese image of the Buddha. It seems possible, then, that the Siamese took hold of the *ketumala* from Ceylon in order to work into it the symbol of the *urna* which, in their case, has rather the form of an inverted question-mark with a spiral tail.

It is not yet definitely decided when this emblem was first used in Ceylon. According to Paranavitana the development of sculpture in Ceylon is as yet very imperfectly understood, for there are very few sculptures which can be definitely dated. It is, therefore, quite possible that some of the known works of art are really older than the dates to which they have been assigned in books on Indian art, and vice versa. Vincent Smith ascribes a seated Buddha from Polonnaruwa to the twelfth century A.D. because it was found in a twelfth-century shrine, but it is quite possible that the image is older than the shrine itself. Conversely, there is a tradition that the great Buddha at Aukana, which has the flame-top, dates from the fifth century A.D., but this may be too early for it. I may add that Vincent Smith assigns this image to the late twelfth century A.D. The great Buddha images at the Galvihara at Polonnaruwa, which are definitely known to have been the work of Parakrama Bahu the Great in the twelfth century A.D., do not appear to have the flame-like top to the *uṣṇiṣa*. Some bronze images which exhibit this development of the uṣniṣa have recently been found, which in other respects should be attributed to a date earlier than the eleventh century A.D.

Now the two most important periods of Ceylon history are: (i) the Anuradhapura period, which dates from (?) 457 B.C. to A.D. 750, and (ii) the Polonnaruwa period, which ranges from A.D. 750 to 1240. Fig. 175 shows an enormous and beautiful stone Buddha at Toluvila, Anuradhapura, assigned to about the sixth century A.D., and, as is clearly discernible, there is no sign of a flame-like instrument on the uṣniṣa. Similarly, in the rock-cut images at Galvihara, which date from the second half of the twelfth century and show exactly the same form of the Buddha, there is no sign of any device rising from the head, but some authorities state that once upon a time they had such, which were later broken off. We cannot, therefore, come to any definite conclusion as to the actual date of the introduction of the flame-like instrument, but I think it is safe to say that it must have occurred sometime during the Polonnaruwa period and more probably in the latter rather than in the earlier half.

It is possible that Rocaraja (or Indraditya) did no more than introduce the new style of Buddha image into Suk'ot'ai, but it is on record that his son, Rām K'amheng, invited the famous priest, Sangharaja, who was preaching the Sinhalese Theravada doctrine at Nakon Sritammarāt, to take up his abode at Suk'ot'ai, that the invitation was accepted, and that Rām K'amheng built a special monastery for him, Wat Arannika, to the west of the city.

The ancient cities of Suk'ot'ai and Sawank'alōk (Sachanalai), as known to Rām K'amheng, are today nothing but deserted ruins, and the modern cities bearing these honoured names are in both cases some miles away from their former sites, the removal being due to a change in course of the river Me Yōm. I have visited both the old and the new cities on several occasions, chiefly for the purpose of examining the kiln-sites, but at the same time I paid some attention to the ancient temples now, alas, desolate.

The modern city of Suk'ot'ai is called T'ani and here at the temples of Rajat'ani and Prachum P'on may be seen rather remarkable collections of standing Buddha images in bronze of several periods, chiefly Suk'ot'ai, U-T'ong and Ayudhya. Claeys illustrates a number of them in his ARCHÉOLOGIE DU SIAM.

It is not possible to give a full description here of old Suk'ot'ai, which is reached by a road some miles long, called P'ra Ruang's road, made of laterite blocks leading from the river bank. Claeys says that there were three concentric walls encircling the city, the inner one built of laterite and the two outer of earth, and that there was an entrance gateway in the centre of each wall. Today most of the walls and of the buildings which they enclosed are lost in the invading jungle, but, in order to give the reader some idea of the type of architecture employed and an aspect of the ruins as they stand at the present time, I have chosen two temples at Suk'ot'ai for illustration, those of Mahā-Tāt and Çri Chum.

The temple of Mahā-Tāt, according to Claeys, originally comprised no less than one hundred and eighty-nine different structures, in the centre being a Tai p'rajedi or stupa with annexes in Khmer style, and to the east of this building a huge assembly hall (vihara), 50 metres (160 feet) long. In the illustration (Fig. 176) is seen this vihara, of which only the lower halves of the columns which supported the roof remain, with the p'rajedi and an enormous standing Buddha in the background. The columns are made of cylindrical laterite blocks encased in cement. Also to be seen at Wat Mahā-Tāt is a Buddhistic scene in stucco on laterite, which is probably somewhat later in style (Fig. 177). Khmer elements, if in a debased form, are still visible in the decoration of the pediment ending in makara heads, but the Death-scene of the Buddha with mourners underneath is typically Tai. Below this scene, in a niche, is a standing figure of the Buddha with an aureole, of a singularly captivating beauty. The poise of the head, the expression on the clear-cut features, and the slender form of the body exercise a subtle fascination which it is hard to convey, but which will be readily appreciated by the sensitive mind.

It was on the site of the palace near this temple that King (then Prince) Mongkut discovered the famous inscribed obelisk of Rām K'amheng in 1833 as well as the stone throne which a few years ago was placed by King Vajirawudh (Rama VI) in the throne hall at Bangkok and now, like our own famous stone which Edward I brought from Scotland, serves as the coronation stone of Siam. It was near by here, too, that I picked up a beautiful fragment of a Sung celadon dish showing the raised fish in the centre.

The temple of Çri Chum (Fig. 178), being in brick and stucco, is almost certainly later in date and may be ascribed to the reign of Dharmaraja I of Suk'ot'ai, the grandson of Rām K'amheng, in the middle of the fourteenth century A.D. The sanctuary containing a gigantic sitting image of the Buddha still stands, but only the columns remain of the former *vihara*. The sanctuary, which is rectangular, is peculiar in style, with its high, narrow, vaulted entrance, through which the figure of the Buddha can be dimly seen; but it appears to have been copied at Ayudhya, when the great bronze image of the Buddha was set up there about a hundred years later. Otherwise I know of no other temple to compare with it in Siam. Except for a little moulding in stucco high up on the walls, like a fringe on a cloth, there is no decoration visible, and the chief interest lies, not in the Buddha image, which in any case is now horribly disfigured, but in the series of sculptures discovered there, illustrating scenes from the Jātakas. One such scene is shown here (Fig. 179), and though the execution is undoubtedly Tai in spirit, it is clear that the influence inspiring it came from Ceylon, if one compares it with the *apsaras* and attendant from Sigiriya of the fifth century A.D. (Fig. 180), and with the later twelfth-century figures from Polonnaruwa in that island. It is also conceivable that the sanctuary of Çri Chum itself was based on some influence from Ceylon. All these frescoes may even be linked up with those in Caves I and XVII at Ajanta, dating from A.D. 500 to 650, of which illustrations are given in Codrington's revised edition of Vincent Smith's HISTORY OF FINE ART IN INDIA AND CEYLON, Plates 180 and 181. These sculptured scenes are now practically hidden in a dark corridor high up in the sanctuary, but it is believed that they were originally set up in the temple of Mahā-Tāt just described, and were later removed to the temple of Çri Chum, when the former fell into disrepair, or, possibly, when some disaster such as fire overtook it.

Sawank'alōk (Sachanalai), the sister-city of Suk'ot'ai, is now, alas, also buried deep in the jungle, and but little remains of its former state. It lies about twelve miles north of the new town on the west bank of the river Me Yōm, near some rapids, and portions of the city wall are met with near the banks of the river.

The main temple of Mahā-Tāt (which simply means 'The Great Pagoda') stands outside the old town, on a peninsula formed by a sharp bend of the river.

The tower of the monastery is Khmer in style but Tai in execution, and these blunted 'P'ra-P'rāng,' as they are called in imitation of the Khmer, are to be found both in the capital, Bangkok, and in various parts of the country (Fig. 181).

The *vihara* is in ruins, only the pillars remaining (laterite cased in cement) and the great image of the Buddha on the altar (Fig. 182).

To the west of the tower is a *stupa* of a most unusual construction

M

in Siam (Fig. 183), though not in Burma, where a counterpart is to be seen in the famous Sule Pagoda in Rangoon, as well as at Pagān, and other places. In the middle of the fourteenth century A.D., the king of Suk'ot'ai found his spiritual mentors in Môn priests from Pegu, and its erection is probably due to their influence.

There was probably a Khmer temple here originally as the gateway (Fig. 184), now much sunk, consists of three enormous round, equidistant laterite blocks joined together and laid horizontally with pointed gable ends, and from the centre rises a pinnacle showing a four-faced figure, probably of Lokeçvara on the analogy of the famous Bayon in Angkor. This does not appear to be Tai, and is almost certainly Khmer in construction.

In the north-eastern corner of the main enclosure is a small shrine containing a beautiful image of the Buddha sitting on the Naga king. It seems to be Tai in style (Fig. 185).

Inside the old city itself I have chosen the best known monument, of which the ruins still exist, to illustrate the type of architecture built by the early Tai sovereigns of Siam. The temple of Chāng Lom, which is attributed to Rām K'amheng, shows clearly its affinity to the Sinhalese style, with its bell-shaped *dagoba* and its elephant terrace. I was fortunate enough to visit this temple on one occasion shortly after the passage of royalty, and so was able to obtain a photograph of it cleared of the jungle (Fig. 186). The fact that it is built of laterite covered with stucco places it near to the Khmer period of domination, before the use of laterite gave way to that of brick; so here we have an interesting meeting between Cambodia and Ceylon in the heart of Siam.

Another temple, that of P'rajedi Chet Teo (The Seven Rows of *Stupas*), though still of laterite construction, is probably rather later in date, if we may judge from a beautiful Tai Buddha image seated on the Naga king after the Khmer fashion, which has withstood all the ravages of six hundred years and still remains in its niched alcove oblivious of time and serenely imperturbable (Fig. 187). The folds of the Naga king have been damaged by thieves in their search for buried treasure, but the image and the magnificent hood are intact. The wide-spreading knees and the hands folded in the lap in the attitude of *samadhi* (Meditation) show the Sinhalese influence, while the features are unmistakably of the Suk'ot'ai school, in its settled and well-defined form of the early fourteenth century A.D.

The first occasion on which I visited the old city of Sachanalai I examined certain other remains of temples, such as Suan Keo Utayan, which stood in a very picturesque setting, and also Somdet Nāng P'ya (Her Majesty the Queen), which had almost disappeared beneath the vegetation but still possessed some mural decoration in stucco in good preservation. I saw, too, the monument called the *Lak Müang* which was always set up at the foundation of a city with (so the ancient story goes) a human sacrifice buried beneath it to propitiate the '*p'ī*,' or spirits, and to bring good fortune to the inhabitants.

Apart from the ruins and objects still standing, our chief source of knowledge of all that pertains to the dynasty of Suk'ot'ai, the first Tai dynasty of Siam, lies in the stone inscriptions of which more than twenty have been found since the days of King Mongkut. These have now been set up in the National Museum, and fifteen of them have been deciphered and translated into French by Coedès. For a study of the evolution of the Siamese script alone they are invaluable, but, in addition, the earlier ones are so full of details of the customs and religion of the princes and their people that a tolerably clear idea can be obtained of the life in Central Siam in medieval times.

I have already spoken of the famous *stela* of Rām K'amheng, the obelisk which dates from A.D. 1292 and forms the Magna Carta of Siam. In this inscription, which is in the earliest form of Tai script, the king records how both he and all his people, high and low, men and women, 'without distinction of rank or sex,' practise the religion of the Buddha with devoutness and always faithfully observe his precepts during the rainy season. At the close of this season there is the grand ceremony of *Kat'in*, or 'presenting robes to the priests,' such as still obtains today, and everyone gives himself over to music and laughter. 'Whoever wishes to play, plays; he who wishes to laugh, laughs; he who wishes to sing, sings.' In the midst of Suk'ot'ai there were temples and statues of the Buddha both great and small, some of the latter measuring 30 feet in height. Rām K'amheng then records how he built the monastery of Arannika specially for the Patriarch, who had come from Nakon Sritammarāt and who had completely studied the Three Baskets (*Tripitaka*). This monastery also contained an image of the Buddha 30 feet high.

The facts so strikingly given in this inscription are supplemented to an unusual degree by another long inscription, also in Tai script, found in Wat Çri Chum but probably belonging to Wat Mahā-Tāt, on which no precise date is discoverable, but which may be ascribed to the reign of Dharmaraja I, the grandson of Rām K'amheng, about the period A.D. 1350–70. After a graphic description of how the Tai dynasty of Suk'ot'ai came into being, the story told is chiefly concerned with a prince who, in imitation of Sakya Muni himself, laid aside his royal robes and way of living and entered a monastery, fully determined to become a future Buddha himself. The great interest from the point of view of this study lies in the many references to Ceylon. For instance, the prince 'loved to wander in the forest, straying here and there and neglecting his food (living on fruit and roots), behaving in every respect after the manner of the monks of Sinhala' (Ceylon). Further, the prince restored the Temple of the Great Relic at Suk'ot'ai (Wat Mahā-Tāt), and the inscription adds that 'when the Somdet P'ra Mahasami [i.e. the priest Sumana, who will be discussed later] came from Sihala [Ceylon] he brought a body of laymen with him and, in his faith, brought also two precious relics of the Buddha.' These relics performed innumerable miracles, which were seen by the laymen of Sihala who threw themselves on the ground in adoration, and the reason for them was to urge all the folk to go to Lankadvipa (Ceylon) to help in furthering the cause of their religion and thereby gain much merit.

It is thus clear that by the middle of the fourteenth century A.D. the Hinayana (Theravada) doctrine of Sinhalese Buddhism was firmly established in the heart of Siam, and, as will be seen later, it received a number of new impulses direct from Ceylon up to the sixteenth century A.D.

I cannot leave the subject of this second inscription without reference to a very singular passage contained in it which is so remarkable that I reproduce it in full. It runs as follows:

When the great brick sanctuary (of Wat Mahā-Tāt) was finished and solemnly opened, a search was made for ancient *stone* images of the Buddha. Homage was paid to them and they were collected together in the Great Sanctuary. In one place a neck or a bust had been found; in another place the hair or an arm or a breast; some-times the head had fallen and was far from the body and it needed *four men* to carry it; sometimes a leg or a thigh had been found, sometimes a hand or a foot. All these stone statues of the Buddha were of large size. They had to be placed on a barrow or a cart to be transported to the Great Sanctuary where they were joined together with lime (cement). Some of these statues were magni-ficent and beautifully decorated, just as if Indra had made them himself. Once restored, they became large, durable, and extremely fine statues of the Buddha. The Great Sanctuary was filled with them and they were placed together in groups or ranged along the galleries.

Were it not that there could be no motive in relating such a story, if fictitious, the whole account would appear to be incredible; but it undoubtedly has a ring of truth about it, and it is hard to know which quality to admire the most in our royal priest, the pietist, the art-lover or the archaeologist, for he seems to have been all three combined in one, and must surely be one of the earliest of whom the record is so clear, at any rate in the East. And the puzzling question remains— What type of ancient stone Buddha image was he likely to find lying about in quantities in deserted ruins in the region of Suk'ot'ai? As far as one may hazard a guess, they must have been of Khmer origin and workmanship. There had scarcely been time by A.D. 1350 for the creation of *ancient* Tai images, and besides, the Tai of Suk'ot'ai and the north seldom worked in *stone*; nor are there any traces of Môn-Indian (Dvāravatī) sculpture in this region. There remain, therefore, only the Khmer; and yet, judging from the evidence available, the Khmer themselves did not penetrate so far north as Sawank'alōk and Suk'ot'ai until the latter half of the twelfth century A.D., so that even their images would scarcely deserve the epithet of 'ancient.' Moreover, the size and plentifulness of these images is so difficult to understand— heads and bodies requiring four men to carry them and enough images to fill the Great Sanctuary and the galleries of Wat Mahā-Tāt at Suk'ot'ai. Where are they now? What has become of this galaxy of beautiful large stone images? There is absolutely no visible sign of them today among the desolate ruins of the temple, and one can only imagine that Indra, seeing the courts and temples forsaken, must have spirited them away.

Two other well-known inscriptions of this period must be mentioned. The first is called the *stela* of Nagara Jum. This is dated 1279 of the *Maha-Sakarāt* (1357 A.D.) and was formerly set up at Wat Parama Tāt near the old city of Kampengp'et on the river Me Ping, between Nakon Sawan and Tāk (Raheng). It records the installation by Dharmaraja I of Suk'ot'ai of a precious and authentic relic of the Buddha obtained from Ceylon, and also of the planting of a branch of the original sacred fig-tree under which the Buddha sat and conquered the army of Mara, the Prince of Evil.

The second is an inscription in the Khmer language set up by the same king of Suk'ot'ai in the Monastery of the Mango Grove, to the west of Suk'ot'ai and outside its walls, and was specially made to commemorate the arrival of a venerable monk from Ceylon in A.D. 1362, his installation at the Monastery of the Mango Grove and the ordaining of King Dharmaraja I himself as a priest. There is also a duplicate (or almost a duplicate) of this inscription in Tai script, which was found some years ago in a temple to the north of Ayudhya.

Thus we have two more clearly defined instances of the influence played by Sinhalese Buddhism in Siam at this time, and I shall have occasion to refer again to the venerable monk of the inscription, since he was destined to play a great part in the spread of Sinhalese Buddhism, and indirectly its artistic influence, throughout the whole country.

Claeys strikes a true note when he says that 'Suk'ot'ai was in reality the centre where Khmer architecture and the Tai contribution brought from the north met and fused together, the crucible from which emerged the true Tai architecture, which still awaits analysis, and the true Tai sculpture, which is more clearly defined.' As regards the sculpture, there are two distinct forms of the Suk'ot'ai style, one of which is distinguishable by the extremely soft rendering of the eyebrows and eyes and by a still relatively large mouth, while in the other the features are more sharply defined and hence take on a more conventionalized form, especially seen in the sharp ridge formed by the eyebrows. Figs. 171 and 188 demonstrate this difference, and, judging from later developments in Siam, the seated figure (Fig. 171) is probably the earlier of the two. Both these examples are in the National Museum, and Fig. 188, about 24 inches high, may perhaps be considered without prejudice the most beautiful example of the Suk'ot'ai style known. It makes an intensely spiritual appeal. Dupont, however, goes further and suggests that, although owing to the use of bronze as opposed to stone there is an almost complete difference between Tai and Khmer art in Siam, yet the half-closed eyes, the gentle smile, and the calm, meditative expression of the Suk'ot'ai figures bring clearly to mind certain Khmer images of the Bayon style, especially certain Bodhisattvas and Taras. He admits that it is too early as yet to do anything but point out certain analogies, but he wonders if there were not actually a rather complex transitional period in which the final examples of the Môn and Khmer periods were linked up with the beginnings of Southern Tai art. This is a very interesting suggestion, as are most of those put forward by Dupont, and we may undoubtedly look for transitional links between the Tai and the Khmer even in North-Central Siam. At the same time, if the influence from Ceylon began to come in about the middle of the thirteenth century A.D., this transitional Tai-Khmer period could not have been of long duration.

The most venerated image of the Buddha of the Suk'ot'ai period still *in situ* is the larger than life-size figure to be seen in the temple of Mahā-Tāt at Pitsanulōk. In Siamese eyes this is considered the most beautiful image known, and is the object of a yearly pilgrimage by large numbers of the people (Fig. 189). An exact replica of this image, which is called P'ra Chinnarāt, was made in the reign of King Chulalongkorn and set up by him in his new temple of Benchamabopit in Bangkok early in this century. The original brother image, P'ra Chinna-Çri, was brought to Bangkok many years ago and is now to be seen in the temple of Bavaranives.

The Suk'ot'ai period is undoubtedly the most important from the Tai standpoint, and the form created represents the 'ideal' in Siamese eyes. To Europeans the Khmer forms are generally considered more pleasing, but that is because the European generally prefers the individualistic or human rather than the symbolic form of art. Each is entitled to its share in our appreciation of beauty, but the more we live with and strive to understand the symbolic form, the more we shall tend to enrich our spirit as opposed to our senses. It has taken me personally a long time to realize this truth, but my own experience has been such that I cannot doubt it now.

CHAPTER XII

THE NORTHERN KINGDOM AND THE
FOUNDING OF AYUDHYA IN THE SOUTH

THE importance of the new school of doctrine and art combined was made manifest throughout Siam almost at once and within a hundred years practically the whole country had accepted it and adapted the Suk'ot'ai ideal to its own immediate needs. As we have seen, Rām K'amheng had taken the first step by inviting the renowned teacher of Sinhalese Buddhism from Nakon Sritammarāt. In A.D. 1362, at the request of Dharmaraja I, a second high priest who had studied in Ceylon arrived at Suk'ot'ai and was provided with a monastery especially built for the purpose. The accounts are rather conflicting as to where this priest came from originally, but I think it may be accepted that he came directly to Suk'ot'ai from Pegu (where another famous teacher-priest named Udumbara Mahāsami resided), and that his name was Sumana. The title Sami, or Mahāsami, is one that was given by the king of Ceylon to foreign priests who came to the island to study the Sinhalese form of Buddhism. The J.K.M. says that Sumana was a native of Suk'ot'ai who went to Pegu to be ordained, but the inscription of Dharmaraja I makes no mention of this. After Sumana had resided at Suk'ot'ai for five or six years his renown reached the ears of the king of Chiengmai, who at that time was Kū Na (or Kilana), and, after repeated requests from the latter, he finally agreed to accept a mission to that country to preach the new form of Buddhism. He set out in A.D. 1369 and was received by the king himself at Lamp'ūn, which was probably still the most important religious centre in the north, and installed there at the temple of P'ra Yün (the Standing Buddha). This temple (Fig. 190) is situated about a mile to the east of the city of Lamp'ūn and is so called because of four standing images of the Buddha which have been set up in niches on the four sides of the building. An inscription in Pali and Tai (Suk'ot'ai script), describing the foundation in detail, was found some years ago in situ, and has been translated by Coedès. The style of the Buddha image is based on that of Suk'ot'ai, though, curiously enough, the arms and hands hang down on both sides of the body, but the style of the temple itself is undoubtedly Burmese, and resembles that of the temple of That-Byin-Nyu at Pagān. One may reasonably conclude from this that it was Sumana himself who superintended the erection of the building, and that he based his plans on a temple he had seen in Burma. There is another small temple at Chiengmai in somewhat the same style, Wat Siriküt, which may be included for comparison (Fig. 191), and here the figure of the Buddha bears a very close resemblance to the Suk'ot'ai school, both in the general style and the particular pose. There is a singular charm about both these temples.

From this time the Suk'ot'ai style of *stupa* architecture and Buddha image spread rapidly throughout the north of Siam, and the countryside is covered with *stupas* in the Burmo-Sinhalese form, though the other temple buildings in the true Tai style appear to owe nothing to Ceylon. The old city of Chiengsen on the Mekōng in the far north was refounded by Sen P'u, the grandson of Meng Rai, in A.D. 1328 when he made it his capital city, but it is now almost completely deserted, and when I first visited it over thirty years ago, one had to cut one's way through the jungle *inside* the city walls; and the District Officer told me that he had actually fired at a rhinoceros almost at his office door. Fig. 192 gives a good impression of the present state of one of the principal temple sites, though it is only fair to say that the Archaeological Department has in places cleared a great deal of the jungle-growth away. The *stupa* is more Burmese than Sinhalese in style, as is witnessed by the successive tiers and angular corners, but the Buddha image is post-Suk'ot'ai and is probably of the late fourteenth or even fifteenth century A.D. I have described this temple and its surroundings in AN ASIAN ARCADY. It was in Chiengsen too, that, bursting through some thick bushes, I suddenly came upon a truly remarkable collection, or 'Council,' of Buddha images of both bronze and stone, headless, armless and legless, lying in their dozens here, there and everywhere. And near by, while digging under the floor of a small sanctuary chapel, I unearthed the only ancient Buddha image cast in silver that I know of (Fig. 193). It is 7 inches high and probably of the fifteenth or sixteenth century A.D. Fig. 194 shows a Buddha head of gigantic size, 18 inches high, which is a fine example of the middle period, say in the mid-fifteenth century A.D. before the general debasement began. This is in my own collection at Oxford.

As regards the temples themselves, the north of Siam is so full of beautiful examples that it is quite impossible to do them full justice here. Indeed, the temple architecture of the Tai needs further careful study and, although Döhring has published an interesting work on this subject, his treatment is more descriptive and purely technical than analytical or artistic. For my present purpose I do not think I can do better than illustrate three of the most beautiful out of all those that I visited in the north. The first two of these are at Nān, while the third is at Lampāng Lūang, a hallowed spot of which I have already spoken. The first (Fig. 195) is quite a small ensemble, but it shows unusually well the type of pillar, pediment, roof-tier, naga-tip and eaves so characteristic of the Tai style. I forget its name. The second (Fig. 196) is the *stupa* of the temple of Cha Heng lying outside the city, across the river and padi-fields. It is approached up a slope guarded by two enormous Nagas, each a hundred yards long, which rear their serpent heads 30 feet high in the air, and is flanked by two magnificent banyan trees, one on either side. When I saw it, the copper casing of the *stupa* shone like gold, and its slender pinnacle soared majestically to heaven against a background of deep blue. All the earth around was swept and clean, and I breathed an air of indefinable peace. There is also at Nān an interesting temple with four images of Buddha back to back in the interior and opposite each image a beautifully carved teak double door. One of these is illustrated in AN ASIAN ARCADY. If these four images are a relic of Brahmanism, it is the only such instance in the north known to me.

The third is the temple at Lampāng Lūang about ten miles south of Lampāng. The original temple is said to have been built by Chām T'ewi herself, but the present buildings were erected in A.D. 1501 in the reign of P'ra Müang Keo of Chiengmai. When I visited them last in 1920 they were being kept in perfect order by the then Chief of Lampāng, as will be seen from the illustration (Fig. 197), which was taken at the time: but I am told that since his death some years ago they have been allowed to fall into disrepair. A more beautiful setting could scarcely be imagined. The giant trees all around speak of its age, and I was reminded at every step of some well-ordered college at Cambridge. The buildings themselves are splendid examples of the architecture of the period, especially the massive, solid *stupa*, the beautiful façade of the *vihara* which is of wood, the pinnacled entrance gateway gleaming white in the sun, and the long eaves of the roof which come down low and lend an air of mystery to the interior. There are no side-walls to the *vihara* and this is a feature of many temples in the north of Siam.

The fifteenth century A.D. was an age of great devotional activity in Siam, and witnessed another strong influx of Sinhalese Buddhism. In A.D. 1423 a body of twenty-five priests from Chiengmai, together with eight from Cambodia, went to Ceylon to receive ordination anew, and were there joined by six Môn priests from Burma. They returned in A.D. 1425, stopped awhile at Ayudhya, Suk'ot'ai and Sawank'alōk on their way home, and finally reached Chiengmai again in A.D. 1430. Strangely enough, the king of Chiengmai at this time, Sām Fang Ken, was a heretic without faith, who adored demons and spirits, and it is possible that it was this deplorable fact that sent the priests to Ceylon to try and revive the people's waning enthusiasm for the true Faith. They established themselves at the temple of Pā Deng two miles west of Chiengmai and soon after their return the priests embarked on a mission throughout the north, visiting Lamp'ūn, Lampāng, Chiengrai and even Chiengsen, where they consecrated a monastery at the foot of the hill Chom Kitti.

Thus was founded the sect of Sihala Bhikkus to whom Rattanapanna, the author of the J.K.M., belonged, and who, by implanting the purest form of Sinhalese Buddhism, gave rise to a great revival of Pali literature and learning in Siam. In A.D. 1442 Sām Fang Ken was deposed by his successor Tilokarāt (after Meng Rai the most renowned king of Chiengmai), who was his sixth son, and sent to the Shan states, where he died a few years later. In this year took place a great ordination of five hundred 'sons of family' (i.e. of important families) on the banks of the river Me Ping, and the revival of Pali Buddhism had taken root. In A.D. 1452 Tilokarāt had the hallowed limits for the future ordination of priests consecrated at the temple of Pā Deng, and in A.D. 1475 a great council was held at Chiengmai for the revision of the Pali scriptures. This revival of Pali literature produced such works as the *Mangaladipani* which, together with the *Dhammapadatthakatha*, forms the basis of the religious system in Siam, north and south, and also in Cambodia. Similar events took place in Burma about the same time, according to the Kalyani inscriptions which were engraved in A.D. 1476 on stone tablets by order of the king of Pegu.

To complete this brief history of Northern Siam, in A.D. 1558 the kingdom of Chiengmai was attacked and conquered by the king of Pegu, and remained, with intermissions, a vassal state of Burma until near the end of the eighteenth century, when the Burmese were finally driven out with the help of the king of Bangkok, to whom Chiengmai then became vassal in turn.

The town of Chiengmai possesses a singular beauty. I was stationed there in 1913 and again in 1915, and completely succumbed to its charms; and when I visited it afresh in 1927 after twelve years' absence, I found it more enchanting than ever, with its brick-red palace-fort surrounded by a lotus-filled moat dating from about A.D. 1350 (which forms the frontispiece to AN ASIAN ARCADY), its shady avenues, its broad flowing river, and its innumerable temples each within its leafy garden, where the tiled roofs and stately *stupas*, the swept courtyards, the green mango-trees and the heavenly blue sky above all combined to induce a feeling of such peace and happiness as it would be hard to match elsewhere. And then, standing sentinel over all, the forest-clad Doi Sut'ep, rising to a height of 5,000 feet at a distance of only a few miles and giving courage to all who 'will look unto the hills.' I saw it from my bedroom window every morning as I opened my eyes.

Most of the important temples in Chiengmai were built during the fourteenth and fifteenth centuries A.D. The temple of P'ra Sing was founded about A.D. 1350 and a crypt added later by King Kilana (Kū Na) to contain the famous Buddha image of that name. The temple of Sūan Dôk was founded in A.D. 1371, and in A.D. 1373 the relic of the Buddha brought to Laoland by Sumana was solemnly installed there. The temple of P'rajedi Lūang (The Royal Pagoda) was begun in 1401 A.D. but not completed until A.D. 1478 by Tilokarāt. It was to this temple that the latter brought the most famous image of all, the so-called Emerald Buddha (now in the Royal Temple at Bangkok), and built a special resting-place for it in A.D. 1481 (Fig. 198). The origin of the Emerald Buddha is obscure, but what is known of its history and cult has been ably set down by Lingat, who ascribes it to the Chiengsen school of the late fourteenth century A.D. King Mongkut stated in a declaration that the statue was made of jade and concluded from this that the stone had been brought from China. Lingat suggests that it may have been hewn out of a stone found in the Nān region, which has been pronounced to be chrysoprase, which the OXFORD DICTIONARY describes as 'an apple-green variety of chalcedony.' The legendary chronicles record that the image was 'born' in India in Açoka's time, was taken thence to Ceylon and later found its way to Angkor. From there it was brought to Ayudhya and finally to Lampāng and Chiengmai. It is not possible to examine this renowned image at close quarters but, judging from the photograph (Fig. 198), it seems to be clearly of local manufacture and probably belongs, as Lingat suggests, to the second period of the northern school. It appears to be about 2 feet high.

I know well the greenish stone produced in the Nān region and consider Lingat's suggestion as most probable.

As a pendant to this survey of art and architecture in Northern Siam, it will, I think, interest the reader to see the kind of folk who still uphold the Buddha, the Law and the Order in that region. Here in this photograph (Fig. 199) you may see for yourself a group of priests, acolytes, and children too young as yet to wear the yellow robe. Remark how their features, both of old and young, recall the Tai type of Buddha features we have been looking at so often—how serious and thoughtful, and yet how calm. But I think I like the Boy-scout best of all.

We must now turn to the south of Siam.

While epigraphical evidence is abundant as to the eclipse of the Khmer at the hands of the Tai in the Sawank'alōk region in North-Central Siam in the second half of the thirteenth century A.D. the course of events in the lower valley of the Menam, especially at Lopburi, during this period is not so clearly defined. Pelliot discusses the question— What happened at Lopburi after the Khmer had been driven out of Suk'ot'ai by Indraditya?—and seems to arrive at the conclusion that Lo (as the Chinese called Lavo or Lopburi) first of all became a vassal state to Hsien (or Sawank'alōk-Suk'ot'ai). This would be the more easily acceptable were it not that in his *stela* of A.D. 1292 recounting the extent of his dominions, Rām K'amheng, although he includes Nakon Sawan, Supanburi, Rajaburi and Petchaburi, expressly omits all mention of Lopburi; and, seeing that Lopburi was the centre of Khmer sovereignty in Siam, it seems hardly possible to account for such an omission if he had actually absorbed it as well.

In his HISTORY OF SIAM Wood remarks: 'It must not be assumed that King Rām K'amheng exercised effective control over all these regions (i.e. those mentioned in the above *stela*). For instance, a Prince of Supan had already by this time attained to a powerful position, and the Tai rulers of Lopburi and the ancient city of Ayodhya (both related to King Rām K'amheng) were either independent or subject to the King of Cambodia.' And again: 'In Siam itself, moreover, a rival power (i.e. rival to Suk'ot'ai) had sprung up which was destined to obtain, in time, dominion over the whole kingdom. This was the Principality of Suwanp'umi (i.e. Supanburi) or U-T'ong, ruled over by an energetic Prince who was descended from the Chiengsen Princes and was probably a distant relation of King Mengrai. Before the end of King Loet'ai's reign (King of Suk'ot'ai, c. A.D. 1317-47), the Prince of

U-T'ong had annexed a large portion of the dominions of the Suk'ot'ai Kingdom. Parts of the Cambodian Empire, moreover, which had never been conquered, even by King Rām K'amheng, were annexed by the Prince of U-T'ong including Lopburi, the old city of Ayodhya and Chantabun.'

Wood cites no references or authorities for his statements that there were at this time *Tai* rulers of Lopburi and old Ayudhya, or that the Prince of U-T'ong had annexed these cities by the middle of the fourteenth century A.D. But it seems reasonable to suppose, from subsequent events, that there were large settlements of Tai in the south who were gradually gathering power and who would not be slow to take advantage of the revolution successfully carried out by Indraditya in the north. Unfortunately, no Tai or Khmer inscriptions have yet been discovered dealing with this eventful period of Siamese history.

The prince of U-T'ong, to whom Wood refers, is well known to history as Rama T'ibodi I, who set up the capital of Siam at Ayudhya in A.D. 1350 near the site of the old city of Dvāravatī and thus established the Ayudhyan dynasty of Tai kings of Siam which endured until the sack of the city by the Burmese and the downfall of the kingdom in A.D. 1767. The city of U-T'ong, the ruins of which lie to the west of the modern city of Supanburi, is of very ancient date, judging from the fragments of sculpture discovered there which resemble those of Dvāravatī, but hitherto it has not been scientifically excavated. The reason for its final abandonment in favour of Ayudhya is said to have been a serious epidemic, but of what disease is not known. Quaritch Wales has given a graphic description in TOWARDS ANGKOR of the conditions obtaining there when the city was deserted.

Prince Damrong has been at some pains to discuss the origins of this prince of U-T'ong and to try and extract the probable truth from the many legends in which his history is wrapped. As a result, he believes that a Tai descendant of King Brahma of Chiengsen named Jaya Çiri, fleeing from the Peguans who had attacked his kingdom in the far north about the year A.D. 1188, came southwards and established himself in the region of P'rapatom. This ruler eventually extended his kingdom to Supanburi (or U-T'ong) which is close at hand and became the founder of the prince of U-T'ong's line. As for the prince of U-T'ong himself, he is thought to have been the son-in-law of his predecessor and not of royal birth himself. The name U-T'ong is popularly supposed to denote 'a golden cradle' because the prince was given a cradle of gold by his father, but Prince Damrong is much more likely to be right in his opinion that U-T'ong is simply the Siamese equivalent of Suvarnabhumi (Supan), which in Pali means the 'land' or 'source' of gold. If these conclusions are correct, then one must assume that during the Khmer rule in South-Central Siam Tai chiefs were allowed to spring up, who held their principalities in fief to the king of Cambodia at Angkor and that, when the Khmer were driven from Sawank'alōk, the latter soon lost their control over Lopburi as well. But they had been masters there for two and a half centuries and the influence of their culture and race is clearly seen in the sculpture of the transition period which has been classed by Coedès under the style of 'School of U-T'ong.' His reasons for adopting this name are given in his own words.

> The name of U-T'ong has been chosen to designate the period to which certain images appear to belong which show a strong Khmer influence allied with various features of a true Siamese art. The greater number of images of this type so far found come from Ayudhya and Lopburi, but they have also been found at Supanburi and as far north as Muang San, in short throughout the territory which formed the nucleus of the Kingdom of Ayudhya. [I cannot trace Muang San on the map, but it probably lies between Supan-buri and Chaināt to the north. U-T'ong images can also be seen now in temples at new Suk'ot'ai (T'ani).] If one were sure that these images were all *posterior* to the foundation of this Kingdom in 1350, they might be naturally classed under the title 'School of Ayudhya, early style.' But it is quite possible that those which came from Supanburi and its neighbourhood are *anterior* to the foundation of Ayudhya, and it seemed that the name of U-T'ong, corresponding to the name of the capital of the principality which was the cradle of the realm of Ayudhya, would be a suitable one for this mixed or transition style which doubtless reflected the political vicissitudes of the country.

In the absence of inscribed and dated images it is difficult to come to a definite conclusion as to when this transition period of sculpture between Khmer and Tai began in the south, but I have been at some trouble to bring together a considerable number of examples of the period, and these show such an extraordinary variety of features, ranging from almost pure Khmer to entirely pure Tai, that I feel the transition must have occupied a fairly long interval of time, and I should not be surprised if it were eventually shown to have had its beginnings early in the thirteenth or even in the twelfth century A.D.

Coedès says that 'of the features of the "School of Lopburi" the sculpture of U-T'ong preserved the form of the face, the band enclosing the hair on the forehead and the male appearance of the torso. One may even perhaps find a far-removed trace of the style of Dvāravatī in the treatment of the arcading of the eyebrows and the lines of the mouth, but on the other hand the use of the flame-pointed uṣnīṣa shows that the influence of Ceylon had already arrived, probably during the period of annexation to the realm of Suk'ot'ai.'

Coedès then develops his views by dividing the sculpture of U-T'ong into two principal groups. The first is represented by a type of image whose elongated oval face is analogous to the style of Suk'ot'ai: this type becomes the direct ancestor of the modern statuary of the school of Ayudhya. The second type shows, on the other hand, a reaction against the style of Suk'ot'ai and exaggerates, sometimes in rather a clumsy fashion, the chief Khmer characteristics. He adds: 'It would seem as if these images were the work of Siamese artists who have tried to copy the Khmer and who, fearing to fall into the style of Suk'ot'ai, have exceeded all reasonable bounds in their imitation of the Khmer style. The face is even shorter than the Khmer, the projecting chin is marked by a dimple, and the shin-bones are marked by a sharp outline.'

Dupont also divides the sculpture of U-T'ong into two groups but regards the question from rather a different angle. According to him the first group is a normal derivative of Khmer art and especially of the Bayon style. The face is broad, the expression soft, and certain details are repeated, such as the band describing a curve on the forehead, and the divided chin. The second group, on the other hand, has obvious affinities with the Tai schools of art. The face is thinner, and the expression is more 'nuancée'; of Khmer influence there only remains the band on the forehead. Dupont finds it difficult to establish priority between these groups and rather pertinently asks—At what stage of development of the Tai schools have we arrived when the art of U-T'ong appears?

Of the two classifications Dupont's appears to me to be the more satisfactory if regarded in a broad sense. For my own part I feel that, taken as a whole, the school of U-T'ong represents a normal development from the Khmer to the Tai throughout lower Central Siam, and that, before a true Tai type was evolved, Tai or Tai-Khmer sculptors were giving such a free rein to their individual tastes and fancies in the delineation of the features such as never occurred before or since in the country. As the Bayon style of Khmer art is now attributed to the end of the twelfth century A.D., it would naturally play an important part in influencing the work of the Tai artists; yet I do not think the latter were bound by any one style, but that they fashioned their images in their own localities entirely independent of one another, until the school of Suk'ot'ai had had time to penetrate this region and cast its all-pervading influence over them.

For the actual type of image produced in this period two figures will suffice. Fig. 200 shows a large image in stone in a temple on the hill of T'ammamun in the Supanburi district, which is undoubtedly Tai-Khmer in style, but is probably late in date as the uṣṇiṣa carries the flame-top derived from Suk'ot'ai. It represents an example of Coedès's second type, in which he considers that the Tai were consciously imitating the Khmer, rather than a natural derivative from the true Khmer image. Fig. 201, on the other hand, shows a bronze image, 20 inches high, which is a good representative example of the transition from Khmer to Tai. The band confining the hair on the forehead, the broad mouth, the arcading of the eyebrows, and the shape of the face all bespeak the influence of the earlier periods, but the treatment of the hair (in tiny round knobs), of the torso, and of the legs, has now become wholly Tai. The set of the arms and hands, however, is still as seen in small Khmer bronze figures from Siam (cf. Fig. 155). The flame-top is missing in this image.

Stone images of this period are comparatively rare and the sculptors, being Tai, modelled mostly in bronze. A noticeable feature is the quality of the bronze composition, possibly due to the presence of gold, which has a smooth texture and nearly always takes on a beautiful patina, thereby giving a most pleasing effect from a purely artistic point of view.

So much for the characteristic types of image of the U-T'ong period. What I propose to do now is to put before the reader four heads which will show the diversity of face-types which appears at this time, and at the same time illustrate the change from features which some might consider purely Khmer to those which are entirely Tai in feeling and which, as Coedès says, form the parent stock from which the national school of Ayudhya was derived. Gradually we leave the realm of concrete personalities and enter that of abstract idealism which governed the Tai so strongly in their representation of the Buddha during their early formative years. How long this period of transition lasted cannot be definitely stated. Dupont thinks it may have lasted until the fifteenth century A.D., and this is possibly true, even if we exclude the conscious imitations referred to by Coedès.

Fig. 202 shows a head, $4\frac{1}{2}$ inches high, which approximates most nearly to the true Khmer type. The rectangular face, the almost straight forehead, the long, thick-lipped mouth, and the uṣṇiṣa without a flame-top are pure Khmer. But the nose, the eyebrows and the treatment of the hair indicate a new influence which has crept in and add a touch of feeling which is Tai. There is no dimple in the chin. The modelling is excellent; there is a poise and a dignity in the head, and a strength in the features which betoken an originality of conception far removed from any conventionalized form. I feel certain that this head must antedate any influence from Suk'ot'ai, and that it is *anterior* to Ayudhya. For a number of years this little head stood on the top of my writing-desk and every morning, when I greeted him, he gave me courage to face another day. It is now in the British Museum.

Fig. 203, 9 inches high, though some of the details, such as the flame-top and the treatment of the hair, are wholly Tai, shows a much stronger resemblance to the Khmer type in spirit. The square face and jaw and the long mouth curling up at the ends lead one to the belief that the artist must have been strongly imbued with Khmer feeling. The modelling is superb, and I consider this head a great work of art. A well-known critic has declared it to be as fine a work of art as ever came out of Egypt. In 1948 it was bequeathed by the late Lord Lee of Fareham to the University of Toronto.

Fig. 204, 8 inches high, is a gilded bronze head which has taken on a beautiful red and green patina, where the gilt has worn off. Its sharply cut outline still shows affinity with its Khmer ancestry, but all the same it is the work of a Tai artist. The delicate nose, the firm mouth and chin, the noble forehead, the half-closed eyes, and the poise of the head, all combine to produce a form full of intense feeling, at once regal and yet meditative, mystic and serene. This head is now in the Barber Institute at Birmingham.

In Fig. 205, 8 inches high, the process of emerging into Tai is nearly complete. The mouth is still large and the nose tends to be flat, but the face is becoming oval, and the eyebrows now arched are sharply marked by incised lines. The hair is formed of pin-points and the tall *Ketumala* shows the Suk'ot'ai influence. This head may be called Tai. It can be seen in the Eastern Museum at Oxford.

Finally, I must include a walking figure of the Buddha of singular charm in the attitude of *Abhaya-mudra* (Dispelling Fear), 11 inches high, which I cannot attribute to any other school than that of U-T'ong (Fig. 206). In South-Central Siam this type of figure is extremely rare, but the form of the *uṣṇiṣa*, the girdle round the waist and the fold of cloth falling from the centre, are obvious links with Khmer statuary, though the features are entirely Tai. The robe hangs closely to the body as if it were wet, and such images are known in Siam as *P'ra piak nam* or the 'Water-soaked Buddha.' Though this image has a certain obvious analogy with the walking figures from Suk'ot'ai, the features are not at all similar to those of that school, and I think we must ascribe it to a period anterior to A.D. 1350. This figure is now in the British Museum.

Although the rise of the Tai and the disappearance of the Khmer meant in general the forsaking of stone for bronze, still at Lopburi itself the old tradition lingered for a long while, and stone images continued to be made even, it is said, until the reign of King Narai in the seventeenth century. This would cover a period of almost four hundred years—which it is rather difficult to credit unless there were a sudden recrudescence of stone sculpture after a longish interval—but there is no doubt that stone sculpture was executed at Lopburi for some centuries after the Khmer had vanished, and the local museum at Lopburi contains a large series of Tai heads which have all been found in the neighbourhood. These heads, which are of life-size or larger in many cases, vary to a great extent in artistic merit, but about the best there is a certain delicacy of feeling and a sensitiveness for form which admirably express the Buddhist spirit.

In a long article in the Siam Society's JOURNAL for January 1951, on 'The Sculpture of Peninsular Siam in the Ayudhya Period,' Luang Boribal Buribhand and A. B. Griswold, the joint authors, express the view that all the four examples of this Tai stone sculpture shown in BUDDHIST ART IN SIAM (Figs. 186–9) should be dated in the seventeenth century A.D. and ascribed to the reign of King Prasat Thong (A.D. 1630–55). I cannot agree with this entirely, and, though of those four Figs. 188 and 189 (Figs. 207 and 208) may be of this period, the other two, in my opinion, are certainly earlier.

Fig. 207, 15 inches high, shows a development of the Tai ideal, and, although the form is becoming conventionalized, there is still an original beauty and nobility of expression combined in this image. Eventually the type becomes stylized to a degree and Fig. 208, $11\frac{1}{2}$ inches high, shows the last stage of the evolution. This particular head is not altogether without merit, but there is a certain smugness of expression, the face is too moon-like in shape, and the features are becoming insignificant. The seeds of decay are clearly shown, and with this type, which is possibly of the seventeenth century A.D., the thousand-year-old school of Lopburi comes to an end. During this long period it has of necessity experienced many vicissitudes of race and character, but, taken all in all, it may well compare with any other school of sculpture in the world.

And now we have reached the last phase of Tai or Siamese art of which I propose to treat, namely, the school of Ayudhya.

All writers on Siamese sculpture are agreed that, once the Tai had firmly established their dominion over the country from Sawank'alōk in the north to Nakon Sritammarāt in the south, the national art which was formed out of a coalescence of all the earlier forces and currents quickly blossomed and as quickly faded, just as we see the brilliant, scarlet blooms of the Flamboyant tree suddenly burst upon us in April in all their glory and then, within one short month, fall to the ground and wither away. It would seem as if, stability once attained, all impulse to create died, and a dead conventional form was soon evolved which has lasted till the present day.

Of the early history of Ayudhya and its kings something must be said. The former capital of Siam, which lies 45 miles north of Bangkok, was built on an island having a circumference of about 14 miles and formed by the confluence of three rivers, the Pā Sāk river and two tributaries of the Menam Chao P'ya. It is said to be on or near the site of the ancient city of Dvāravatī, and the full title of Ayudhya still contains that name. It remained the capital of Siam until A.D. 1767 when it was sacked and almost completely destroyed by the Burmese; and although a new administrative provincial capital has sprung up on the island within modern times, yet the centre of it today is filled with nothing but picturesque ruins, but faintly recalling the glories of the past, when Ayudhya was said by seventeenth-century writers to be as fine and large a city as London. Kaempfer, the German physician, writing in A.D. 1690 in the first volume of his HISTORY OF JAPAN, is not quite so enthusiastic, but gives on the whole a graphic and, what reads to the writer as, an exact description of the city in those days. He says that 'the streets run in a streight line along the canals; some of them are tolerably large, but the greater part very narrow and all, generally speaking, foul and dirty. Some also are overflow'd at high water. Considering the bigness of the city, it is not very populous and in some parts but thinly inhabited, particularly on the West side on account of its remoteness, and towards the south by reason of the morassy ground, over which people make shift to get upon planks or paltry bridges....There are abundance of empty spaces and large gardens behind the streets wherein they let Nature work, so that they are full of grass, Herbs, Shrubs, and Trees that grow wild.'

After describing the three royal palaces, he takes notice of the temples. 'They are in great number, for as the whole country is stocked with Priests and monks, this city abounds in all parts with Temples, the courts of which keep a regular proportion with the streets and are full of pyramids and columns of divers shapes and gilt over. They do not equal our churches in bigness, but far exceed them in outward beauty by reason of the many bended roofs, gilt frontispieces, advanced steps, columns, pillars and other ornaments. Within they are adorned with many images as big as the life and bigger, skilfully formed of a mixture of plaister, rosin, oyl and hair, the outside of which is first varnished over black then gilt.' He then adds: 'In a Peguan temple out of the city there sits on an eminence such an Idol strongly gilt, the proportion of which is such that it would be of 120 foot in length if standing.'

I have no space for more, but this seems to me to give a picture of Siam of all times—as it was in A.D. 1350 and 1690, and as may still be seen today—magnificence, beauty and squalor all happily and naturally mingled together. But it is not without significance that, in the making of large Buddha images for the temple, stone gives way first to brick and stucco and finally to 'plaister, rosin, oyl and hair'!

Wood says that at the time of Rama T'ibodi I, in the second half of the fourteenth century A.D., Ayudhya was a very small city, with a wall of mud, and that the buildings, including the royal palace, were constructed of timber. The brick wall, of which parts may still be seen, was built by King Chakrap'at (A.D. 1549–65) and the palace, of which only the foundations now remain, dates from the time of King Trailokanāt (A.D. 1448–88). The principal ruins to be seen today are those of the vast temple of Çri Sarap'et, which also dates from the second half of the fifteenth century A.D. (Fig. 209). The two largest pagodas in this temple, both in the Sinhalese style, were built of brick and stucco by King Rama T'ibodi II in A.D. 1491 to receive the ashes of his father, Trailokanāt, and his elder brother, Boromoraja III, who died after a reign of only three years. Near by may also be seen one of the largest bronze images of the Buddha in the world (Fig. 210), known as P'ra Mangala Pabitra. It is about 50 feet high including the base, and is made of sheets of copper-bronze fastened on to a core of brick. From the purely conventional style portrayed, it is clearly of late date, possibly sixteenth century, and is not of great artistic value. There is, however, still a sense of dignity and proportion about the image which makes it sufficiently imposing, and any comparison with that at Kamakura in Japan will not be to its disadvantage. The right arm, the fingers of the left hand, and the point of the flame-top have been restored within recent years. This image is a good representative example of the conventional style into which the school of Ayudhya eventually developed.

There had at one time been another gigantic image of the Buddha, ordered in A.D. 1499 for the temple of Çri Sarap'et by Rama T'ibodi II. This image was also about 50 feet high, and the pedestal was 24 feet long. It was covered with gold plates weighing nearly 800 lb., and took more than three years to complete. It was destroyed by the Burmese in 1767 and, when the first king of the Bangkok dynasty found it impossible to restore the broken fragments, he had them buried beneath a pagoda in Wat Jetup'on in Bangkok.

When he first assumed the throne, Rama T'ibodi I was probably only acknowledged as King or Overlord from Lopburi southwards to Singora, but it was not long before he attacked Cambodia and, in spite of an initial reverse, succeeded in capturing its capital, Angkor, in A.D. 1352; whereupon its puppet king became vassal to Ayudhya. His successor, Boromoraja I, carried the work of consolidation still further by invading the realm of Suk'ot'ai in A.D. 1371, and finally in A.D. 1378 capturing all its principal cities from Kampengp'et northwards to Pitsanulōk and Sawank'alōk. This was the end of the independent kingdom of Suk'ot'ai, and the succeeding chiefs became vassal to Ayudhya, until in A.D. 1438 this territory was incorporated in the kingdom of Siam. In A.D. 1393 the vassal king of Cambodia endeavoured to break his bonds and attacked Siam, but was routed and deposed in favour of a grandson who was placed under the tutelage of a Siamese general and garrison. Again, in the reign of Boromoraja II (A.D. 1424–48), war broke out with Cambodia, and this was the final act of the drama. Angkor was captured and sacked after a siege of seven months in A.D. 1431, its vassal king died and the king of Siam set up his own son as king of Cambodia. A large quantity of bronze images of animals were brought back to Siam by the king and may still be seen at P'rabāt. The capital of Cambodia was later removed to Pnom-penh and thence to Lovek, and the great Khmer empire sank into insignificance and ruin. Much mystery is often made today over the disappearance of Angkor. There is no mystery. Thus by the time of the accession of Trailokanāt in A.D. 1448 the kingdom of Siam had absorbed its neighbour, Suk'ot'ai, had broken the power of Cambodia and had set up its dominion over most of modern Siam. There only remained the northern state of Chiengmai to be brought to heel, but, although Trailokanāt spent most of his long reign in attempts to conquer it, the task proved beyond his powers, and it was left to the Burmese king, Bureng Naung, in the middle of the following century to put his iron heel on Chiengmai and to bring the line of Meng Rai to an inglorious end. The northern region was, in fact, not finally incorporated in the kingdom of Siam until A.D. 1874, when a Siamese High Commissioner was sent to reside at Chiengmai for the first time. An interesting fact referred to by Wood is that in A.D. 1463, owing to the constant attacks by Chiengmai, Trailokanāt removed his capital northwards to Pitsanulōk and appointed his elder son to be governor of Ayudhya. Pitsanulōk remained the capital until his death in A.D. 1488.

Ayudhyan remains in brick and stucco of the fifteenth and sixteenth centuries A.D. are still to be seen at Lopburi in juxtaposition to the older Khmer temples, of which they are mostly conscious imitations. Their extremely dilapidated state is probably due as much to the depredations of robbers seeking the supposed treasures buried in their hearts as to the hand of time. Outside the temple of Mahā-Tāt are the two towers seen in Fig. 211. In spite of their debased style there is still something monumental about these structures, though their chief attraction is perhaps due to their crumbling condition. Near by is the p'rajedi seen in Fig. 212 which was originally built in the pointed Sinhalese style, but which is now chiefly remarkable for the stucco panel of seven Buddhist disciples preserved on one of its sides. Above them can just be seen the mutilated figure of the Buddha with one disciple on either side. Considering the limitations of the materials used, the artist has achieved a delightful rhythm and harmony in working out his conception. This is the finest fragment of Ayudhyan decorative sculpture still in existence.

Of the sculpture of the Ayudhyan period not much to its credit has hitherto been written. Coedès goes so far as to say that the mediocrity of the school of Ayudhya has caused him to exclude it altogether from his work on the National Museum, while Dupont gives it very little space in his essay on Siamese art. According to him, 'all attempts at classification are impossible, chiefly because the general decadence of Tai art does not entice one to further study of it.' These are hard sayings which are possibly justified if we regard Tai art from A.D. 1600 onwards. But the earlier manifestations are not without their artistic value, and even if the first joy of creative genius has subsided, there is still much to appreciate in the earlier products of the national school. From our brief historical survey, it is easy to see how Suk'ot'ai and Cambodia met at Ayudhya to form the basis of that school. The part played by Suk'ot'ai, being of Tai origin itself, was a natural evolution, to which was added, as in the buildings of the period, a conscious imitation of the Khmer style which was clearly much admired by the Tai kings. The student will be able to judge for himself how far the combination of these two elements succeeded in producing a work of art from the figure shown (Fig. 213). It may be taken as typical of the period, and the characteristics mentioned above are clearly marked. The features, which are unmistakably Tai, represent an abstract ideal and show a softness and a roundness of expression altogether foreign to Khmer traditions. The modelling of the head is good and still shows careful handling, but the lower part of the torso and the legs and feet are stiffly conventional and the broad flowing robe seems, as it were, stuck on to the body. The diadem with its crowning point, the large necklace with its hanging pendant, the bracelets on the upper part of the arms, the girdle round the waist and the broad fold of cloth running down from its centre are all copied directly from the Khmer. Dupont is in some doubt whether the crown and diadem are derived from the art of the Bayon period in Cambodia, or from the more ancient crowns of the temple of Angkor. But this type of crown is known to me in certain examples of Khmer art from Siam itself, and I do not think it necessary to look any further for the origin of the Tai inspiration. Dupont states, further, that the clothing reproduces exactly that found on Buddha images from Prah Khan (a temple adjoining the city of Angkor), and that the ornaments equally point to a Khmer influence. There can be no doubt of this, and I would even say that the Tai artist probably had a Khmer model in his mind when the first examples of this type were evolved. As I have said already, it is not to my mind a question of Khmer influence, but of conscious and direct imitation whether from Siam or Cambodia itself. Coupled with this I show a head until recently in my possession, Fig. 214, which shows how the type developed. This gilt bronze head, 20 inches high, is the finest of its kind, artistically, known to me. The soft lines of the eyebrows, the delicate nose, the sensitive mouth, and the downcast eyes, set in a face of perfect proportions, represent the totality of the Siamese conception of their ideal Being. There is a majesty as well as beneficence about this head which cannot be denied and which demands respect from any beholder.

At a later date, probably in the sixteenth century A.D., the crown, diadem and ornaments were abandoned and the type shown in the gigantic image at Ayudhya became the national style. It speaks for itself, and one can understand why students find no inclination to push their researches further.

My last illustration of the school of Ayudhya is of some interest as it shows a large head of the Buddha, $17\frac{1}{2}$ inches high, made of a sweet-scented wood (mai chan hôm) found in the eastern district of Siam (Fig. 215). The face is covered with lacquer, and the hair is formed of lacquer knobs; the eyes are filled with mother-of-pearl, a decoration, in itself witness of decadence, which came into fashion in the seventeenth century A.D. to which this head probably belongs. Small wooden images of the Buddha are to be found everywhere throughout the country sometimes coated with silver, but figures of such size carved out of wood are uncommon.

In the Bronze Hall of the National Museum at Bangkok are ranged, one on either side, two rows of Brahmanic statues of life-size, or greater in some cases, of Tai workmanship, which date from the Ayudhyan period. One of these is illustrated here, Fig. 216. It is a bronze image of Çiva in his aspect of Teacher, 6 feet 8 inches high, which was cast and set up by a prince, who called himself Çri Dharmaçokaraja, at Kampengp'et in the year A.D. 1510. It shows how, even at that late date, Khmer influence still exercised a fascination over the Tai, and the other statues in the Museum, of Vishnu and other male and female deities, all bear witness to this same fact. The statue shown here is of special interest as it bears a long inscription in Siamese on the top of the pedestal, running round the feet, recounting how the prince made this statue for the protection of all human beings, and how he had repaired the temples, roads and canals in his territory. For all the work he has carried out he offers the merit acquired to their majesties, the two kings, i.e. King Boromoraja of Ayudhya, and his son, Prince Jetta (afterwards King Rama T'ibodi II), who was then Crown Prince, ruling at Pitsanulōk. The prince who ordered the image must have been a local chief, probably descended from the once royal house of Suk'ot'ai.

The presence of these figures in the heart of Siam does not mean that there was a sudden outburst of Brahmanism at the beginning of the sixteenth century A.D. consequent on a decadence of Buddhism.

On the contrary, the creator of the Çiva image hopes that it will exalt both the Buddhist and Brahman religions and cult of the gods, so that they may not fall into obscurity and darkness. Throughout the history of Siam the religion of the Buddha has been no hindrance to the worship of the Brahmanic gods, and still today P'ra In (the god Indra) is the Protector of the Buddha, and watches over all his works. Buddhism is, indeed, the most tolerant of all religions and it is only a few years ago that I heard King Prajadjipok pay a moving tribute to a Christian Mission in his country and say that as long as they contributed to the happiness of his people and the maintenance of good government, so long would he welcome their presence in Siam.

I have now reached the end of my tale. I do not pretend to have solved all the intricate problems involved in tracing the development of sculpture and architecture in Siam: few countries, indeed, offer so rich a field of research. But as far as I can I have endeavoured to fit together all the fragments so far discovered into the pattern of my mosaic picture, and to indicate the lines of any future search for those pieces still missing.

As I said at the beginning, I have made no attempt to treat of modern trends or problems in any of the countries of South-East Asia: enough to study the past if we are to understand the present. It has been clearly shown that they have one and all derived their culture from India, each adapting it to its own needs and imbuing it with its own local genius. Now, after a long sleep, Asia is on the march, and it is safe to say that the meeting of the two great civilizations, India and China, embracing nearly half the human race, will prove to be one of the most momentous events of the future. What kind of a synthesis will be the outcome?

BIBLIOGRAPHY

Containing a list of selected works dealing with History, Art and Culture as a groundwork for the study of the Background of South-East Asia.

I. INDIA

BACHHOFER, L. *Early Indian Sculpture*. 2 vols. The Pegasus Press, Paris, 1929

BHATTACHARYYA, B. *Indian Images I*. The Brahmanic Iconography, Calcutta and Simla, 1921

The Indian Buddhist Iconography, London, 1924

BINYON, L. *Examples of Indian Sculpture at the British Museum*. London, 1910

BURGESS, J. *The Ancient Monuments, Temples and Sculptures of India*. 2 vols. London, 1897

BURGESS, J., and FERGUSON, J. *Cave Temples of India*. London, 1880

CAMBRIDGE HISTORY OF INDIA, Vol. I. Cambridge, 1922

CHANDA, R. P. *"Beginning of the Sikhara of the Nagara (Indo-Aryan) Temple."* Rupam No. 17, 1924

CODRINGTON, K. DE B. *Ancient India (to the Guptas)*. Ernest Benn, London, 1926

V. A. Smith's *History of Fine Arts in India and Ceylon* (Revised). Clarendon Press, Oxford, 1930

COHN, W. *"Indische Plastik."* Die Kunst des Osten, Berlin, 1921

CONZE, E. *"Buddhism."* London, 1951

COOMARASWAMY, A. K. *The Aims of Indian Art*. Essex House Press, Broad Campden, 1908

History of Indian and Indonesian Art, E. Goldston, London, 1927

"The Indian Origin of the Buddha Image." *Art Bulletin*, New York University, Vol. IX, 1927

Elements of Buddhist Iconography. Cambridge (U.S.A.), 1935

COUSENS, H. "The Ancient Temples of Aihole and Pattadakal." *A.S.I.A.R.*, 1907–10

"Buddhist Stupas at Mirpūr Khas, Sind." *A.S.I.A.R.*, 1909–10

CUNNINGHAM, SIR A. *A.S.I.A.R.*, Vols. I to XXIII (1862–87), especially Vol. IX (pp. 40–6), and Vol. XVII (pp. 25–9). Calcutta

The Bhilsa Topes, London, 1854

FERGUSSON, J. *A History of Indian and Eastern Architecture*. London, 1910

FOUCHER, A. *The Beginnings of Buddhist Art*. London, 1918

l'Iconographic Bouddhique de l'Inde. Paris, 1900–5

The Influence of Indian Art on Cambodia and Java, Vol. III. Calcutta, 1922

GANGULY, M. *Orissa and Her Remains, Ancient and Mediaeval*. Calcutta, 1912

GANGULY, O. C. *South Indian Bronzes, Historical Survey of South Indian Sculpture*. London, 1915

GRÜNWEDEL, A. *Buddhist Art in India* (English Edition). London, 1901

HAVELL, E. B. *Handbook of Indian Art*. John Murray, London, 1920

JOUVEAU-DUBREUIL, G. *Archéologie du Sud de l'Inde*. 2 vols. Geuthner, Paris, 1914

Pallava Antiquities. Probsthain, London, 1916

Ancient History of the Deccan. Pondicherry, 1920

KRAMRISCH, STELLA. *Indian Sculpture.* Heritage of India Series. Calcutta, 1933
 A Survey of Painting in the Deccan. Royal India Society, London, 1937
VAN LOHUIZEN DE LEEUW, J. E. *The Scythian Period.* Leyden, 1947
LONGHURST, A. H. "Ancient Brick Temples in the Central Provinces." *A.S.I.A.R.*,
 1909–10
MARSHALL, SIR JOHN. *Guide to Sanchi,* Calcutta, 1918
 Guide to Taxila. Calcutta, 1918
 Monuments of Ancient India (cf. *Cambridge Hist. of India,* Vol. I)
MENDIS, G. C. *Early History of Ceylon.* Y.M.C.A. Publishing House, Calcutta, 1935
MITTON, J. E. *Lost Cities of Ceylon.* John Murray, London, 1916
REA, A. *Pallava Architecture.* A.S.I., Madras, 1909
THOMAS, E. J. *Life of Buddha.* Kegan Paul, London, 1927
VOGEL, J. PH. "The Mathūra School of Sculpture." *A.S.I.A.R.*, Calcutta, 1906–7,
 1909–10

II. BURMA

ANCIENT MONUMENTS IN BURMA (Amended List). Government Printing Press,
 Rangoon, 1921
ARCHAEOLOGICAL PHOTO-NEGATIVES OF BURMA (Office of Supt. Archaeo-
 logical Survey, Mandalay). Government Printing Press, Rangoon, 1935
BURMA RESEARCH SOCIETY—Journal of, Rangoon.
DUROISELLE, CH. "Stone Sculptures of the Ananda Temple Pagān." *A.S.I.A.R.*,
 1913–14
 "The Ari of Burma and Tantric Buddhism." *A.S.I.A.R.*, 1915–16
 "Explorations at Pagān and Hmawza" (old Prome). *A.S.I.A.R.*, 1924–29
GLASS PALACE CHRONICLE OF KINGS OF BURMA (Tr. by Pe Maung Tin and
 G. H. Luce). Oxford University Press, 1923
HALLIDAY, R., and BLAGDEN, C. O. "Les Inscriptions Môn du Siam." Vol. XXX.
 B.E.F.E.O., Hanoi, 1930
HARVEY, G. E. *History of Burma.* Longmans, Green & Co., London, 1925
MARCHAL, H. *l'Architecture Comparée dans l'Inde et l'Extrême-Orient.*
 Etudes d'Art et d'Ethnologie Asiatiques II, Paris, 1944
PARMENTIER, H. *l'Art Architectural Hindou dans l'Inde et en Extrême-Orient.* Van
 Oest, Paris, 1948
PHAYRE, SIR A. *History of Burma.* Trübner, 1883–4
RAY, NIHAR-RANJAN. *Brahmanical Gods in Burma.* University Calcutta, 1932
 Sanskrit Buddhism in Burma. University Calcutta, 1932
SCOTT O'CONNOR, V. C. *Mandalay and Other Cities of the Past in Burma.* Hutchin-
 son, London, 1907
THOMANN, TH. H. *Pagān, ein Jahrtausend Buddhistischer Tempelkunst,* Heilbronn,
 1923
U TIN (S. D. O. PAGĀN). *J.B.R.S.*, Vol. IX, Pt. 1

III. JAVA AND INDONESIA

BASTIAN, A. *Indonesien.* 5 vols. Berlin, 1884–94
BERNET-KEMPERS, A. J. *The Bronzes of Nalandā and Hindu-Javanese Art.* Ned-
 Indie O. en N. Amsterdam, 1933

BLOM, J. *The Antiquities of Singasari*. Leiden, 1939

CAMPBELL, D. MACLAINE. *Java: Past and Present*. 2 vols. London, 1915

CHAILLEY-BERT, J. *Java et ses habitants*. Paris, 1900–07

COLLET, O. J. A. *L'Ile de Java sous la domination française*. Brussels, 1910

COOMARASWAMY, A. K. *History of Indian and Indonesian Art*. London, 1927

CRAWFURD, J. *History of the Indian Archipelago*. Edinburgh, 1820.
  A Descriptive Dictionary of the Indian Islands and Adjacent Countries. London, 1856

GANGOLY, O. C. *The Art of Java*. Calcutta, 1927

GROUSSET, R. *L'Art Pāla et Sena dans L'Inde Extériéure*. Paris (Musée Guimet), 1932
  De L'Inde au Cambodge et Java. Monaco, 1950

KROM, N. J. *Inleiding Tot de Hindoe-Javaansche Kunst*. 2 vols. (In Dutch.) The Hague, 1920
  Hindoe-Javaanshe Geschiedenis. (K.I. Voor de Taal . . . en Volkenkunde van Ned-Indie.) The Hague, 1931.
  L'Art Javanais dans les Musées de Hollande et de Java. *Ars Asiatica*, Vol. VIII. Paris, 1926
  The Life of Buddha on the Stupa of Barabudur. The Hague, 1926
  Archaeological Description of Barabudur, 2 vols. The Hague, 1927
  A History of the Netherlands–Indies. (In English.) Bulletin Colonial Institute. Amsterdam, 1938–9

LOEBER, J. A. *Das Batiken, eine Blüte Indonesischen Kunstlebens*. Oldenburg, 1926

MONEY, J. W. B. *Java*. 2 vols. London, 1861

MUS, P. "Barabudur." *B.E.F.E.O.*, 1935

PFYFFER ZU NEUECK, J. J. *Skizzen von der Insel Java*. Brussels, 1837

PONDER, H. W. *Java Pageant*. London, 1934

RAFFLES, SIR STAMFORD. *The History of Java*. 2 vols. London, 1817
  with CRAWFURD, J. *Description Géographique, Historique et Commerciale de Java et des autres Iles de l'Archipel Indien*. 2 vols. Brussels, 1824

SCHELTEMA, J. F. *Monumental Java*. Macmillan, London, 1912

SCIDMORE, E. R. *Java, the Garden of the East*. New York, 1897

STOCKDALE, J, J. *Sketches, Civil and Military, of the Island of Java and its Immediate Dependencies*. London, 1812

STUTTERHEIM, W. *Rama-Legenden und Rama-Reliefs in Indonesien*, 2 vols. Munich, 1924
  Pictorial History of Civilization in Java. Weltevreden, 1926

VERNEUIL, M. P. *L'Art à Java. Les temples de la période classique Indo-Javanaise*. Paris, 1927

VOGEL, J. PH. *Buddhist Art in India, Ceylon and Java*. (Translated from Dutch.) Oxford, 1936

WALCOTT, A. S. *Java and Her Neighbours*. New York, 1914

WITH, KARL. *Java—Brahmansche und Buddhistische Architectur und Plastik*. Hagen I.W., 1920

IV. CAMBODIA AND INDO-CHINA

AYMONIER, ETIENNE. *Le Cambodge*, 3 vols. E. Leroux, Paris, 1900–03

DE BEYLIÉ, L. *L'Architecture hindoue en Extrême-Orient*. Leroux, Paris, 1907

BRIGGS, LAWRENCE P. "The Ancient Khmer Empire." Philadelphia, 1951 (Vol. 41, Pt. I, of the *Transactions of the American Philosophical Society*).

CHATTERJEE, BIRAM RAJ. *Indian Cultural Influences in Cambodia.* Calcutta, 1927

CHHABRA, B. CH. "Expansion of Indo-Aryan Culture during Pallava Rule. *J.A.S.B.*, 1935

COEDÈS, G. "Etudes cambodgiennes." *B.E.F.E.O.*, XI à XLIV, 1911–51
 Pour mieux comprendre Angkor. Adrien-Maisonneuve, Paris, 1947
 Les Etats hindouisés d'Indochine et d'Indonésia. de Boccard, Paris, 1948

CORAL-RÉMUSAT, G. DE. *L'art Khmer.* Ed. d'art et d'historie, Paris, 1940. (*Études d'art et d'ethnologie asiatiques*, I.)

DUPONT, PIERRE. "Musée Guimet. Catalogue des Collections Indochinoises." *B.C.A.I.*, 1931–34

ECOLE FRANÇAISE D'EXTREME-ORIENT. *Mémoires archéologiques.* I. *Le temple d'Içvarapura*, 1926. II. *Le temple d'Angkor Vat.*, 1929–32

GLAIZE, MAURICE. *Les monuments du groupe d'Angkor.* Saigon, Portail, 1948

GROSLIER, G. *Recherches sur les Cambodgiens.* Challamel, Paris, 1921
 La Sculpture Khmère ancienne. Crès, Paris, 1925
 Les Collections Khmères du Musée Albert Sarraut à Phnom Penh. Paris, 1927 (*Ars Asiatica*, XVI).

LAJONQUIÈRE, L. DE. *Inventaire descriptif des monuments du Cambodge.* Leroux, Paris, 1902–12

MARCHAL, H. *Guide archéologique aux temples d'Angkor*, Van Oest, Paris, 1928
 L'architecture comparée dans l'Inde et l'Extreme-Orient. Paris, Ed. d'art et d'Histoire, 1944. (*Etudes d'art et d'ethnologie asiatiques*, II.)
 Le décor et la sculpture Khmers. Paris, Ed. d'art et d'histoire, 1951. (*Etudes d'art et d'ethnologie asiatiques*, III.)

PARMENTIER, H. *L'art Khmer primitif*, 2 vols. Van Oest, Paris, 1927
 L'art Khmer classique: monuments du quadrant nord-est, 2 vols. Paris, Ed. d'art et d'Histoire, 1939
 L'art architectural hindou dans l'Inde et en Extrême-Orient. Paris, Ed. d'art et d'Histoire, 1948

STERN, PHILIPPE. *Le Bayon d'Angkor Thom et l'évolution de l'art Khmer.* Geuthner, Paris, 1927

WALES, H. G. QUARITCH. *The Making of Greater India.* Quaritch, London, 1951

V. SIAM

BANERJI, R. D. "The Eastern Indian School of Mediaeval Sculpture." *A.S.I.*, Delhi, 1933

BEGLAR, J. D. "Report on a Tour in the Central Provinces in 1873–4." *A.S.I.A.R.*, Vol. VII, 1878

CHAVANNES, E. "Une Inscription du Royaume de Nan-Tchao." *J.A.* (Vol. XVI), Paris, 1900

CLAEYS, J. Y. "L'Archéologie du Siam." *B.E.F.E.O.*, Vol. XXXI. Hanoi, 1931

COEDÈS, G. "Le Royaume de Çrivijaya." *B.E.F.E.O.*, Vol. XVIII (6), Hanoi, 1918
 "Tablettes Votives Bouddhiques du Siam." *Études Asiatiques.* Paris, 1925 and *J.S.S.*, Vol. XX (1), 1926.

Recueil des Inscriptions du Siam, Part I (1924) and Part II (1929). National Library (Part I) and Royal Institute (Part II), Bangkok

"Documents sur l'Histoire Politique et Religieuse du Laos Occidental." *B.E.F.E.O.*, Vol. XXV (1), Hanoi, 1925

"Le Musée National de Bangkok." *Ars Asiatica* (G. Van Oest), Vol. XII. Paris, 1928

"Les Inscriptions Malaises de Çrivijaya." *B.E.F.E.O.*, Vol. XXX. Hanoi, 1930

"Documents sur la Dynastie de Sukhodaya," *B.E.F.E.O.*, Vol. XVII (2). Hanoi, 1917

"Excavations at Pong Tük." *J.S.S.*, Vol. XXI (3). Bangkok, 1928

"On the Origin of the Sailendras of Indonesia." *J.G.I.S.*, Vol. I (2). Calcutta, 1934

"Notes sur quelques sculptures provenant de Çrideb (Siam)." *Mélanges Linossier*, Musée Guimet, Paris.

"New Architectural Discoveries in Siam." *I.A.L.*, Vol. II (1). London, 1928

"Indian Influences in Siamese Art." *I.A.L.*, Vol. IV (1). London, 1930

DAMRONG RAJANUBHAB, H.R.H. PRINCE. *History of Siam Prior to the Ayudhya Period. J.S.S.*, Vol. XIII (2). Bangkok, 1920. (Translated by (Sir) J. Crosby, K.C.M.G., K.B.E., C.I.E.)

DUPONT, P. "Art de Dvāravatī et Art Khmer." *Revue des Arts Asiatiques*. Paris, 1935

KRAMRISCH, STELLA. "Pāla and Sena Sculpture." *Rūpam*, No. 40, Calcutta, 1929.

LAJONQUIÈRE, LUNET DE. "Essai d'Inventaire archéologique du Siam." *B.C.A.I.* Paris, 1912

LE MAY, REGINALD. "Introduction to Study of Sculpture in Siam." *Burlington Magazine*, London, 1929, and in *I.A.L.*, Vol. IV (2), 1930

"A Visit to Sawankalōk." *J.S.S.*, Vol. XIX (2). Bangkok, 1925

A Concise History of Buddhist Art in Siam. Cambridge, 1938

LINGAT, R. "Le Culte du Bouddha d'Émeraude." *J.S.S.*, Vol. XXVII (1). Bangkok, 1934

PARANAVITANA, S. "Religious Intercourse between Ceylon and Siam in the Thirteenth to Fifteenth Centuries." *J.R.A.S.* (Ceylon), Vol. XXXII, Colombo, 1932

PETITHUGUENIN, P. "Notes Critiques pour servir à l'Histoire du Siam." *B.E.F.E.O.*, Vol. XVI (3). Hanoi, 1916

SAINSON, C. *Histoire particulier du Nan Tchao*. Leroux, Paris, 1904

SALMONY, A. *Sculpture in Siam*. Ernest Benn, London, 1925

WALES, H. G. QUARITCH. "A Newly-Explored Route of Ancient Indian Cultural Expansion." *I.A.L.*, Vol. IX (1). London, 1935

WOOD, W. A. R. *A History of Siam*. T. Fisher Unwin, London, 1926

VI. JOURNALS

AMERICAN ORIENTAL SOCIETY (*J.A.O.S.*)

ARCHAEOLOGICAL SURVEY OF CEYLON, ANNUAL REPORT (*A.S.C.A.R.*)

ARCHAEOLOGICAL SURVEY OF INDIA, ANNUAL REPORT (*A.S.I.A.R.*)

BURMA RESEARCH SOCIETY, Rangoon (*J.B.R.S.*)

COMMISSION ARCHÉOLOGIQUE DE L'INDO-CHINE, Paris (*B.C.A.I.*)

ÉCOLE FRANÇAISE D'EXTRÊME-ORIENT, Hanoi (*B.E.F.E.O.*)
ÉTUDES ASIATIQUES, Paris
GREATER INDIA SOCIETY, Calcutta (*J.G.I.S.*)
INDIA SOCIETY, LONDON, *Indian Art and Letters* (*I.A.L.*) (now Royal India, Pakistan and Ceylon Society)
JOURNAL ASIATIQUE, Paris (*J.A.*)
MUSÉE GUIMET, ANNALES DU, Paris
ORIENTALISCHE LITERATUR-ZEITUNG, Berlin (*O.L.Z.*)
REVUE DES ARTS ASIATIQUES, Paris
ROYAL ASIATIC SOCIETY (*J.R.A.S.*)
ROYAL ASIATIC SOCIETY, Ceylon Branch
ROYAL ASIATIC SOCIETY, Malayan Branch
RŪPAM, Calcutta (ceased publication)
SIAM SOCIETY, Bangkok (*J.S.S.*)
TOUNG PAO, Paris

INDEX

MAP AND ILLUSTRATIONS

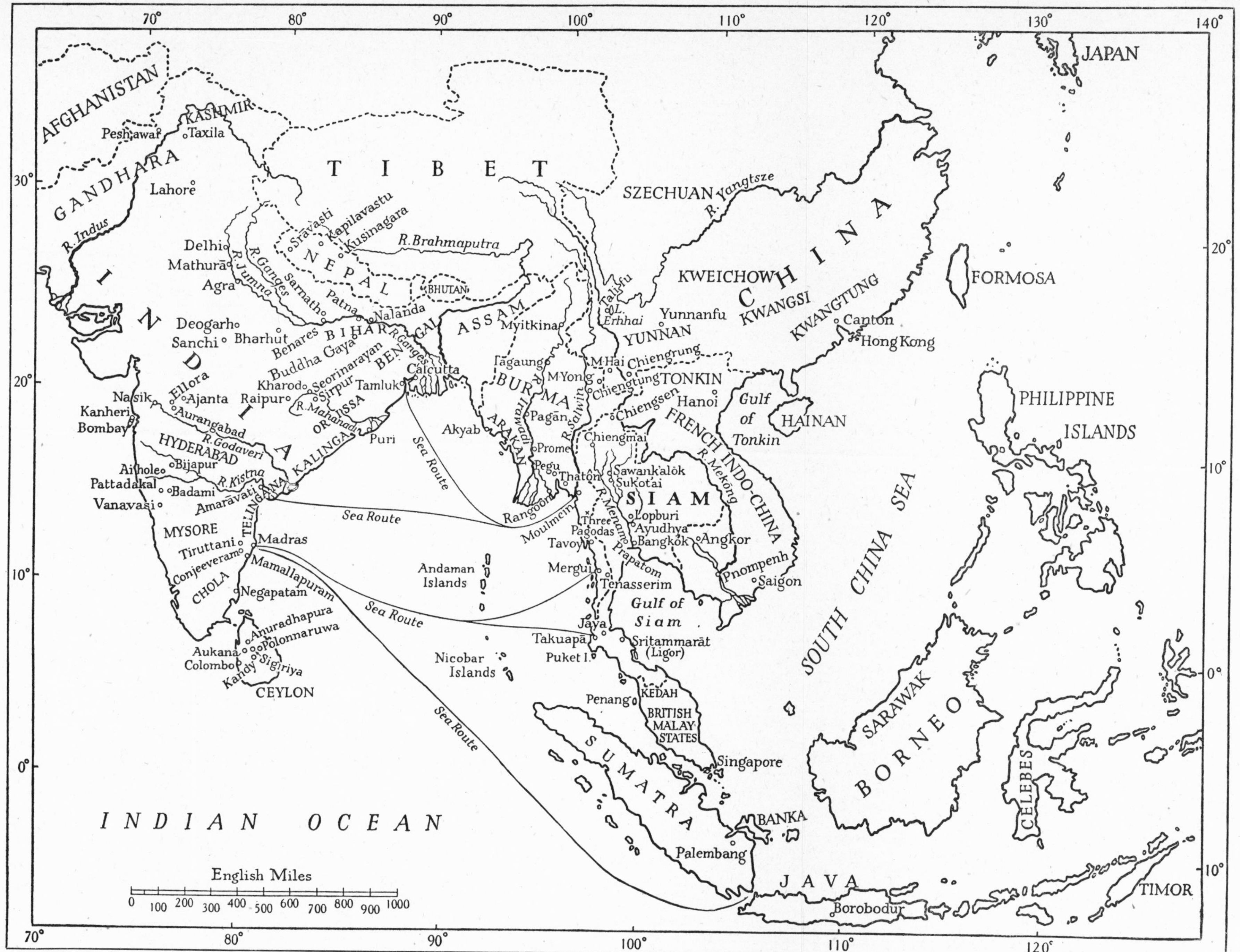

Map 1.—Relations and Sea Routes between India and the Indo-Chinese Peninsula

Map 2.—South East Asia

Fig. 1. Stone Stela. Buddha with two
Disciples. Inscription in Pyu and Sanskrit

Fig. 2. Gold seated Buddha from Khin Ba's
mound at Old Prome

Fig. 3. Stone Stela. Group of Pyu

Fig. 4. Round Silver Relic
Casket from Khin Ba's
mound

Fig. 5. Square Silver
Relic Casket from Khin
Ba's mound

Fig. 6. Silver Dvārapāla
(Guardian) from Khin
Ba's mound

Fig. 7. Bronze standing
Buddha, South Burma,
Gupta style

Fig. 8. Hard clay Tondo
showing Musicians with
Drunken Dancer, South
Burma, early Indian style

Fig. 9. Nan Paya Temple at MyinKaba near Pagān

Fig. 10. Brahmanic Bas-relief inside Nan
Paya Temple

Fig. 11. Hindu Temple of Nat Hlaung
Gyaung at Pagān

Fig. 14. Stupa of Shwesandaw, built by Anawratha, south of Pagān

Fig. 12. General View of Pagán, showing Ananda Temple

Fig. 13. General View of Pagān, showing many Temples

Fig. 15. Ananda Temple, built by Kyanzittha

Fig. 16. Portrait Figure of Kyanzittha in Ananda Temple

Fig. 17. Portrait Figure of Shin Arahan in Ananda Temple

Fig. 18. Temple of Mahābodhi at Pagān

Fig. 19. Stone seated Buddha. Pāla period from Nalandā, Bihar. (Brit. Mus.)

Fig. 20. Bronze seated Buddha, from Pagān, Pāla style

Fig. 21. Bronze seated Buddha. Later pure Burmese style

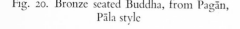

Fig. 22. Temple of
Thatbyinnyu at Pagān

Fig. 23. Temple of
Shwegu at Pagān

Fig. 24. Chapata Stupa at Pagān

Fig. 25. Temple of Gawdaw Palin at Pagān

Fig. 26. Mingalazedi Stupa at Pagān

Fig. 27. Bronze standing Buddha, early
Indian style, found at Pong Tük, West Siam.
(Nat. Mus., Bangkok)

Fig. 28. Bronze standing Buddha, early
Indian style, found in North-east Siam.
(Nat. Mus., Bangkok)

Fig. 29. Bronze standing Buddha, early Indian
style, found in Annam, French Indo-China

Fig. 32. Stone Pillar, with inscribed Môn characters, from Lopburi, Central Siam. (Nat. Mus., Bangkok)

Fig. 30. Bronze standing Buddha, Gupta style, found at Pong Tük, West Siam. (Nat. Mus., Bangkok)

Fig. 31. Stone standing Buddha (headless), Gupta style, Môn, found at Lopburi, Central Siam. (Nat. Mus., Bangkok)

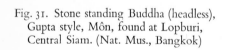

Fig. 33. Stone standing Buddha,
Gupta period, from India. (Brit. Mus.)

Fig. 34. Stone standing Buddha, Gupta
style, early Môn, outside Temple at
Bangkok

Fig. 35. Stone seated Buddha, Gupta style, early Môn, at Pr'apatom,
Lower Central Siam

Fig. 36. Stone Bas-relief of Buddha and Devotees, Gupta style, early Môn, from P'rapatom, Lower Central Siam. (Nat. Mus., Bangkok)

Fig. 39. Stupa at P'rapatom, North Indian style

Fig. 37. Stone 'Wheel of the Law,' early Indian style, early Môn, from P'rapatom. (Nat. Mus., Bangkok)

Fig. 38. Stone Deer (to represent Buddha), from P'rapatom, early Môn. (Nat. Mus., Bangkok)

Fig. 40. Quartz Head of Buddha, early
Môn. (Author's Collection)

Fig. 44. Head of Buddha
in Terra Cotta, Môn.
(Nat. Mus., Bangkok)

Fig. 41 Stone standing Buddha, Môn.
(Nat. Mus., Bangkok)

Fig. 46. Bronze standing Buddha, Môn.
(Nat. Mus., Bangkok)

Fig. 45. Stone seated Buddha
on Nāga King, late Môn
period.
(Nat. Mus., Bangkok)

Fig. 42. Stone Head of Buddha, Môn. (Author's Collection)

Fig. 47. Bronze standing Buddha, Gupta period, from Kedah, Malay Peninsula

Fig. 50. Stone Brahmanic deity

Fig. 49. Stone Brahmanic deities, Pallavā style, from Region of Takūapā. South Siam

Fig. 48. Stone standing Viṣṇu, pure
Indian style, from Region of Jaya,
South Siam

Fig. 51. Stone standing Viṣṇu,
Pallavā style. (Nat. Mus., Bangkok)

Fig. 52. Bronze Torso of Lokeçvara, Pāla style. (Nat. Mus., Bangkok)

Fig. 53. Stone seated
Lokeçvara, Pāla period,
from Bodhgaya, Bihar

Fig. 54. Bronze standing Lokeçvara,
Pāla style. (Nat. Mus., Bangkok)

Fig. 55. Bronze seated Buddha, on Nāga King, Môn-Khmer style.
(Nat. Mus., Bangkok)

Fig. 56. Arjuna group of Temples, Dieng Plateau, Java

Fig. 57. Chandi Bhima, Dieng Plateau, Java

Fig. 58. Monster Mask used on lintel of doorway at Chandi Arjuna

Fig. 59. Bronze Çiva and Parvati, from
Dieng Plateau

Fig. 65. Typical stone Buddha at
Borobodur

Fig. 60. Stupa of Borobodur, Central Java

Fig. 61. Circular platform with ring of small stupas, Borobodur

Fig. 62. Gateway to Stupa,
Borobodur

Fig. 63. Stone relief portraying life of Buddha. Gallery at Borobodur

Fig. 64. Stone relief portraying previous life of Buddha. Gallery at Borobodur

Fig. 66. Chandi Kalasan, south-
west of Prambanan

Fig. 67 Chandi Mendoet, near Borobodur

Fig. 68. Stone Buddha inside Chandi Mendoet, Gupta style

Fig. 69. Stone seated Maitreya in Chandi Plaosan, Central Java, Sailendra style

Fig. 70. Stone standing Çiva in Chandi Banon, south-east of Borobodur, Sailendra style

Fig. 71. Stone seated Lokeçvara,
Sailendra style

Fig. 72. Stone seated Ganeça,
decorated with skulls, Sailendra
style

Fig. 73. Stone standing Çiva at
Prambanan

Fig. 74. Stone relief at Loro-Jonggrang, Prambanan

Fig. 76. Stone group of three
figures at Loro-Jonggrang

Fig. 75. Stone relief
at Loro-Jonggrang,
Prambanan

Fig. 77. Stone Viṣṇu in Chandi Belahan, Eastern
Java

Fig. 79. Stone seated Prajnaparamita, style of
Singhasari. (Leyden Mus., Holland)

Fig. 78. Stone Durga slaying the
bull, style of Singhasari, Eastern Java

Fig. 81. Gateway to Chandi Djago, relief showing
local Javanese style

Fig. 82. Stone standing Hari-Hara, style
of Majapahit. (Batavia Mus.)

Fig. 80. Stone standing Bhrkouti
from Chandi Djago, Pāla style, from
Singhasari

Fig. 83. Temple of Panataran, South-eastern Java, style of Majapahit

Fig. 84. Temple of Panataran, stone relief in Javanese style

Fig. 85. Bronze seated figure of Sri, goddess of glory and fertility

Fig. 86. Stone standing Hari-Hara,
pre-Angkor, from Southern Funan.
(Pnompenh Mus.)

Fig. 87. Stone standing Hari-Hara, pre-Angkor,
from Southern Funan. (Pnompenh Mus.)

Fig. 88. Stone seated Ardhanari (Çiva and Uma in one form), pre-Angkor.
(Nat. Mus., Bangkok)

Fig. 89. Stone Torso of Yakṣi, pre-Khmer. Found at Çri-Deb. (Nat. Mus., Bangkok)

Fig. 91. Stone Torso of god, pre-Khmer.
Found at Çri-Deb. (Nat. Mus., Bangkok)

Fig. 90. Stone standing Viṣṇu, pre-Khmer.
Found at Çri-Deb. (Nat. Mus., Bangkok)

Fig. 92. Fragment of stone inscription in
Sanskrit. Found at Çri-Deb.
(Nat. Mus., Bangkok)

Fig. 93. Stone standing Buddha, pre-Angkor, from South Cambodia. (Pnompenh Mus.)

Fig. 94. Stone seated Buddha, pre-Angkor, from South Cambodia. (Pnompenh Mus.)

Fig. 95. Sanctuary shrine at Kharod, Central Provinces, India, Gupta period

Fig. 96. Sanctuary shrine at Lopburi, Khmer period

Fig. 97. Brick relief of Buddha 'turning the wheel of the law,' at Tāt Panom, North-east Siam

Fig. 100. Brick relief of horseman in 'flying gallop,' at Tāt Panom, North-east Siam

Fig. 99. Brick relief of rider seated on elephant, at Tāt Panom

Fig. 98. Brick relief of rider standing on elephant, at Tāt Panom, North-east Siam

Fig. 101. Isolated single Sanctuary Shrine
at Sambor Prei Kuk, Cambodia

Fig. 102. Temple of Prah Ko,
showing six towers, Cambodia

Fig. 103. Temple of Ta-Keo,
showing five towers, Cambodia

Fig. 104. Sanctuary Temple on Pnom Bakheng, Angkor

Fig. 105. Temple at Banteai Srei, near Angkor

Fig. 106. Reconstructed Sanctuary Tower
at Banteai Srei

Fig. 110. Apsaras in niche at Banteai
Srei

Fig. 107. Pediment at Banteai Srei

Fig. 108. Pediment at Banteai Srei

Fig. 109. Pediment at Banteai Srei

Fig. 112. Small ruined Temple at head of Stairway, P'ra Vihara

Fig. 111. Main Stairway at P'ra Vihara

Fig. 113. Entrance to second Temple at P'ra Vihara

Fig. 114. Exterior of fourth Temple at P'ra Vihara

Fig. 115. Large rectangular third Temple at P'ra Vihara

Fig. 116. Bird's Eye View of P'ra Vihara

Fig. 117. General View from the air of the Great Temple at Angkor

Fig. 118. View of Approach to Great Temple at Angkor

Fig. 119. Tower of Great
Temple at Angkor

Fig. 120. Sunken Courtyard with Pillared Cloister at Angkor

Fig. 122. Figures of Apsaras on Exterior at Angkor

Fig. 123. Figures of Apsaras on Exterior at Angkor

Fig. 121. Scene on Bas-relief in Inner Gallery at Angkor

Fig. 124. Carving on Pillar at Angkor (enlarged)

Fig. 125. General View of the Bayon Temple in Angkor-Thom

Fig. 126. Face of Lokeçvara on Tower of
Bayon

Fig. 127. Southern Entrance Gate to City of
Angkor-Thom

Fig. 128. Causeway lined with Gods and Demons

Fig. 131. Dancing Devas on Pillar of Bayon Temple

Fig. 129. 'Near View' of Figures of Gods on Causeway

Fig 130. Figures of Demons on Causeway

Fig. 132. Legendary Scene on Bas-relief in Bayon Temple

Fig. 133. Bas-relief Scene in Bayon Temple

Fig. 134. Bas-relief Scene in Bayon Temple

Fig. 135. Bas-relief Scene in Bayon Temple

Fig. 136. Bas-relief Scene in Bayon Temple

Fig. 137. Bas-relief Scene in Bayon Temple

Fig. 138. Stone seated Buddha, from Pimai, North-east Siam. (Nat. Mus., Bangkok)

Fig. 139. Stone seated Buddha, from Lopburi, Central Siam. (Nat. Mus., Bangkok)

Fig. 140. Bronze seated Buddha, from Lopburi, Central Siam

Fig. 141. Stone Head of Buddha, from Lopburi. (Author's Collection)

Fig. 142. Exterior of Temple, or Palace, at Panom Rung, North-east Siam

Fig. 143. Main Sanctuary inside Temple, or Palace, at Panom Rung, North-east Siam

Fig. 144. Carved Lintel over Doorway at Pimai, North-east Siam

Fig. 145. Carved Lintel over Doorway at Pimai, North-east Siam

Fig. 146. Exterior Moulding at Pimai, North-east Siam

Fig. 147. Temple of Mahā-Tāt at Lopburi, Central Siam. Another view of Fig. 96

Fig. 148. Temple of P'ra Prāng Sām Yot at Lopburi, Central Siam

Fig. 152. Stone Head of Bodhisattva from Lopburi, Central Siam

Fig. 149. Stone Buddha seated on Nāga King inside Temple of P'ra Prāng Sām Yot at Lopburi

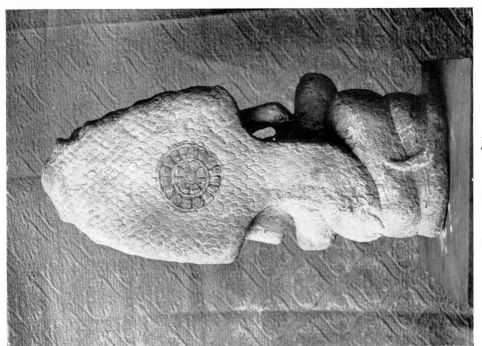

Fig. 151. Reverse of Fig. 150

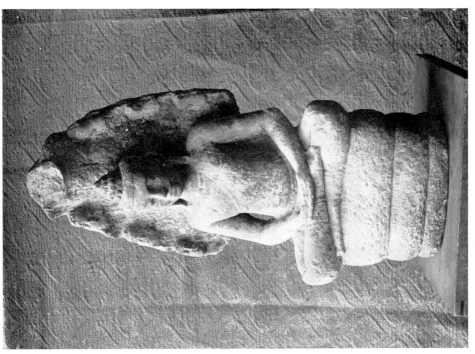

Fig. 150. Stone Buddha seated on Nāga King. (Author's Collection)

Fig. 153. Stone Head of Buddha, from Lopburi. (V. and A. Mus., London)

Fig. 154. Bronze standing Buddha, outside Temple of Benchama Bophit,
Bangkok

Fig. 156. Bronze Figure of Young Woman, showing Hair-dressing

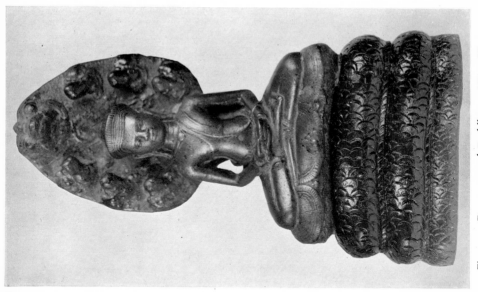

Fig. 155. Bronze seated Buddha on Nāga King

Fig. 157. Chinese Temple at Müang Hai in Yunnan, South China

Fig 158. Temple of Wat Sing at Chiengmai, North Siam

Fig. 159. Temple of Kukut at Lamp'ūn, North Siam

Fig. 160. Temple of Si Liem at Nang Hoi near Lamp'ūn, North Siam

Fig. 161. The Great Stupa at Lamp'ūn, North Siam

Fig. 162. Bronze seated Buddha, Chiengsen style, from North Siam

Fig. 164. Stone standing Buddha, Pāla period, from Bodhgaya, Bihar. (Now at Chiengmai)

Fig. 163. Bronze Head of Buddha, Chiengsen style

Fig. 165. Stone seated Bodhisattva, Pāla period, from Bodhgaya. (Brit. Mus.)

Fig. 166. Bronze seated Bodhisattva from Northern Siam

Fig. 167. Stone Figure of 'Death of Buddha,' Pāla period, from Bodhgaya, Bihar

Fig. 168. Temple of Chiengman in Chiengmai, North Siam

Fig. 169. Temple of Chet Yôt near Chiengmai, North Siam

Fig. 170. Stucco Figure on exterior of Temple of Chet Yôt

Fig. 171. Bronze seated Buddha, from
Suk'ōt'ai, Central Siam.
(Nat. Mus., Bangkok)

Fig. 172. Bronze walking Buddha,
from Suk'ōt'ai. (Nat. Mus., Bangkok)

Fig. 173. Bronze seated Buddha known as P'ra Sihing. (Nat. Mus., Bangkok)

Fig. 174. Bronze seated Buddha, from Ceylon

Fig. 175. Stone seated Buddha, from Anuradhapura, Ceylon

Fig. 176. Temple of Mahā-Tāt in ruins at Suk'ōt'ai

Fig. 177. Stucco Scene of 'Death of Buddha' at
Temple of Mahā-Tāt, Suk'ōt'ai

Fig. 186. Temple of Chang Lom at Sawank'alōk

Fig. 178. Temple of Çri Chum at Suk'ōt'ai

Fig. 179. Jataka Scene with inscription on stone in Temple of Çri Chum at Suk'ōt'ai

Fig. 180. Apsaras and attendant from Sigiriya, Ceylon

Fig. 181. Temple of Mahā-Tāt at Sawank'alōk

Fig. 182. Ruined Vihara of Temple of Mahā Tāt, Sawank'alōk

Fig. 184. Sunken Gateway of Khmer style at Sawank'alōk

Fig. 183. Stupa of Môn style at Sawank'alōk

Fig. 185. Stone seated Buddha on Nāga King at Sawank'alōk

Fig. 187. Stone seated Buddha on Nāga King at Sawank'alōk

Fig. 189. Bronze seated Buddha at Pitsanulôk, Central Siam

Fig. 188. Bronze Head of Buddha, from Suk'ôt'ai. (Nat. Mus., Bangkok)

Fig. 190. Temple of P'ra Yün, near Lamp'ūn, North Siam

Fig. 191. Temple of Sirikut at Chiengmai, North Siam

Fig. 196. Stupa of Temple of Cha Heng, near Nān

Fig. 192. Temple at Old Chiengsen, North Siam

Fig. 193. Silver seated Buddha, found at Old Chiengsen, North Siam

Fig. 198. 'Emerald' (Chrysoprase) seated Buddha, from North Siam. (Royal Temple, Bangkok)

Fig. 199. Group of Priests and Acolytes, from North Siam

Fig. 194. Bronze Head of Buddha, from
North Siam. (Author's Collection)

Fig. 206. Bronze walking Buddha, early
Ayudhya style. (Brit. Mus.)

Fig. 205. Bronze Head of Buddha,
Tai-Khmer, U-T'ong style

Fig. 195. Temple at Nān, North Siam

Fig. 197. Temple of Lampāng Lūang, near Lampāng

Fig. 200. Stone seated Buddha, Supanburi, Khmer-Tai style

Fig. 201. Bronze seated Buddha. Khmer-Tai style

Fig. 202. Bronze Head of Buddha, Khmer-Tai, U-T'ong style. (Brit. Mus.)

Fig. 203. Bronze Head of Buddha,
Khmer-Tai, U-T'ong style
(Toronto Mus.)

Fig. 204. Bronze Head of Buddha,
Khmer-Tai, U-T'ong style
(Barber Institute)

Fig. 207. Stone Head of Buddha, Tai,
from Lopburi

Fig. 208. Stone Head of Buddha, Tai,
from Lopburi

Fig. 209. Temple of Çri Sarap'et at Ayudhya

Fig. 210. Bronze seated
Buddha, at Ayudhya

Fig. 211. Two Towers in Tāi style at Ayudhya

Fig. 213. Bronze standing Buddha, Tāi-Khmer style, at Ayudhya, in Temple at Bangkok

Fig. 212. Stucco Panel of Buddhist Figures on Stupa at Ayudhya

Fig. 215. Lacquered Wooden Head of Buddha, Ayudhya style. (Author's Collection)

Fig. 214. Gilt-Bronze Head of Buddha, Tai-Khmer style, Ayudhya

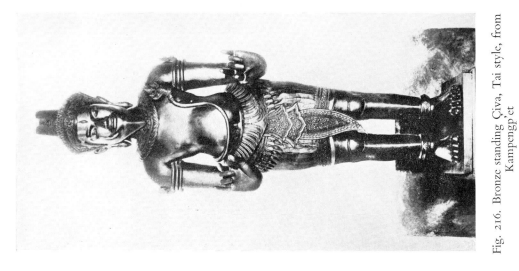

Fig. 216. Bronze standing Çiva, Tai style, from Kampengp'et